The MOOSEWOOD RESTAURANT KITCHEN GARDEN

The MOOSEWOOD RESTAURANT KITCHEN GARDEN

— Revised —

CREATIVE GARDENING for the ADVENTUROUS COOK

David Hirsch

TEN SPEED PRESS
Berkeley | Toronto

Ten Speed Press
Box 7123
Berkeley, California 94707
www.tenspeed.com

Distributed in Australia by Simon and Schuster Australia, in Canada by Ten Speed Press
Canada, in New Zealand by Southern Publishers Group, in South Africa by Real Books,
and in the United Kingdom and Europe by Airlift Book Company.

Cover and text design by Toni Tajima
Illustrations by Ann Miya

Library of Congress Cataloging-in-Publication Data
Hirsch, David P.
    The Moosewood Restaurant kitchen garden ; creative gardening for the
    adventurous cook / David Hirsch.—Rev.
       p. cm.
       Includes bibliographical references and index.
    ISBN-10: 1-58008-666-7 (pbk.)
    ISBN-13: 978-1-58008-666-0 (pbk.)
    1. Vegetable gardening. 2. Kitchen gardens. 3. Herb gardening. 4. Organic gardening.
    5. Cookery (Vegetables) 6. Cookery (Herbs) 7. Moosewood Restaurant. I. Title.
    SB324.3.H57 2005
    635—dc22   2005001136

Printed in the United States of America
First printing, 2005

1 2 3 4 5 6 7 8 9 10 — 09 08 07 06 05

This book is dedicated to
the memory of David Deutsch.

Acknowledgments for the Original Edition

I would like to thank the following:

Allan Warshawky, with whom I shared my first garden, and so much more, at Lavender Hill.

My friends and fellow Moosewood members, for their wisdom (culinary or otherwise), warmth, and cocreation of an enjoyable livelihood—especially Bob Love, for recipe testing; Susan Harville and Nancy Lazarus, for editorial assistance; and Ned Asta, for aesthetic considerations.

Arnold and Elise Goodman, for their thoughtful and caring advocacy as our agents.

Sydny Miner, who edited with encouragement and clarity.

Ashley Miller, Linda Burton, and Karen Orso, for various information.

Steve Edminster, who intrepidly word processed my scribbly handwriting.

David Deutsch, for editorial process, daily support, and sweet companionship.

Acknowledgments for This Revision

My colleagues at Moosewood for their love and collaboration these last 28 years!

Linda Dickinson, Sara Robbins, Wynnie Stein, and Lisa Wichman for testing recipes, as well as Nancy Lazarus, for consummate editorial support.

Arnold and Elise Goodman, literary agents who are part of the Moosewood family.

Ann Miya, illustrator, and Toni Tajima, book designer, for giving new life to the look of this book.

Meghan Keeffe, my editor with just the right touch.

Albert, the nicest cat ever.

My late parents, Sydell and Herb, as well as siblings: Phil, Karen, and Carol Hirsch and their families.

John Campione, my loving partner; we found each other just in time.

Contents

Introduction • 1

VEGETABLES • 7

HERBS • 97

EDIBLE FLOWERS • 145

DESIGN • 157

GARDENING TECHNIQUES • 183

RECIPES • 217

Resources • 284

Bibliography • 287

Index • 290

Introduction

THE FIRST EDITION of this book appeared in 1992. I have been enthusiastically gardening since then, and I recently realized that I could add a considerable amount of new and updated information to more accurately reflect my knowledge of the subject. As I write this in 2004, Moosewood Restaurant is in its thirty-first year, and we have expanded beyond the restaurant into the world of organic food products and the authorship of nine cookbooks. I am very proud to have been a part of our presence in the ever-evolving culture of American cuisine.

It's now been more than 30 years since I moved to the country outside of Ithaca, New York, when a "back to the land" movement was at its height. Until then I had worked in New York City, in an upper-floor office facing the Hudson River. Through the winter and early spring, I would get up from my drawing board and gaze wistfully at the sunset, wishing I were somewhere "out there." Not necessarily in New Jersey, looming on the horizon, but somewhere. The then-popular vision of a country lifestyle was a romanticized mixture of simplicity and directness. Although halcyon days of festivity and coming together awaited us in our new lives, so did the normal everyday difficulties of sustaining a livelihood and nurturing relationships. Few of us who have stayed in the countryside became the self-sufficient farmers we'd hoped; rather, we are simply people who prefer the open spaces and delight in the privilege of relating closely with the earth.

My first encounter with Moosewood Restaurant, aside from dining there, was as a gardener with a surplus of fresh basil. We negotiated a barter arrangement: herbs for meals. A few months later, I heard from my neighbor

Linda Dickinson—who was then and remains a member of the collective—that Moosewood was looking for new employees. It seemed to be a job I was suited for. I had always loved to cook. As a teenager, I watched Julia Child on television and took notes. The flexible work schedule was another incentive: I'd have time to work on a cabin I was building and to garden.

That was in the fall of 1976, which I guess makes me one of the collective's senior members. I immediately felt at home. I enjoyed learning and contributing to the ever-changing cooking repertoire and appreciated the casual yet structured worker-management environment. After the series of brief jobs and the pleasurable seminomadic existence that had begun after I graduated from architecture school in 1968, cooking at Moosewood became my first and only job of any duration.

Gardening and cooking are two of my favorite pastimes. Both are physical, sensual activities that offer tangible, relatively immediate rewards. I find it very satisfying to be involved in the entire process of creating food, from planting to cooking. The child in me enjoys gardening's playing-in-the-dirt, messy aspects, while my adult side favors the more aesthetic considerations of garden design and food preparation. An interest in architecture makes me curious to explore spatial possibilities in gardens, what different environments feel like, and how gardens can open up, frame, or enclose a given site. I think for most gardeners there's an unconscious connection to the archetypal myth of re-creating our own little Eden—a bountiful, sumptuous place of beauty where you gather the harvest.

The reality, of course, is quite different. But determined gardeners don't give up. I've endured early frosts, hail, snow, swarms of grasshoppers and gypsy moths, herds of deer, and the usual onslaught of assorted bugs, beetles, mites, grubs, voles, caterpillars, and larvae. Through it all, the gardener perseveres and learns to accept that not every seed sprouts and even the most carefully nurtured plant may die. And yet, as clichéd as it may sound, it is still miraculous to see, in a matter of short weeks, a 10-foot-tall sunflower emerge from a $1/4$-inch-long seed.

Time in the garden always goes quickly for me. My life has grown busier in the last few years, so garden time feels more precious. Yet, like other zealous gardeners, I find there's always time and room for new beds and borders that will need care. Even when there isn't.

Over the years, I've supplied the restaurant with herbs, flowers, and rare specialty produce. New types or varieties can be tested both in the garden and in the restaurant, stimulating curiosity and interest in both pursuits. This year, along with old favorites, my garden includes Thai basil, scarlet runner beans, escarole, lemon verbena, pearl onions, anise hyssop, Tangerine Gem marigolds, Merlot and Anuenue lettuces, Garden of Eden pole beans, *shungiku* (edible chrysanthemum), and Lady Bell early red peppers.

There is no one Moosewood kitchen garden. We buy from a number of local individual gardens and small farms that supply us (as well as other restaurants and markets) throughout our brief, bountiful growing season. In addition, several of the Moosewood staff have gardens that provide the restaurant with herbs, edible flowers, and vegetables.

With very few exceptions, we use fresh produce year round, with a particular emphasis on locally grown foods. Anyone who has tasted homegrown tomatoes, corn, or peas knows that store-bought vegetables just can't compare. Produce from afar must be bred, grown, and harvested with an eye to its perishability, appearance, and yield rather than aesthetic appeal and taste. Superior quality and flavor result from harvesting foods as close to ripeness and the kitchen as possible. In addition, the nutrient and vitamin content of freshly picked food is always higher. Home growing can also expand your cooking repertoire to include interesting vegetables and herbs that may not be available in local markets or simply are impractical to grow commercially.

At Moosewood, we try to cook with as much organically grown food as possible, and also to avoid packaged foods prepared with preservatives. Public consciousness about pesticides, herbicides, and food additives is certainly increasing, and we look forward to a time when an even higher percentage of agriculture is devoted to organic farming. In the last few years, the organically grown sector of both raw and packaged foods has shown more growth than any other food-related area.

I'm a confirmed organic gardener because I feel there's an undeniable connection between our own physical and spiritual health and how we treat the earth. Growing at least part of your own food and purchasing organic produce gives your body a break from the plethora of pesticides and herbicides used in most of commercial agriculture. Eating from the lower end of the food chain—plants, grains, seeds, nuts, and dairy products, with little or no meat— reduces the consumption of unwanted toxins. Meat from livestock whose diet consists of grains grown with herbicides and pesticides contains toxins in greater concentration than the grain itself. There are also the ecological concerns. It takes 9 pounds of grain to make 1 pound of meat. Grazing livestock creates deforestation and soil erosion in many parts of the world.

COMMUNITY SUPPORTED AGRICULTURE

The Community Supported Agriculture (CSA) movement (www.csacenter. org) is an important resource for folks who don't have the space or time to garden. Introduced to the United States from Europe in 1984, CSA provides a direct link between consumers and farmers. Members receive a share of the farm's harvest as crops are ready throughout the season. Each CSA has its own guidelines: some require volunteered time, others ask for pick-up at the farm, some deliver to your door. All require some financial commitment at the season's start. Members often can request the kinds of produce they'd like to have. Some CSAs offer dairy, meat, and other products. The movement's popularity is due in part to the availability of produce just as fresh as from one's own garden. At this writing, there are more than a thousand small farms supported by shareholders in the United States, and a handful in Australia, Canada, Ghana, Hungary, and New Zealand.

Small farms go out of business every year. The large corporations running the huge farms that supply the bulk of what Americans eat may be more concerned with their profits than with the effects their farming methods will have on the environment for decades to come. CSA helps support farmers' sustainable practices by ensuring fair compensation and guaranteed outlets. Local economies benefit by keeping money in the community. Members have access to fresh, tasty, nutritious food that has a more personal connection to their lives. In fact, the first co-ops in Japan that inspired this movement were called *teikei*, roughly translated as "food with a face on it."

SUSTAINABLE CUISINE

Food professionals concerned with the health and productivity of our communities have become interested in the idea of sustainable cuisine. Organic farming is at the center of this movement, but issues of food distribution and worker compensation are addressed as well. Our reliance on fossil fuels to transport food thousands of miles has global implications of enormous import. Fair compensation for all involved in the industry, from workers picking crops to dishwashers, needs to be addressed. Moosewood is a member of Chef's Collaborative (www.chefscollaborative.org), an association of food professionals that works to promote sustainable cuisine by education, inspiration, and mutual support.

Our restaurant kitchen is surprisingly small and basic. Most of the techniques necessary to produce our meals are straightforward and can be applied in the home kitchen. What I think defines our style as "Moosewood" is the use of fresh foods prepared daily for an ever-changing menu that reflects the variety of the seasons. Our eclectic mix of recipes has been influenced by both international and American regional cooking styles and reflects the rich diversity of flavors and tastes that can be achieved with a full range of vegetables, herbs, grains, beans, nuts, and soy and dairy products. Many cuisines that we have drawn from, particularly those of Asia, traditionally feature superb meatless, protein-sufficient dishes.

This book is a guide for cooks and gardeners who want to feel the compounded pleasure of growing and cooking their vegetables and herbs, even if their garden is a windowsill of potted herbs. I hope to share our enjoyment of these two creative, life-sustaining processes.

In the chapters to follow, you will find discussions of vegetables, herbs, and edible flowers (pages 7–155) that we have enjoyed using at the restaurant. Each entry includes ornamental aspects, growing requirements, harvest information, and culinary tips. This revised edition has been expanded to include updated material throughout, with more attention to heirloom varieties and specific entries that reflect knowledge gained in the years since the original was published.

I have always admired gardens that are sensitive to their environment and reflect individual personal style. The Design chapter (page 157) is intended to help outline planning decisions for new or experienced gardeners. In it are examples of various possibilities for kitchen gardens in a range of sites. The Gardening Techniques chapter (page 183) is a guide to basic information especially useful to first-time gardeners. Beginners may find it helpful to read these chapters before learning about individual vegetables, herbs, or flowers. Recipes are included (pages 217-283), many of which are new to this edition; all are Moosewood or personal favorites that feature specific herbs and vegetables.

Since this book is not intended to be a complete garden primer, the curious gardener may be interested in consulting other resources. The Resources (page 284) and Bibliography (page 287) will provide you with a wide selection of gardening and cooking information as well as other resources that I have found to be helpful.

Vegetables

W HEN WE'RE RUSHING ABOUT THE KITCHEN, chopping and cooking vegetables, we seldom think about a seed being sown. Yet that is how the process starts for cooks and gardeners alike.

The growing season begins with choosing which seeds to sow. Seed catalogs list a confusingly wide array. To learn which varieties perform best in your region, talk with gardeners in the neighborhood, at a local farmers' market, or at a cooperative extension office; you'll also find help in gardening and lifestyle magazines, such as *Horticulture, Organic Gardening, Sunset*, and *Martha Stewart Living.* An often overlooked source is your local newspaper's gardening column. Ultimately, your own experience will combine with outside information to form a unique and individual body of knowledge.

Included in the Resources (page 284) are seed and nursery catalogs that I have found to be reliable and informative. Many clearly indicate such valuable information as how many feet of row a given quantity of seed will plant, the best season for sowing, which varieties are disease resistant, and which plants are widely adaptable or will thrive only in a specific region.

Gardeners with limited space or time may choose to buy seedlings at a local nursery or garden center. This can be particularly helpful for plants that require an early start indoors—such as onions, leeks, or spring broccoli—or that need specific conditions, such as heat-loving eggplant. I always buy a few greenhouse-started tomato plants to get a jump on the season, in addition to starting my own plants from seeds. Local nurseries usually sell plants that have been grown successfully in your area.

In this chapter, I recommend varieties of plants that have proven—in either my experience or that of trusted sources—to be vigorous and healthy as well as culinarily appealing. Unless specifically noted, these varieties are widely available. The seed companies that I suggest in this chapter have been particularly useful in my years of gardening. I realize there are many other worthwhile sources; however, in the interest of being concise, I have limited my recommendations to a few that cover diverse geographic regions. I have included a wider selection in Resources (page 284).

Admittedly, some of my prejudices have influenced what appears or does not appear in this book. There is no discussion of celery, which I find far too difficult to grow and not that much better tasting than store-bought. Nor will you find ordinary radishes, whose chief asset, in my opinion, is the speed at which they produce many more than one could want.

Each year brings new vegetable varieties, usually improved for vigor, resistance to disease or pests, shipping ability, physical appearance, or a desirable trait, such as a leafier dill with fewer flowers. Rarely, a genuinely new type of vegetable appears, like the snap pea.

Hybrids do have their distinct advantages as improved, often disease-resistant, high-yield varieties. Since their seeds may be sterile or revert to manifesting an undesirable characteristic of a parent's strain, they can be reproduced only by a controlled pollination of the original parent selections and not from their own seeds. Hybrids are usually more expensive and need to be purchased, because the process just described is not one the home gardener can easily replicate. Do not confuse ordinary hybrids with the kind of interspecies breeding that has been done in genetically modified foods.

There is a continuing effort to preserve heirloom and other open-pollinated varieties that are in danger of being lost forever as new hybrid plant varieties push them out of the marketplace. Open-pollinated varieties produce seeds that are true to type, meaning they're replicas of themselves. Over the years, farmers have selected the most desirable plants and saved their seeds for the next year's crop. Heirlooms are specific strains that have been planted by farmers and gardeners for generations. The criteria that farmers and gardeners followed for saving heirlooms didn't include modern marketing concerns like uniformity, transportability, or ease of growing in the widest possible range of climates. Rather, factors like taste and good performance in a specific region were of more importance.

In North America, immigrants brought their treasured foods in the form of seeds to provide a link to their past. Aware that the seeds might be taken from them, many gardeners and farmers hid them in places like clothing hems or suitcase linings. Indigenous Americans shared their bounty of crops not known in pre-Columbian Europe with the first European settlers. The contributions of these two complex groups helped to create a rich and diverse selection of food plants that far exceeded that of any previous culture. We hope that recent and future immigrants will continue this tradition, although outwitting Customs officials is likely a lot rougher now than in the nineteenth and early twentieth centuries.

The concern in preserving heirloom varieties is to prevent the loss of a broad genetic base, as more old varieties are lost when fewer are grown. A narrow, less diverse source of food crops may not be as adaptable to changes in climate, insect population, and disease.

Many of the heirloom or open-pollinated varieties are still desirable plants for home gardeners, and in the last decade or two, the work of dedicated preservationists all over the world has resulted in an expanded market for heirlooms. Heirlooms now have their own cachet: seed catalogs highlight varieties, garden shows on television discuss them, and farmers' markets flag the oldies but goodies. Many of the recommended vegetables that follow in this chapter are heirlooms; my short-list favorites are

- Pole beans: Kentucky Wonder
- Runner beans: Scarlet Runner
- Beets: Chioggia
- Broccoli: Romanesco
- Cabbage: Early Jersey Wakefield
- Carrots: Touchon
- Cauliflower: Early Snowball
- Cucumbers: lemon
- Eggplant: Rosa Bianca
- Garlic: Spanish Roja
- Kale: Russian Red
- Lettuce: Forellenschluss
- Asian greens: tatsoi
- Peas: Lincoln
- Potatoes: Yellow Finn
- Squash: Waltham Butternut
- Tomatoes: Brandywine

There are no hard-and-fast rules as to which type—hybrid or open-pollinated—will be a better plant. For example, although Brandywine tomatoes have remarkable flavor, one wet and cool summer they did terribly in my garden while the hybrids came through just fine. One standout exception is sweet corn. Hybrid varieties are markedly superior: sweeter and with a longer window for harvesting. I have also had particularly successful crops with hybrid members of the cabbage family and onions, spinach, and carrots. Purchased seeds saved from year to year will be most viable if kept in a cool, dry place below 70°F but above freezing. Most seeds will keep between 3 and 5 years, but buy fresh corn, leek, onion, parsley, and parsnip seeds every year.

The following vegetable listings include "Culinary Tips." In most cases, measurements and detailed instructions are not given; the tips are meant to be a guide or a jumping-off point for a cook's inspiration.

Gardeners may find that their soil becomes more fertile as the seasons go by as a result of good gardening practices that include the addition of compost, decomposing organic mulches or manures, and crop rotation. With good soil, you may get good results placing plants closer together than indicated in the "Starting" discussion for each vegetable that follows. Those with very limited garden area may want to choose varieties that are suited to close spacing; see Container Gardening (page 177).

ASIAN SPECIALTY VEGETABLES

The cuisines of Asia have strongly influenced Moosewood's cooking style for a variety of reasons:

- The vegetables' fresh, clean flavor is enhanced with just a few seasonings, such as soy sauce, ginger, garlic, and sesame oil.
- Because the vegetables are cooked quickly, they retain nutrients and texture.
- Traditional vegetarian protein sources such as tofu, tempeh, and wheat gluten products provide nutritional balance for meatless dishes.

The vegetables listed below will not only widen your cooking and gardening repertoires but also provide greens and roots that are rich in flavor, vitamins, minerals, and other nutrients. All except daikon are quick to harvest, at 20 days for baby greens and 40 to 50 days for full-sized plants.

Chinese cabbage resembles green cabbage but with thinner, frilled, lettuce-like, crisp leaves. Both napa (which is blocky and barrel-shaped) and Michihli (taller and cylindrical, also called celery cabbage) have a sweet, mildly tangy taste; napa varieties store better. Most crops are started from late spring for summer harvest, to midsummer for fall harvest. Chinese cabbage does best with the declining day length after the summer solstice. In areas where lettuce is a difficult summer crop, try Chinese cabbage for better heat tolerance.

Daikon, an important ingredient in Japanese cooking, is a crisp, white radish 12 to 18 inches long. *Daikon* means "big root" in Japanese. They're sweet yet hot and spicy. Varieties are available for spring, summer, and fall planting. Tokinashi (Seeds of Change) is a good, mellow variety for spring planting in most areas and early-fall planting where winters are mild. Miyashige (Johnny's and Seeds of Change) has done well for me with plantings in July and August for fall harvest. As with other root crops, a stone-free soil as well as adequate watering in dry times will give the best quality.

Edible chrysanthemum *(shungiku)* is grown for its young tender leaves' aromatic flavor, which recalls the pungent fragrance of ornamental garden chrysanthemums. Plants not picked as greens for cooking can be left to produce delicate orange and yellow button flowers that are also edible.

Flowering mustards are grown for their budded flowering shoots, similar in appearance to the botanically related Italian broccoli raab. Mustards do best in cool spring or fall weather in areas with mild winters. Hon Tsai Tai has purple-red flowering stems with a mild turnip-mustard flavor. Gai Lon (Chinese kale) is a green variety with similar flavor.

Mizuna is a mild Japanese mustard with fringed, lacy foliage and white stems. The leaves make an attractive edible garnish as well as adding ornament to the garden. Plants can be harvested all season from one sowing: pick the outer leaves and keep plants well watered. *Mibuna* is a related green with smooth leaves; use as you would mizuna.

Pak choi (bok choy) is used widely in Chinese dishes, where it lends a crunchy texture and sweet but mildly pungent flavor. An excellent variety is Mei Qing Choi: widely available, it's a "baby" type with pale green stems and darker green, veined leaves. The compact plants are mature at 6 to 8 inches tall and make an attractive edging plant. In addition to being a good size for small households, they're heat- and cold-tolerant. Standard varieties are about 15 to 18 inches tall and somewhat resemble Swiss chard.

Tatsoi (spoon mustard) has a flavor similar to that of its fellow cabbage family member, pak choi. Its abundant, small, deep green, spoon-shaped leaves radiate from a central rosette. One of my favorite greens for both salads and quick stir-frying, it's also an attractive, low-growing plant for edging beds or borders. Tatsoi is heat- and cold-tolerant, which allows for a long growing season. I've harvested tatsoi well into December by covering late summer-sown plants with a plastic tunnel (page 203) in mid-fall.

STARTING

All of the above vegetables thrive in soil within a pH range of 6.0 to 7.5. Early spring planting is possible for daikon, edible chrysanthemum, mizuna, pak choi, and tatsoi. Chinese cabbage varieties for spring planting should be seeded in the garden after the last frost, or started indoors in peat pots 3 to 4 weeks before the last frost is expected. Plant seedlings after the danger of frost has passed, because seedlings exposed to frost and cold may bolt to seed before forming heads, although the mature plants can handle frost at harvest time.

Chinese cabbage, daikon, and the standard-sized pak choi are seeded in rows 18 inches apart, with plants thinned to 6 inches apart for daikon and 10 to 12 inches for cabbage and pak choi.

Smaller-sized pak choi, mizuna, flowering mustards, chrysanthemum, and tatsoi are seeded in rows 12 inches apart, with plants thinned to 4 to 6 inches apart. All of the above can also be sown thickly in 6-inch-wide bands for a cut-and-come-again crop of baby greens. Cut 4- to 6-inch-tall plants 1 inch from the soil and keep well watered for second and possibly additional cuttings.

Fall crops are possible for all of the above, as they can tolerate light frosts. Winter crops can be grown in the South or Pacific coastal areas, or by anyone with a cool greenhouse or protected cold frame.

CULTURAL REQUIREMENTS

Flea beetles have been a major problem in growing all but the chrysanthemums in many parts of North America. They can be effectively controlled with row covers (page 202) applied before seedlings emerge, and with the insecticides pyrethrum and rotenone.

HARVEST

Chinese cabbage heads can be stored refrigerated or in a cool cellar for several weeks.

Daikon roots that are harvested in the fall can be stored like carrots (page 31).

Flowering mustard stems that are flowering should be harvested to encourage the production of new stems.

Edible chrysanthemum greens should be picked while plants are quite small, up to 6 inches tall.

Mizuna plants should be picked whole when 6 to 12 inches, or individual smaller leaves can be picked for a long season of harvest.

Pak choi, once harvested, can be stored in the refrigerator or a cool cellar for several weeks.

Tatsoi may be harvested as individual leaves or whole plants.

CULINARY TIPS

There's no reason to limit Asian greens to Asian dishes. The tender, young, raw greens of Chinese cabbage, mizuna, pak choi, and tatsoi can be used in all manner of green salads or added to soups. I've also used them as a nutritious green addition to dishes as diverse as pizza and omelets.

Bob Love is a former Moosewood cook with a wonderful facility for the cuisines of Southeast Asia, where he lived for many years. Try his fast and delicious stir-frying technique for greens: Prepare the greens by thoroughly washing and then chopping coarsely. Cut garlic cloves into pieces large enough to be removed with a slotted spoon or mesh strainer. Heat some oil in a wok and fry the garlic until it's golden; remove and reserve. Stir-fry the greens until they're tender: older and bulky greens will take 5 to 10 minutes; young or delicate, soft greens may be cooked in 1 or 2 minutes. The rinse water that clings to the leaves should provide sufficient moisture. Add a few splashes of soy sauce, Chinese oyster sauce, rice wine, and rice vinegar. Sprinkle the reserved crisp garlic over the completed dish.

Daikon radishes are traditionally used in salads, soups, stews, dips, and pickled condiments. Pickled daikon is used to cleanse the palate.

Grated daikon is an excellent addition to a dipping sauce for spring rolls, tempura, or grilled kabobs. Combine $1/2$ cup vegetable stock or water with 2 tablespoons soy sauce and 2 tablespoons sake or cream sherry. Simmer for 5 minutes. Remove from the heat and add 1 teaspoon each of honey and apple juice, $1/4$ cup grated daikon, and 1 teaspoon grated fresh gingerroot.

ASPARAGUS

Garden-grown asparagus is tender, sweet, and a delightful surprise to those who've only tasted it from the market. It's an unusual vegetable in that it's a perennial; yearly maintenance is all that is necessary to keep plants bearing well. The mature plants make a lush 4- to 6-foot screen or hedge for the summer landscape. The lacy foliage provides a handsome background for lower-growing flowers, herbs, or vegetables. Because all of their energy goes to producing spears, the nonflowering male plants give higher crop yields than the female plants, which produce seeds. Jersey Giant and Supermale are two newly developed varieties of this "macho" breed. Purple Passion is reputed to be sweeter and more tender than the green varieties, with some sacrifice in yield. Asparagus cultivars are bred differently for mild and cold climates; check with your local county cooperative extension agent for varieties suitable for your climate. This is a crop for gardeners with room to spare; two 20-foot-long rows will supply four people with fresh spears through the growing season.

STARTING

Most gardeners buy 1-year-old crowns (roots) from the local garden center or by mail order and plant in early spring. Choose a spot where the tall, fern-like foliage will not shade sun-loving plants or be disturbed by rototilling or deep cultivation; this should be a permanent bed. Asparagus grows well throughout the continental United States and southern Canada, except in Florida and the Gulf Coast. Soil should be well drained and fertile, with a pH range between 6.0 and 7.0.

Dig an 8-inch-deep trench, piling the soil to one side. Space trenches 4 feet apart, measured center to center. Remove large stones and supplement the new bed with compost, well-rotted manure, or peat moss to ensure a nutrient-rich home for the 10- to 15-year lifespan of the plants. Refill the trench with 2 inches of soil and supplement, then space the crowns 15 inches apart on top of this bed, with their long, snaky roots pointing down. Cover the plants with 2 inches of soil. As the new shoots emerge, simply fill in with more of the supplemented soil until the crowns are covered with 6 inches of soil, completing the job by early summer. This keeps the plants from pushing themselves to the surface as they grow.

CULTURAL REQUIREMENTS

Yearly maintenance includes providing adequate moisture, nutrients, and protection from invasive weeds. Asparagus is a heavy feeder; it will thrive if the soil fertility is kept high with early-spring and post-harvest applications of compost or well-rotted manure. Additional organic mulch applied during the growing season helps to maintain moisture and keep weeds from being a problem. If grasses or other perennial weeds do become well established in your asparagus bed, the best time to deal with the problem is late fall. Cut down the ferns after the first hard frost, then cultivate or till shallowly to remove as much of the weed roots as possible. The asparagus roots are fairly deep and shouldn't be disturbed. Apply a generous mulch of 2 to 3 inches, using the cut ferns as well.

CULINARY TIPS

- Snap off the tough bottom end by bending a spear with both hands until it snaps. Or, if you have the time and patience, peel the lower stem end to remove the tough, fibrous portion.

- At Moosewood, we don't use any special pots for cooking asparagus. Spears can be blanched in boiling water for 2 to 3 minutes, or steamed for slightly longer.

- The wonderful, delicate flavor of fresh asparagus calls for the simplest preparations. Steam and toss either with butter and lemon or with sesame oil and a little grated fresh ginger.

- Asparagus adds class to any salad or marinated vegetable dish.

- Stir-fry sliced asparagus with just one or two other ingredients, such as tofu and mushrooms.

- Serve cooked spears with a smooth and tangy dressing that's half yogurt and half homemade garlic Herbed Mayonnaise (page 266).

- When using chopped asparagus in a soup or stew, add the tips toward the end of cooking time for best appearance and texture.

- Roasting asparagus is a simple method of preparation that yields remarkably succulent stalks, especially if they're fat and fresh. Preheat the oven to 400°F, brush the spears with olive oil to lightly coat, sprinkle with salt, and bake in a single layer on a low-rimmed flat baking sheet for 20 to 25 minutes, rolling the spears once during baking. If desired, a little pressed or minced garlic can be added to the oil.

HARVEST

At the start of the second year, after one full year of growth following planting, a few spears may be cut for sampling. Spears are ready to be cut when they're 6 to 8 inches tall and the tips are closed tight. Snap off the spears at ground level and refrigerate any not consumed immediately. During the third year, harvest for a period of only 3 weeks. In succeeding years, harvest can continue for up to 6 weeks or until the newly emerging stalks are less than 1/2 inch in diameter. Pick often (two or three times a week), as stalks will leaf out and slow down production of new spears.

BEANS

A satisfying crop for the kitchen gardener, beans produce abundantly, yielding more per square foot than most other vegetables. They're valuable in garden rotations because legumes add nitrogen to the soil by way of beneficial nitrogen-fixing bacteria that live in nodules on the roots of bean plants. The familiar immature seedpods (snap, green, or string beans) or mature seeds (dried beans) are one of the world's most important food sources.

Bush bean plants average about 2 feet tall, need no support, and are usually green, wax, or French filet types. If, like me, you garden where spring is unstable, you'll find that Provider is far ahead of the pack for best germination and growing in cool temperatures. Roc d'Or (Johnny's, Seeds of Change) is a buttery wax bean that is also tolerant of cool conditions. French filet beans, another bush type, are long and slender and must be picked when they're no more than 1/4 inch in diameter. Vigilant gardeners will be rewarded with tender beans of delicate flavor. Triumph de Farcy is an heirloom variety we have enjoyed. Morgane (Cook's) is an exceptional filet bean because of its unusually high yields coupled with good flavor. Purple bush beans are easier to pick as they stand out against the green foliage, and they are attractive on a platter of multicolored raw vegetables for dips or salads. When cooked, however, they turn green. Royal Burgundy is a tasty purple bean that also tolerates cool soils. Roma II is a Romano or Italian bean with thick, rich, "beany"-flavored pods, my favorite of all the bush beans.

Pole beans give the highest yield for the amount of space required and can be grown along fences, trellises, or poles. Garden catalogs offer a nice selection of ornamental towers that can be used to support bean vines. Gardeners with access to sturdy sapling trees can cut three or four and trim them into 6- to 8-foot-long poles to make "tepees," lashed together at the top and set a few inches into the ground. Portable trellising (page 55) is another option. The Fortex pole bean heads my list; it's a pole bean with the tenderness of filet beans, but it can be picked over a much longer period. Unlike filet beans, Fortex has great quality even as the beans mature from 6 to 11 inches long. Trionfo, or Trionfo Violetto, is a vigorous, attractive Italian heirloom with lavender flowers, purple-veined green leaves, and tasty purple beans. I've grown it on a fence that separates a vegetable garden from a perennial flower garden. The lush foliage with dark beans makes a handsome backdrop for the multihued perennial flowers. Another heirloom, Kentucky Wonder, has been grown for generations and is still worthy because of its distinctively delicious "beany" flavor. Make sure to pick the pods when they're no bigger than 6 to 7 inches long to avoid stringy texture.

Runner beans are well known for their ability to quickly cover arbors, trellises, and fences with dense foliage and festive blossoms on 8- to 12-foot-long vines that are a bit more shade tolerant than most beans—perfect for creating screens for shade or privacy. Northern or cool-weather gardeners will have success with runner beans, but they perform poorly where daytime temperatures are regularly above 85°F. Runner beans are a flourishing crop for me in the cooler weather of late summer to frost. Scarlet Runner, with bright scarlet-orange flowers that make a dazzling edible garnish, and Painted Lady, with bicolored red and white blooms, are two excellent heirloom varieties. Pick the beans when they're young and tender, at 4 to 6 inches long. Dwarf Bees (Territorial) is an unusual runner bean because of its bush habit, but with the same vermilion flowers as the taller varieties.

Shell beans include green soybeans, limas, French flageolet, and many other varieties traditionally popular both here and abroad. Shell beans are picked when the pods are halfway to maturity—harvest them when the bean seeds inside are fully formed but still tender and not yet dried. Home gardeners can enjoy the tender, buttery sweetness of freshly shelled beans that are rarely available in markets. Green soybeans or edamame have gone from relative obscurity outside of Asia to becoming a popular, healthful snack everywhere. Easier to digest than dried soybeans and surprisingly sweet, edamame, like all soybeans, are a complete source of protein and are high in fiber, vitamins, and calcium. Envy (Johnny's) is a good choice for quick-bearing plants in short-season areas, while Sayamusume (Fedco, Seeds of Change, Territorial) is a higher-yielding variety that matures about 10 days later. Lima beans excel in growing seasons with long, hot summers, but Jackson Wonder (Fedco, Territorial) is an heirloom bush variety that also succeeds in areas with more temperate weather. Chevrier (Cook's) is a flageolet bush bean with a delicate flavor similar to baby limas, but it's easier to grow in cool climates. The pastel green–shelled beans make a delightful side dish. Tongue of Fire (Johnny's) has red-striped, cream-colored pods with large, delicious beans. Seeds for this were originally collected in Tierra del Fuego, at the tip of South America. There are many other varieties of shell beans to explore; three favorites are cannellini, the classic minestrone bean with subtle, delicate flavor and tolerance of cool-weather growing; Jacob's Cattle, a pretty maroon-and-white speckled bean excellent for baking; and Speckled Bays (or Taylor's Horticultural), creamy red-striped beans that are among the earliest to mature. Beans that have fully matured can be dried and stored for winter use. Kitchen gardeners with lots of space may want to grow their own kidney, pinto, black, navy, or other kinds of beans for drying.

Tepary beans are ancient beans found in the Southwest and Mexico. Teparys thrive in dry conditions with heat and alkaline soils—the plants will actually yield fewer beans in rich, moist soil. Teparys' roots grow twice as deep in the same amount of time as conventional beans to allow them to tap deeper reserves of moisture. They are also adapted to flower and bear beans quickly, before summer heat and drought intensify. The dried beans are as versatile in cooking as any other bean. Mitla Black (Fedco, Seeds of Change), from the Mitla Valley of Oaxaca, Mexico, is reputed to be more tolerant of moister climates.

STARTING

After the last expected frost date, sow seeds in well-drained, warm soil between pH 6.0 and 7.5. Soils cooler than 65°F will result in poor germination and possible seed rot. For bush types, sow seeds 1 inch deep, 2 inches apart, in rows 24 to 36 inches from other plantings. Pole types should be sown 1 inch deep with six to eight seeds per pole, thinned later to the four strongest vines. Alongside a fence or trellis, plant seeds 3 to 4 inches apart. Northern gardeners should start lima bean seeds indoors in peat pots or soil cells at 70°F or higher. Outdoor seeding, when soil and air temperatures are warm enough for good germination, may be too late to mature a crop of beans before the cooler weather returns.

❧ CULINARY TIPS ❧

❧ Only the stem of green or wax beans must be trimmed; the curly end is tender. The fastest way to trim beans is to line up about ten at a time on a cutting board and slice off the stem ends. Folks with more leisure can snap off one stem at a time, bean by bean.

❧ The year's first tender pickings are at their best quickly blanched or steamed and tossed with plain or herbed butter (pages 271–273) or a tasty olive oil. When there's abundance, use them as supporting players in soups, stews, stir-fries, and casseroles, and marinated in salads.

❧ All beans have edible flowers. Scarlet runner blossoms make showy garnishes that add a sweet flavor to salads and sanwiches.

❧ Fresh shell beans such as limas, cannellini, or flageolet are simmered in stock or water for 15 to 30 minutes or until just tender.

Flageolets are traditionally simmered with thyme, bay leaf, onions, cloves, parsley, garlic, and tomatoes.

❧ To cook dried beans more quickly and produce a tender bean, withhold salt until the beans are almost done.

❧ To preserve nutrients in dried beans, cook them in their soaking liquid. To minimize gastric disturbance, soak beans for 3 to 4 hours and change the water before cooking.

❧ Purée cooked dried beans with olive oil, garlic, and savory herbs. Serve on a bed of steamed kale or other greens.

❧ For a classic Japanese edamame snack, boil the soybean pods for 15 to 20 minutes, until completely tender. Sprinkle with coarse salt and, like peanuts, pop the beans from the pod into your mouth.

Nitrogen legume inoculant, a harmless and beneficial bacteria, will greatly increase the yield of all beans by encouraging nitrogen-fixing bacteria to grow on the plants' roots. Lightly dust the seeds with the inoculant, moisten, and plant as usual, or simply pour a small amount into each seed hole or row as you sow.

To avoid vast quantities of snap beans maturing at once, plant 3- to 4-foot rows 1 to 2 weeks apart as late as 2 to 2½ months before the first frost date.

CULTURAL REQUIREMENTS

Overfertilizing beans results in lushly foliaged plants with few beans. The nitrogen-fixing properties of the plants themselves allow for lighter fertilization. Avoid working around bean plants after a heavy dew or rainfall to help prevent the spread of a damaging foliage rust disease encouraged by such damp conditions. Rotate bean beds from year to year to thwart any overwintering diseases or pests. It may be necessary to guide the young vines of climbing varieties; they're easily distracted and will ramble everywhere if left to their own devices.

HARVEST

The bean plant's speedy, prolific growth may surprise the inexperienced gardener. A few days away from the bean patch and you return to find a mess of big, tough beans. Fresh snap beans should be picked often, ideally every other day. Climbing varieties offer the advantage of some of the harvest's being at eye level. I don't like to bend over the plants while picking bush varieties, so I leave sufficient room between rows to lounge comfortably on the mulch while hunting for beans amongst the foliage.

Shell beans are picked fresh when the pods are full, still green, and somewhat lumpy, with the beans firm but not dry. Beans to be dried for winter storage should be picked when the pods are papery dry and the seeds have fully matured to a firm, dense consistency. If it's rainy and damp at harvest time, hang the whole bean plant upside down in a dry, warm spot to fully dry. Remove all bean plant debris from the garden to avoid potential diseases and insects from overwintering. It can be composted if the heap is hot enough to kill harmful organisms (page 188).

BEETS

Beets provide a double harvest: nutritious greens and ruby roots. The earthy sweetness and brilliant color of the roots are unique among vegetables. Keith Barton, a good friend and passionate vegetable gardener, gave me seeds for Bull's Blood, an heirloom beet prized for its showy and delicious, large, purple-red leaves. Grow as a cold-tolerant fall crop for greens and baby beets, or add some of the seeds to a mesclun seed mix for a shot of lustrous color. Bull's Blood can take the summer heat, so it can be added to flower borders as a dark foil for lighter-foliaged plants. Detroit Dark Red is a reliable beet with deep red, sweet flesh. For good flavor and uniquely colored roots, try the beautiful heirloom Chioggia beets with their alternating interior rings of deep rose and creamy white. Golden beets, vibrant orange, make a dazzling borscht.

STARTING

Beet seeds can be sown 1 month before the last hard frost, when the soil is workable. Encourage germination by soaking the seeds in water for 12 hours prior to planting. Seedbeds should be worked about 8 inches deep, well spaded, and freed of clods and stones that cause misshapen roots. A soil pH between 6 and 7 will give the best results. For succession planting, sow seeds ½ inch deep in rows 12 to 18 inches apart every 2 weeks until midsummer.

CULTURAL REQUIREMENTS

Thin seedlings to 4 to 6 inches apart, using the thinnings as edible greens. Beets resent extreme heat and need ample water during hot, dry periods to prevent the development of woody, tough roots. In areas with very hot summers but relatively frost-free winters, grow beets as a fall and winter crop.

HARVEST

Beets are ready to harvest from 8 weeks on; the optimum sizes for tender, juicy roots are from 1 to 3 inches in diameter. Flavor will deteriorate if the roots remain in the ground after maturity. Store in a cool root cellar (35°F to 40°F) for the winter months. Cut off the greens, leaving a 1- to 2-inch stub of stems.

❧ CULINARY TIPS ❧

- ❧ Dismayed by the poor quality of winter tomatoes at Moosewood, we frequently use tender, shredded raw beets to garnish tossed salads.

- ❧ Young, tender beet leaves of 3 to 4 inches make a fine salad green.

- ❧ Cook unpeeled, scrubbed beets whole. When the roots are slightly cool, it's easy to slip off the skin and cut into the desired shape. This avoids messy peeling and bleeding of raw beets.

- ❧ For a perfectly pink Scandinavian salad, we mix cooked beets with new red potatoes and then toss with sour cream, mayonnaise, snipped dill, and chives. Serve on a bed of ruby lettuce.

- ❧ Joan Adler, our resident cooked-greens enthusiast, likes to serve steamed beet greens tossed with an Herb Butter (page 271) and topped with diced, cooked beet-root.

- ❧ Sauté beet greens with garlic and oil; toss with soy sauce and a few drops of rice vinegar.

- ❧ Try roasting whole baby beets alone or with new potatoes, pearl onions, and small globe carrots.

BROCCOLI

We can thank Italian immigrants to North America for this very nutritious vegetable, which was fairly uncommon here in the nineteenth century. Like other members of the brassica or cabbage family, broccoli is a nutritious cool-season crop. Here in the Northeast, typical summers are cool enough to plant broccoli from mid-spring until midsummer. Most seed houses carry a blended mix to help stagger the harvest with early-, mid-, and late-season varieties. This helps to avoid a glut of broccoli with all the plants forming heads at once. Small Miracle is a good choice for gardeners with limited space; they can be planted 8 inches apart and yield 6- to 8-inch heads. Romanesco types, heirlooms often listed with broccoli, are actually more related to cauliflower. This unique and strikingly ornamental vegetable has a mild flavor and a cone-shaped head of chartreuse florets spiraling in a pattern that can only be described as psychedelic. Romanesco plants need high fertility and grow large, taking up an area about 3 feet by 3 feet. Minaret (Cook's) is a Romanesco variety that is more compact. Broccoli seed sprouts have received a lot of attention for their healthful effects, reputed to be more concentrated than the mature vegetable. For these, always purchase seed strictly intended for sprouting; even organic seeds may not be graded for human consumption.

Broccoli raab (also called broccoli rabe and rapini), is a vegetable that asserts its presence with its full flavor and distinctive edge of bitterness. More closely related both botanically and in flavor to turnip greens, broccoli raab is a quick-to-harvest cooking green that is grown for its young flowering shoots. In areas where spring can quickly turn to summer, broccoli raab is better grown in the increasingly cooler weather of fall. As is true for its brassica family cousins, light frosts will mellow and sweeten broccoli raab's flavor.

STARTING

Broccoli seeds should be started indoors about 2 months before the last frost for spring planting. Seeds need warmth to germinate, ideally 65° to 75°F; however, seedlings can tolerate cooler weather and do best around 60°F. Transplant the 1- to 2-inch seedlings to individual pots or soil cells.

Place seedlings in the garden in fertile soil of pH 5.5 to 7.0, 3 to 4 weeks before the last expected frost. Space plants 18 inches apart in rows 30 inches apart. See pages 207 to 210 for protection from cabbage-family pests and diseases; though nasty and prevalent in certain regions, these are easy to control.

Broccoli plants eventually become quite large, at least 2 feet square. However, interplanting with a row of early spring greens, such as spinach, lettuce, or a dwarf snow pea, works well. Seed the greens down the middle of a double row of broccoli, 15 inches from each side. By the time the broccoli is nearing full size, the greens will have matured and can be pulled.

Midsummer or (in warmer climates) fall planting for fall or winter crops can be direct seeded or started indoors. Seeds can be sown directly in the garden, 1/2 inch deep, and thinned to stand as above. Seedlings are more tolerant of summer heat than are older plants, which could bolt (go to seed) without forming usable heads.

Broccoli raab is easier to germinate in cool soil than broccoli, so it can be direct seeded from early spring to late summer, $1/4$ to $1/2$ inch deep, in rows 12 to 18 inches apart. If flea beetles are prevalent, protect with a fabric row cover at planting time.

❧ CULINARY TIPS ❧

❧ Broccoli leaves and stems are frequently tossed into the compost. However, stems pared to remove the leathery peel and small leaves are as delicious as the familiar flower head.

❧ Cabbage worms are the offspring of white butterflies that lay their eggs on plant leaves. Broccoli harvested from unprotected plants (page 208) should be soaked in salt water before cooking to avoid the embarrassment of serving the well-camouflaged green worms. Soak the broccoli heads in well-salted water for 15 minutes. Dead worms will float to the top. Rinse the broccoli and prepare as usual.

❧ Broccoli is crisper if stir-fried or steamed. Boiled or blanched broccoli tends to hold moisture and be soggy.

❧ Slightly undercook broccoli, as it tends to continue cooking even when removed from the heat.

❧ Lemon juice and vinegar turn broccoli a drab olive color if allowed to sit for more than a few minutes. For marinated dishes, we reserve the lemon or other acidifying agent until right before serving.

❧ Cooked broccoli goes well with gomasio, a seasoning made of toasted sesame seeds ground with sea salt. This staple of macrobiotic cooking is available at natural food stores or Asian markets, or can be made fresh at home with a *suribachi* and *surikogi*—a Japanese mortar and pestle.

❧ Broccoli imparts a strong, unpleasant taste if cooked too long in slowly simmered soups or sauces. Add it toward the end of the cooking time.

❧ Broccoli raab is nicely paired with pasta, which mellows its assertiveness. Sauté the sprouted stems and leaves with garlic and olive oil until tender, then toss with drained pasta and Parmesan or Romano cheese. Add some roasted red pepper strips for color and contrasting sweetness. Alternatively, skip the pasta and serve the raab with some creamy white beans mashed with a little olive oil and lemon juice.

CULTURAL REQUIREMENTS

Broccoli and raab thrive in a cool, fertile, well-mulched and well-watered soil. The addition of limestone and/or wood ash helps to keep the soil alkaline and deters clubroot and root maggots. Crop rotation of cabbage family members (broccoli, brussels sprouts, cabbage, cauliflower, collards, kale, kohlrabi, mustard, turnips) is crucial to disease control; select a spot where none of the above has grown for 2 to 3 years.

Cabbage family members are heavy feeders that benefit from applications of compost or organic fertilizer two or three times during the growing season.

HARVEST

Broccoli heads should be harvested while buds are fully formed yet tight. After the central head is cut, plants will continue to send up smaller side sprouts for several weeks of extended harvest.ds.

Broccoli raab sprouted stems should be cut, including leaves, just before the buds open. For spring-planted raab, cut the entire plant before hot weather.

BRUSSELS SPROUTS

The first time I saw brussels sprouts growing, I was amazed at its odd growing habits. Mature plants look like exotic miniature trees with clusters of sprouts hugging a fat, stocky stem topped with big, umbrella-like leaves. Rows of the leafy, blue-green columns add architectural, visual interest to the garden and provide nutty, sweet sprouts from fall into winter. Oliver (Fedco, Johnny's) is an early-maturing variety that is adaptable to adverse conditions.

STARTING

Brussels sprouts require a long growing season of 90 to 110 days from seedling to harvest. Start seeds in June, indoors or out, and transplant in July to a permanent spot, 18 inches apart in rows 3 feet apart.

CULTURAL REQUIREMENTS

Brussels sprouts have the same needs as broccoli (page 22). Maximize space by interplanting early-maturing vegetables or herbs between rows of brussels sprouts.

HARVEST

Sprouts are ready when they're the size of Ping-Pong balls, about 1 inch in diameter. Pick the lowest sprouts and leaves first. Removing these will encourage the plant to grow new ones at the top. The flavor greatly improves after one or two light frosts. Plants can stand in the garden until temperatures stay below freezing, at which point you should remove the leaves and cut the sprout-filled stalks. Store in a cool place for 4 to 6 weeks.

✂ CULINARY TIPS ✂

- ✂ For faster cooking, cut an X in the bottoms of the biggest sprouts.
- ✂ Cut brussels sprouts in half for an unusual stir-fry addition.
- ✂ Cooked rounds of carrots, parsnips, or sweet potatoes will add sweetness and color to cooked brussels sprouts.
- ✂ Serve cooked sprouts topped with crisp bread crumbs that have been toasted in Herb Butter (page 271).
- ✂ Cheese sauce and brussels sprouts is a classic combination.

CABBAGE

Cabbage was a mainstay in the kitchen gardens of the past because of its excellent keeping qualities. I was initially hesitant about growing cabbages: could homegrown be so much better than store-bought and warrant the amount of space and growing time? Yes! Especially the early-maturing summer heirloom varieties like Early Jersey Wakefield, with its crisp, tender heads that are compact and shaped like upside-down ice cream cones, and sweet, juicy leaves that make the best salads and cole slaws. Small-headed varieties, with heads about 6 inches across, are useful if space is at a premium; they're cute and can be grown as close as 8 to 12 inches apart. Gonzales green (Johnny's, Territorial) and Red Express red (Johnny's) are two mini cabbages I particularly enjoy, because I'm usually cooking for one or two. Savoy cabbage makes attractive heads with blue-green, waved and crinkled leaves that are more tender than—and not as thick as—those of most green cabbage. Melissa (Fedco, Territorial) is my choice for both flavor and appearance. The big mature heads are beautiful when rain or dew beads on the ruffled leaves. Ruby Perfection (Fedco) is a red cabbage that has long-term storage potential and vivid, red-purple color, with flavor that sweetens in cold weather. The flamboyant, frilled-leaf heads of ornamental cabbage brighten the darkening days of late fall. Mature plants are very frost tolerant. Seed in the late spring.

STARTING AND CULTURAL REQUIREMENTS

Cabbage does best in a cool, moist growing season. Seed starting and cultural requirements are similar to those for broccoli (pages 23 to 25). Maintain moist soil conditions, especially in hot weather. The cabbage feeder roots grow close to the surface, so avoid weeding or digging deeply into the surrounding soil.

HARVEST

Harvest when heads are firm, solid, and the desired size, or before hard frosts. Heads left too long are more likely to split, especially if moisture has been uneven. Early-maturing cabbage is juicier than the later, storage types; however, they should be eaten soon after picking for best quality. My former neighbor Irene Brown taught me about the mini heads that emerge from the base of cut cabbage plants. If you don't need the garden space, allow these small "sprouts" to remain and grow 3 or 4 inches across. They are great for soups or cooking whole. Late-season varieties are best for storage in a cool, dry root cellar or pit. To hold mature cabbage heads in the garden during cool but not freezing weather for later harvest, twist the whole plant sharply—by breaking some of the roots, you stop the growth of the head. Cabbage tastes sweeter when harvested after a light frost.

❧ CULINARY TIPS ❧

❧ Use a stainless-steel knife for cutting red cabbage; an iron knife or cleaver will turn it a washed-out blue.

❧ For a sweet, mild flavor, steam or sauté cabbage over low to moderate heat. High heat breaks down sulfur components in the cabbage, resulting in a strong taste and smell.

❧ Sauté onions, apples, raisins, and cabbage in butter for a fall side dish.

❧ Use savoy cabbage for a light, mild flavor. The large, ruffled leaves make nifty beds for platters of salads or dips as well as snazzy wrappers for stuffed cabbage rolls.

❧ We make a light, tangy cole slaw with the young, tender vegetables of early summer: shredded cabbage, carrots, kohlrabi, and turnips, with Dill–Red Onion Vinaigrette (page 263). Red cabbage makes a lavender-pink cole slaw.

❧ L. D. (the dean of Moosewood cooks) has a simple, delicious family recipe for sweet-and-sour cabbage: Slow-cook cabbage and onions in butter until they are decidedly brown (not burnt). Toward the end of the cooking time, add sugar and vinegar to taste.

❧ Cooks in tropical locales of Latin America and Southeast Asia use cabbage for salads as it's more heat tolerant than lettuce. There's no need to limit cabbage to traditional cole slaws. Try shredded cabbage with your favorite dressing.

CARROTS

Freshly dug carrots are crisp, sweet, and juicy. Their ferny foliage softly edges a border or bed. This extremely versatile vegetable excels whether cooked, juiced, or eaten as is. They're high in potassium, fiber, vitamin C, and the antioxidant beta carotene. For best flavor and yield, look for varieties that are compatible with the planting season (spring or summer) and your soil type—blunt, short varieties are better for stony or clay soils. Like other root vegetables, carrots' flavor tends to be best when they mature in cool weather. Nelson, however, is a good variety for spring planting with harvest in warm weather at the baby stage or full size. It will do well where summer temperatures are moderate. Parmex (Cook's, Johnny's) is a small, rounded carrot we like to roast whole. Its size makes it ideal for gardens where the soil is not as deep nor friable as would be right for bigger carrots. Touchon (Cook's), a French heirloom of the Scarlet Nantes type, has done reliably well for me sown in spring and summer. Nantes types are among the best for sweet taste and smooth texture. With fine-grained flesh and practically no core, they can't be easily harvested by machine; growing your own gives you the chance to try something not often available commercially. Bolero (Johnny's, Territorial) is another Nantes type that stores exceptionally well and has good flavor. Gardeners in mild winter climates, or with a greenhouse, can try Napoli (Cook's, Johnny's), a variety of especially sweet carrots for fall sowing and winter harvest. Those for whom size is everything will note that Japanese Imperial Long (Seeds of Change) holds the record for giant roots, up to 3 feet in length in sandy soils. A new variety I'm interested in growing is Yellowstone (Fedco, Cook's, Territorial), a vibrant yellow carrot reputed to have good flavor and storage potential.

STARTING

Carrots are a bit more high maintenance than many of their vegetable colleagues. For all but the "baby" varieties, good soil preparation is essential. The ideal soil for carrots is a loose, deep, sandy loam with pH 5.5 to 6.5.

Enriching the soil with bonemeal, wood ash, and rock phosphate will increase available potassium and phosphorus to yield sweeter and more flavorful roots. Avoid manure that is not thoroughly aged and decomposed, as it will damage the roots. I also supplement with well-rotted compost and dig out as many rocks as I can. Many carrot varieties now come in pelleted seeds, much easier to see and plant, so fewer seedlings are wasted in the thinning process. Sow seeds 1/2 inch deep, 1 to 2 inches apart in rows 12 to 16 inches apart, or in a band 1 foot wide, in well-dug, stone-free soil. Seeds should be no more than 2 years old. To avoid soil compaction, do not work in wet, cool soil; plant in a raised bed or stand and kneel on a plank laid alongside the seedbed to distribute your weight. Clumped soil will lessen the yield of good-sized, straight carrots. Ensure a good supply by making successive plantings every 3 weeks until early August or until daily temperatures consistently exceed 88°F.

CULTURAL REQUIREMENTS

Carrots can take up to 3 weeks to germinate. Maintaining a consistently moist soil surface is critical, as well as avoiding crusting of the soil. Using a fine spray or mist with a hose or watering can is essential when there's no rain. In addition, try one of the following:

- Cover the seedbed with straw or moistened burlap. Straw can stay, but burlap should be removed as the carrots germinate.
- Sow radish seeds with the carrots. They germinate quickly, break up the soil surface, and keep a crust from forming. (This method has its drawbacks for those of us who don't care for radishes, but there's always the compost heap.)
- Germinate seeds before planting by placing them between two damp paper towels; store in a dark place until the tips of the first leaves just emerge from the seeds. Handle carefully and plant as above without breaking the tiny seedlings.
- For faster germination, wait until soil has warmed to at least 65°F. Many sources indicate early-spring planting for carrots, but in my experience the seeds just sit and wait for some warmth. The higher temperatures call for more attention to maintaining consistent soil moisture since heat will quickly dry the seedbed.

- Top the seedbed with a 1-inch-deep layer of sifted compost, vermiculite, or perlite that has been well soaked before seeding. These will hold moisture longer than sandy soils.

Mulching will keep weeds down and the moisture level high. Plants should be thinned to stand 2 inches apart. Although it's difficult, when it comes to thinning carrots, beginning gardeners must be ruthless. An overcrowded carrot bed will yield only disappointment.

HARVEST

Around the maturity date, pull up a carrot and check it. Carrots are mature when they're bright orange (pale carrots lack flavor) and the appropriate length for that variety. Harvest may continue for about 3 weeks after maturity; later, cracking and quality loss may occur. Containers filled with sand work well for winter storage. Cut the tops and store the roots in a cold, but not freezing, humid location. Stored carrots will not be as tasty as fresh ones. Late-maturing carrots grown in cold-winter areas can be mulched with a foot or so of dry straw to prevent them from freezing. Push aside the straw for midwinter harvests. Gardeners in snow country should mark the row with a sunflower stalk or some other tall marker.

❧ CULINARY TIPS ❧

- Carrots will retain more nutrients if they are scrubbed and not peeled. They will stay crisper longer if the green tops are removed immediately upon picking.

- Add grated carrots to cornbread, muffins, pancakes, and yeasted and quick breads for color, sweetness, and nutrition.

- We serve raw carrot salads as light accompaniments to rich dishes or as part of multifaceted combination plates.

- Add marsala wine to sautéed carrots for a fragrant glaze.

- Parboil carrots to be roasted or grilled to reduce cooking time.

- Carrots puréed in soups, stews, or sauces impart a golden hue and a hint of sweetness.

- Juiced carrots are very popular at the restaurant. One of the best healthful pick-me-ups, they're even tastier when accented with of one or more of the following juices: fresh ginger, parsley, orange, lemon, lime, celery, or beet.

CAULIFLOWER

Cauliflower grows best in cool weather, with ample rainfall or irrigation. Choose varieties that suit your growing season, with plants maturing in spring, late summer, or fall. Snow Crown is an all-season type that I've grown dependably in both summer and fall. Early Snowball is an heirloom with tasty white heads I like to grow as a fall crop. Purple-headed types, such as Violet Queen, add an unusual color as a raw vegetable for salads or dips but turn green when cooked. Johnny's Selected Seeds has the orange-headed variety, Citrus, as well as a deep purple one, Graffiti; both are distinctive because they hold their color when cooked.

STARTING AND CULTURAL REQUIREMENTS

Seed starting and cultural requirements are the same as for broccoli (page 23). For large, standard-sized heads of 7 to 10 inches across, individual plants should be spaced 18 inches apart in rows 2 to 3 feet apart, yielding one head per plant. Gardeners with limited space could opt for smaller heads of 3½ to 5 inches across by spacing plants 8 to 12 inches apart each way. Heads exposed to sunlight and heat will turn somewhat yellow unless protected by a technique called blanching: Simply tie the plant's large outer leaves over the newly emerging white head. (Purple varieties do not require blanching.) Bear in mind, though, that a "wrapped" head makes a cozy hideout for pests, so carefully open and check the growing heads periodically.

HARVEST

Harvest while the head is crisp and compact, before it opens up and becomes "ricey." Although cauliflower is similar in culture to broccoli, it doesn't develop side shoots when the head is cut. Pull out harvested plants.

❦ At Moosewood, we frequently include cauliflower in our marinated vegetable salads. Use lemon juice or a clear vinegar as the acidifying element. Steamed until tender but crisp, cauliflower holds its shape, doesn't discolor, and absorbs the marinade.

❦ Roseanne Trapani, a friend who is an excellent Italian cook, introduced me to a favorite side dish: steamed florets dipped in beaten egg, then in herbed bread crumbs, drizzled with oil or garlic butter, then baked on a baking sheet at 350°F until golden.

❦ Cauliflower curries are a regular feature of Moosewood menus. The florets absorb the seasoning and hold up well in slow cooking.

❦ A mixture of caraway seeds and chopped fresh dill with yogurt or sour cream gives steamed cauliflower a Scandinavian flavor.

❦ Vary a standard cheese sauce for cauliflower by adding chopped shallots, tarragon, and parsley.

❦ Serve composed platters of alternating florets of cauliflower, purple cauliflower, and broccoli, stems cut at varying lengths and assembled, floret side up, to form a dome.

❦ Susan Harville is a Moosewood author with a special interest in Italian cuisine. Pasta with cauliflower is one of her at-home favorites. Put up a big (1 gallon or more) pot of water to cook pasta. Choose a bite-sized shape, such as ziti or shells, and cut the cauliflower into pieces of similar size. Cut garlic cloves into pieces big enough to scoop out with a slotted spoon. Sauté the garlic in olive oil, remove when just golden, and reserve. Start to sauté the cauliflower in the seasoned oil when the pasta goes into the pot. Spoon on a little of the hot pasta water to help steam the cauliflower. Toss the drained pasta with the cauliflower and reserved garlic, top with freshly grated Parmesan cheese, and serve.

COLLARDS AND KALE

When we say "Eat your greens," this is the stuff we're talking about. High in vitamins A, B, C, and E as well as iron, calcium, potassium, phosphorus, and magnesium, this duo is a powerhouse of nutrition. They're a good source of calcium for people avoiding dairy products. Kale and collards are at their sweetest and tastiest in cool weather, especially after the first light frosts.

Collards and kale are related closely enough to be grouped together. Both will survive subfreezing temperatures with renewed growth in the spring, when the plants soon flower and go to seed. In my Zone 5 garden, their winter survival seems to depend upon adequate snow cover to protect the plants from temperatures of 0°F and below.

Collards resemble a nonheading cabbage, but with a slightly different flavor. They are a popular winter green in the South. Although not as showy as kale, collard plants with large green or blue-green wavy leaves have an architectural presence, growing up to 3 feet tall. Collards withstand dry and hot summers better than kale. Champion bears sweet, dark green leaves over a long season.

Kale is not only a healthful vegetable but also a desirable ornamental, with its wavy, curly, crinkly, or smooth foliage. Different varieties offer a palette of colors—greens ranging from pastel to dark, blue-green, purple, and red. Red Russian is an heirloom variety with purple-red veins and stems and flat, green-gray leaves. It is hands down my favorite because, unlike other kales, its young leaves are tender and not bitter in the warmth of summer. Redbor is an exciting, showy kale, an upright plant with tightly curled, deep purple, almost magenta leaves. I've used Redbor as the centerpiece in a large container with herbs and edible flowers. Add Red Russian and Redbor seeds to custom mesclun mixes (page 76); the young leaves contribute color and mild flavor. Winterbor is a particularly hardy, vigorous ruffled-leaf kale good for fall and winter harvests. Lacinato or Dinosaur kale is an heirloom Italian variety with long, narrow, heavily quilted, deep green leaves. The nickname comes from its ability to add a "Jurassic Park" quality to gardens. I've interplanted it with flowers where its almost black leaves make a great visual foil for bright colors.

STARTING AND CULTURAL REQUIREMENTS

Both collard and kale seeds should be sown at least 3 months before the first frost, in soil of pH 6.0 to 6.8, $1/2$ inch deep, in rows 20 to 30 inches apart. For an early crop, I start Red Russian Kale indoors 1 month before the soil is ready to plant. Thin kale plants to 12 inches apart, collards to 24 inches. Both can be grown all winter in mild climates. Cultural requirements are the same as for broccoli (page 23).

HARVEST

Harvest the young leaves of both collards and kale without disturbing the uppermost point of new growth. The very hardy plants can be picked when there's snow on the ground but before temperatures are consistently below freezing.

❧ CULINARY TIPS ❧

❧ Add shredded or chopped greens to soups, stews, or stir-fries for additional heartiness, flavor, and nutrition.

❧ Stir-fry greens with garlic and olive oil, Mediterranean-style, or with ginger and a splash of soy sauce, Asian-style, for a quick and savory side dish.

❧ Add sautéed greens to pasta, pizza, mashed potatoes, or rice. Season with an Herb Butter (page 271).

❧ Sara Robbins, a Moosewood cook with an extended family in the South, makes tasty greens using well-washed collards with the tough stems and leaf spines removed. Coarsely chop the leaves and simmer in water to cover until tender. Drain. Toss with butter, salt, black pepper, vinegar, and Tabasco or other hot pepper sauce. The piquant flavor of this dish is a good complement to rich foods.

CORN

The unsurpassable quality of home-grown sweet corn makes it one of the most popular garden vegetables. But gardeners with limited space may well decide not to plant corn. It's unlike other vegetables in that you can't raise just a few corn plants: pollination requirements for good yields demand sowing seeds in blocks of at least 4 feet by 6 feet. If you have access to farmers' markets or roadside stands, there is good news in that newer corn varieties hold their sweetness fairly well after picking.

Though seed catalogs list a staggering number of varieties, there are just three basic types of sweet corn: normal, sugar enhanced, and supersweet or extrasweet. Genetic differences determine each variety's sweetness and tenderness and the rate at which sugar is converted to starch following picking.

Normal sweet corn quickly converts to starch after picking. Isolation from other varieties of corn is not necessary. Golden Bantam, premiered in 1902, remains an open-pollinated yellow corn prized for its sweet-corn flavor. The gardener must be vigilant at harvest time, because open-pollinated corns become tough and lose flavor more quickly at maturity than hybrids. Silver Queen is a time-tested, late-maturing white corn variety of superb tenderness and flavor.

Sugar enhanced (se) and Everlasting Heritage (EH) gene varieties have increased sugar and tenderness. Isolation from other varieties of corn is not necessary. Sugar Buns is my favorite early corn of this type. It's sweet, with a good "corny" flavor that some of the sugar-enhanced varieties lack. Bodacious, maturing a bit later, is equally good.

Supersweet or extrasweet corn has a "shrunken" (SH 2) gene named for the shriveled appearance of the dried kernel. This corn has the highest sweetness —about twice the sugar content of the older varieties—and the slowest conversion of sugar to starch. Northern Xtra-Sweet (Johnny's) is an early corn that tolerates cooler conditions better than other supersweets. Kandy-Plus

(Cook's, Fedco) is my favorite choice for a main-season corn. With good-sized ears on healthy plants and balanced sweetness and corn flavor, this one defines summer.

As delectable as the supersweets are, they have special requirements:

- Plantings must be separated by at least 25 feet from non-supersweet corns to avoid cross-pollination. Alternatively, stagger planting dates to ensure a minimum 12-day difference in projected maturity.
- Soil temperature should be quite warm—ideally 75°F, but no less than 60°F.
- The "shrunken" seeds need more moisture for germination than do other types.

When choosing a corn variety, check with other gardeners or a county cooperative extension agent to find the best variety for your location. Where springs are cool, choose early varieties that are bred for higher germination in cooler soils. Northern gardeners should look for short-season varieties that will mature before the first frosts. Gardeners in climates with long, hot summers can grow just about any corn from the dozens offered in catalogs.

Seeds of Change (page 286) in New Mexico is a good source of traditional corn varieties from the Americas. If I had the space and a longer, hotter growing season, I'd be curious to try some of their multicolored corns grown for flour, meal, or ornament. Hopi Pink or Hopi Purple Flour, Mandan Red Flour, and Oaxacan Green Dent are all a treat to cook with. They achieve their best color when they are fully mature and the husks are dry and crackly. Ears can be left to dry on the stalk, even after several frosts. Or, after the husks have begun to dry, move the husked ears to a dry, warm location to complete the process.

STARTING

Corn seeds will rot or germinate poorly in cold, wet soil. Because I garden organically, I don't use seeds treated with fungicides to allow for earlier planting. However, I have several techniques to enable earlier corn planting that I'll use depending on the kind of spring we have; all are worth trying. Apply all three if it was a very cool spring and you want a crop sooner than later. Note, too, that the second and third steps are not sequential; you might mulch about the same time as starting seeds.

First, if the garden is mulched over the winter, pull back the hay or mulch to allow the soil to warm.

Second, a covering of black or IRT plastic mulch (page 201) will prewarm the soil. Cover the seedbed 2 weeks before planting; then either remove the plastic or cut slits in rows where the seeds are to be sown or the seedlings planted.

Third, to get a head start in colder climates, sow seeds indoors in a seedling flat composed of cells no smaller than 2 inches in diameter. Keep in a warm, well-lit spot until seedlings are 2 to 3 inches tall and the weather is settled and frost free. Plant hardened-off seedlings as directed below.

Outdoors, plant corn seed in rich, fertile soil of pH 6.0 to 7.0, 1 inch deep (1$^1/_2$ inches in very hot weather), 4 inches apart, in rows 30 inches apart. Thin seedlings to eventually stand 6 to 10 inches apart. To ensure pollination, three or four parallel rows must be planted simultaneously. In the small garden, plant rows that are just 3 to 4 feet long. Corn can also be grown in a minimum of four hills, 2 feet apart, to make a square. Sow six seeds per hill, thinned to the three strongest seedlings. Corn plants have deep, extensive roots that require generous space.

All plant growth slows during the shorter days of late summer. Schedule midsummer plantings to provide extra days. For example, in an area with an expected first frost of October 15, plant an 80-day variety no later than July 5, allowing 20 extra days for 100 days total.

❧ CULINARY TIPS ❧

- ❧ Try roasting corn for a different, nutty flavor. Pull off the outer husk but leave the inner leaves, and bake at 375°F for 15 minutes.

- ❧ To grill ears of corn, leave the inner husks on and soak in water for $^1/_2$ hour. Drain and grill over a low fire for about 1o minutes, occasionally rolling the ears about for even cooking.

- ❧ Add corn kernels to omelets, cornbread, muffins, waffles, and pancakes for flavor, color, and texture.

- ❧ Make simple corn fritters with 2 cups of corn kernels sliced off the cob, 2 beaten egg whites, $^1/_4$ cup cracker or matzoh meal, $^1/_4$ cup milk, and a pinch of salt. Drop onto a lightly oiled, hot skillet, turning once. Serve with maple syrup.

- ❧ Butter is always great with ears of corn, but try them Southwestern style with a spicy mayo seasoned with lime juice and a few shakes of hot sauce, or with just a squeeze of lime and a sprinkle of cayenne.

- ❧ Baby corn (the small secondary ears) is a nice addition to stir-fries, or it can be quickly steamed as a side dish or added to Asian noodle or rice salads.

CULTURAL REQUIREMENTS

The rapid, lush growth of a towering corn plant requires ample moisture and fertile soil. Shallow cultivation is necessary to avoid damaging surface roots. When the weather turns hot and soils begin to dry, apply mulch to maintain moisture and choke weeds. Suckers, the side growth at the base of plants, do no harm and need not be removed from corn plants. In windy locations, you can prevent toppling by hilling up 2 to 3 inches of soil at the plant base.

Native Americans traditionally planted corn, squash, and beans together. Beans and squash are good companions for corn because they shade out weeds if their vines are encouraged to run in the corn rows. This is only an effective technique where the beans and squash can be planted later than the corn and with adequate spacing. If planted at the same time or earlier, the vigorous bean and squash vines can smother the young corn seedlings.

To aid pollination for small plantings, clip off the pollen-bearing tassels atop each plant and shake them over or lay them across the corn silks. (This will also relieve old frustrations for those who were never chosen to be on the cheerleading squad.)

Sweet corn is apparently at the top of the list of raccoons' favorite foods. If they're in your area, they'll find the corn, maybe just as it's ready to pick. If a dog that'll spend the night out near the garden isn't an option, try an electric fence. Install two to three strands at 4-inch intervals starting at ground level. Remember to turn it off when people are around.

HARVEST

Harvest corn when the silks are brown and dry and the kernels are full. Peeking is okay but should be limited since loose husks invite pests and birds. Regular varieties of sweet corn should be picked while the cooking water is boiling. Supersweets will keep their flavor and sweetness refrigerated for up to 10 days. Some of these varieties are actually sweeter 24 hours after picking than at harvest.

Healthy corn plants will produce a second or even third ear, lower on the stalk than the first one. For Asian-style "baby" corn, harvest these smaller secondary ears just as the silks emerge.

Cornstalks should be removed and shredded or composted after harvest to discourage disease and pest tenancy.

CUCUMBERS

Cucumbers add a refreshing, cooling note to salads and chilled soups. Sweet, firm, and crisp, with an edible, unwaxed peel, garden-grown cukes are far superior to supermarket fare. They are also remarkably easy to grow and quite prolific. The four basic cucumber types are slicing, pickling, burpless, and mideastern. Look for disease-resistant varieties.

American slicing cucumbers grow on 4- to 6-foot-long vines and are best used fresh. Spacemaster is a dwarf variety, suitable for containers and small gardens, with vines that have a 2- to 3-foot spread. Marketmore 76 (Johnny's, Fedco) has been successful for me, with sweet fruit and vigorous, healthy vines. The lemon cucumber is a favorite heirloom variety from the 1890s, not often seen in markets. The round, thin-skinned, 3-inch fruits are exceptionally mild, sweet, and good for snacking. As the name suggests, these cukes are ready when they turn from green to lemon yellow.

Pickling cucumbers are specifically bred to make crisp, flavorful pickles. Pick the cukes while small, no longer than 4 to 5 inches. French cornichon types should be picked when 1½ to 2 inches long. Homemade Pickles (Cook's, Territorial) makes great dill pickles when picked at 5 inches long.

Burpless varieties, with ancestry in Asia, produce thin-skinned, sweet cukes that are slow to mature and develop seeds. Try them if you've had trouble digesting cukes. The larger fruit can be up to 15 inches long. For a classic Chinese variety that is crisp and sweet with almost no seeds, try Suyo Long (Johnny's, Fedco).

Mideastern (Beit Alpha) varieties are particularly juicy, thin-skinned, and nonbitter cucumbers. Pick when 4 to 5 inches long, before seeds have hardened. Amira (Cook's, Fedco, Territorial) is a refreshing, delicious cuke of this type that is not generally available commercially because it doesn't ship well.

- A remedy for bitter cucumbers is to cut off the stem end and peel the cucumbers, including a thin layer of the white flesh just beneath the skin.

- Stuff seeded cucumbers with an Herbed Cheese Spread (page 276).

- We like to serve cucumber salads as a refreshing counterpoint to hot, spicy dishes. Toss cucumber slices with one of the Vinaigrette Dressings (page 262).

- Chilled potato or tomato soups get a refreshing lift from puréed or diced cucumber.

- Toss linguini or thin Asian noodles with sesame or peanut butter dissolved in warm water and combined with minced garlic, chopped fresh cilantro, scallions, mild vinegar, hot chiles, diced cucumbers, and soy sauce.

- To keep the crispness of cucumber slices that will be dressed with a marinade or dressing, generously salt the cucumber slices, place them in a colander, and weight with enough pressure to squeeze out excess juice for about 15 minutes. Rinse and drain the slices before proceeding with the recipe. This will also remove any bitterness.

STARTING

In short-season areas, start cucumber seeds indoors one month before the last possible frost date or when garden soil temperatures are consistently 65°F or higher. Seedlings resent transplanting, so start seeds in peat pots or soil cells. Use dark plastic mulches (page 201) to increase soil warmth.

Outdoors, sow seeds or plant seedlings in rich soil of pH 5.5 to 7.0 in rows with plants 12 inches apart, or in hills 4 feet apart with three plants per hill. Train vines to grow up a trellis or fence; this will conserve garden space, hasten ripening, and in particular prevent fruit rot. Rows that run from east to west will get the most available sunshine for quick growth and ripening.

CULTURAL REQUIREMENTS

Young seedlings are very frost tender. Hot caps or plastic jugs with the bottom removed make good covers for early spring or cold nights. Young seedlings can be protected from cucumber beetles with a floating row cover, which must be removed as the plants climb a fence or trellis and to allow for pollination.

With a water content of 95 percent, cucumbers require consistent watering during dry periods.

HARVEST

Harvest cucumbers often: like their cousin zucchini, they grow at an amazing rate, especially in the heat of summer. Pick cukes when they are no larger than the size indicated for that variety. All are at their best when the seeds haven't fully developed and the skin is uniformly green (except lemon types) without pale or yellow patches. At season's end, remove the vines to prevent them from harboring diseases and pests.

EGGPLANT

The eggplant is a decidedly ornamental vegetable, with its shiny, pendant fruit and star-shaped, lavender leaves. Plant them along garden paths where they can be appreciated up close, or tuck a few plants into sunny flower beds. Eggplant is a warm-weather grower; most varieties won't set fruit with temperatures under 70°F.

The most familiar types are the Mediterranean eggplants, cylindrical with fat bottoms. Rosa Bianca (Fedco, Seeds of Change) is an Italian heirloom we treasure during the short time it's available here in Ithaca. The white fruit are streaked with lavender, and the flesh is very mild, with an unusually creamy texture when cooked. Violetto di Firenze (Cook's), another heirloom, is a lustrous lavender striped with cream. Imperial Black Beauty is the classic deep purple eggplant for growing where summers stay warm. This heirloom's fruits can be up to 3 pounds each.

Asian varieties, smaller and more slender, are worth growing in short-season areas because they set fruit in cooler weather and mature early. I've had good results with Orient Express (Johnny's). Pingtung Long (Cook's, Fedco) is a Taiwanese heirloom reputed to be early, vigorous, and prolific.

- ❧ Presalting eggplant before cooking is a common technique to remove bitter juices. Ripe eggplant from the garden should not need this treatment. Exceptions include dishes for which a dry eggplant is desired, such as breaded, fried slices for eggplant parmigiana. Lightly salt slices and place in a colander, with some plates or other weight on top to express juices. Allow to drain for about 1 hour. Rinse, pat dry, and proceed with your recipe.

- ❧ Eggplant is one of the few vegetables that we prefer to slightly overcook. Crunchy eggplant ranks with raw potatoes for unappetizing texture and taste.

- ❧ Skinning eggplant will yield a more delicate flavor and texture, but it's an optional step in most recipes. When the eggplant will be pureed, as in baba ganouj, remove the skin.

- ❧ Marinate strips of steamed or baked eggplant in one of the Vinaigrette Dressings (page 262).

- ❧ We could bake and stuff eggplant with a different filling every day of the week. Place eggplant halves cut side down on an oiled baking tray, cover with aluminum foil, and bake in a 350°F oven until the flesh is tender—about 45 minutes for a full-sized eggplant. Turn the halves over and mash the flesh a bit with the tines of a fork. Pile filling on top. Bake again to heat through. Here are a few filling possibilities:

  - Couscous, pine nuts, currants, scallions, mint, and parsley
  - Sautéed mushrooms, bread crumbs, tarragon, and Dijon mustard
  - Bulgur, tomatoes, bell and chile peppers, cilantro, and olives
  - Sautéed tofu, rice, shiitake, soy sauce, ginger, and garlic
  - One of the Herbed Cheese Spreads (page 276) and rice
  - Sautéed chopped fennel bulb and basil, croutons, and Parmesan cheese

- ❧ Mix puréed roasted eggplant (page 231) with lemon juice, tahini, and minced garlic to make baba ganouj, a dip for pita bread and veggie sticks.

STARTING

Eggplant seeds germinate best in soil temperatures between 80°F and 90°F. If necessary, sow seeds indoors 8 to 10 weeks before planting, using heating cables, mats, or lamps for consistent warmth. After germination, 70°F soil temperatures will suffice. Transplant to the garden when nights are consistently above 50°F, in soil of pH 6.0 to 7.0, 24 inches apart, in rows 30 inches apart. Grow eggplants where other night-shade-family plants (tomatoes, potatoes, peppers) have not grown for 2 years.

CULTURAL REQUIREMENTS

Plastic mulches (page 207) and heat-retaining fabric row covers help extend the warm conditions in which eggplant thrives. Young plants are quite the magnet for flea beetles if they're in your area. Fabric row covers will help with that too, but remember to periodically remove them in the daytime so that pollination can occur.

HARVEST

Pick eggplants as soon as they're ripe; they'll be glossy and full. A dull finish indicates overripe eggplants of inferior flavor and quality. Use a sharp knife to cut the fruit from the brittle, easily damaged stems.

FENNEL

Fennel, also known as Florence fennel or *finnochio*, is another vegetable introduced to North American markets by Italian immigrants. Its popularity has broadened recently with an increased appreciation of Italian cooking. Feathery, divided foliage tops celery-like stems that widen at the base to form a bulb. The bulb has a sweet anise or licorice flavor with a background taste of celery. Some markets sell it as anise, which is actually a different species. I enjoy using fennel in all manner of savory dishes with Mediterranean leanings, for its subtle but unusual flavor and delicate sweetness. Zefa Fino is the most widely available variety. Make sure the seeds you buy are for bulbing or Florence fennel and not for the herb *Foeniculum vulgare*, also known as fennel (page 117). The herb yields feathery fronds of foliage but no edible bulb.

STARTING

Sow seeds in late spring (for cooler climates) or late summer to early winter (for warmer climates), allowing 3 growing months before harvest. Seedlings can take light frosts. Plant seeds in rich soil, 1/2 inch deep, in rows 18 inches apart. Thin plants to 8 inches apart. Transplants must be started in peat pots or soil cells to avoid disturbing the roots, which will cause plants to bolt to seed.

CULTURAL REQUIREMENTS

Fennel does best in moderate temperatures and quickly bolts to seed in hot, dry weather. Keep plants well watered during dry spells. When the stalks are a foot tall, blanch the stems by hilling up the soil around the base. This will result in a more tender vegetable.

HARVEST

Bulbs are ready for harvest when they're 2 to 3 inches in diameter. The fibrous, tough stalks can be discarded or used to flavor soup stocks. We like to use the tender foliage sprigs as a garnish.

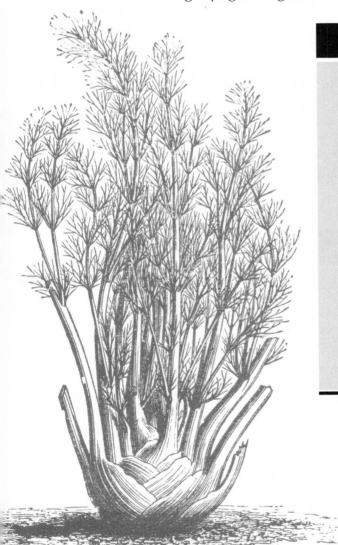

CULINARY TIPS

- Thinly sliced raw fennel bulb is a classic ingredient of antipasto platters. Include in tossed salads for an unusual touch.

- Combine thin slices of fennel and orange sections with a few drops of lemon juice and chopped mint and lemon balm leaves for a refreshing salad.

- Blanch fennel halves for 5 minutes in water or stock, drain, top with Parmesan and mozzarella cheeses and chopped oregano or marjoram, then broil.

- Add fennel to soups, sauces, stews, and roasted and marinated vegetables for a light anise flavor.

- Wedges or thick slices of fennel are delicious grilled.

KOHLRABI

An odd-looking member of the cabbage family, kohlrabi looks like a leafy turnip growing above ground. Its nutty-sweet flavor and crisp apple–like texture make this unfamiliar, underappreciated vegetable well worth growing. The flavor is best when grown in the cooler seasons of spring, late summer, fall, and winter.

Early White Vienna is an excellent heirloom variety, the ancestor of many modern hybrids. Gigante is an unusual kohlrabi that can achieve a diameter of 8 to 10 inches, compared to the typical 2 to 3 inches. It takes about twice as long to put on the added girth: roughly 130 days compared with 60 for Early White Vienna.

STARTING

For summer harvest, sow seeds in early to late spring in soil of pH 6.0 to 7.5, $1/2$ inch deep, in rows 18 inches apart. Thin plants to stand 4 to 6 inches apart. Sow again in mid- to late summer for fall harvest. In warm-winter areas, sow in late fall for winter harvests.

CULTURAL REQUIREMENTS

Kohlrabi is a cool-weather crop; its culture is the same as for broccoli (page 23).

❧ CULINARY TIPS ❧

❧ Peeled and grated kohlrabi is a crunchy, sweet addition to leafy and raw vegetable salads. Mix with grated carrots, apples, or beets and dress with a Vinaigrette Dressing (page 262) or Herbed Mayonnaise (page 266).

❧ Thin kohlrabi slices make an excellent crudité with other vegetables for dips.

❧ For a simple side dish, steam slices and top with butter and chives or dill.

HARVEST

Kohlrabi "bulbs" (which are actually thickened stems) are ready for harvest when 2 to 3 inches in diameter. Thicker stems will be tough and fibrous. An exception is the previously mentioned Gigante, which will generously serve a large gathering of kohlrabi fanciers. With all kohlrabi, cut the plants instead of pulling, to spare neighboring roots.

LEEKS

Leeks are the gentlest and sweetest members of the onion family. Their subtle flavor harmonizes with and creates good background for more dominant notes. Long popular in Europe, leeks command high prices in U.S. markets and are still considered a specialty vegetable. They're not difficult to grow but require some special attention noted below. The 2- to 3-foot-tall plants have blue-green, straplike foliage that contrasts nicely with the rounder, softer foliage forms of lettuce, cabbage, and other vegetables and herbs. Leeks vary in their speed to maturity and hardiness. Generally, those noted as summer or early leeks are quicker to mature and less hardy than later leeks that can overwinter. Lincoln (Fedco, Johnny's) is a reliable early leek that is ready in the hot days of August here in Ithaca. I like to use them with newly dug potatoes to make Vichyssoise. Blue Solaise (Cook's) is my first choice for a hardy leek. The deep blue-green leaves on husky plants get streaked with violet as the cold weather deepens.

STARTING

In cold-weather areas, start leek seeds indoors from February to March, sowing seeds ¼ inch deep in flats. Seeds can be sown outdoors in early spring, in soil of pH 6.0 to 8.0, in rows 18 inches apart; however, germination can be slow and uneven.

CULTURAL REQUIREMENTS

Leeks are more tender if the stems are blanched, or protected from direct sunlight. This can be accomplished in a number of ways:

- Sow seeds or plant transplants in a trench 6 inches wide by 6 inches deep. As the plants grow, gradually replace the soil that was removed.

- Plant seedlings 2 inches lower than they were grown in the seed flat. Bank the stems with compost, well-rotted manure, or hay. Continue throughout the growing season.
- Plant seedlings in 6-inch-deep holes, burying all but 1 to 2 inches of green leaf. Don't firmly tamp the soil around the plants, but allow it to fill in by the action of rain or irrigation.

Regardless of which blanching method you use, the stalks should eventually be banked with 10 inches of soil (measured from the root zone up).

Mulching leeks keeps the soil evenly moist and weed-free. Provide consistent irrigation or watering during dry periods.

HARVEST

Leeks can be harvested at any time. The whites and the greens of young leeks can be used like scallions. More mature plants, however, have tough, leathery outer leaves, so only the white blanched stem and tender inner greens are eaten.

Early leeks should be harvested before temperatures plunge to the mid-20s Fahrenheit. Hardier leeks can be harvested into freezing weather and overwintered if protected or grown in mild winter climates. Be sure to harvest them all before warmer weather returns in the spring; otherwise, a tough, fibrous flower stalk will develop in the center of the leek. When desired, leave a few to flower. Like those of other Allium family members, the leek's ornamental blooms are elegant globes of tiny florets. When temperatures consistently remain below freezing, harvest leeks and store refrigerated or in a cool cellar. You can also cover the row with about a foot of hay or straw to prevent the ground from freezing hard. Mark the row with an old cornstalk or sunflower stem, or you might find

- It's important to rinse leeks carefully, as soil and grit tend to lodge in the multilayered stem. Cut off the roots and tough leaves, slice the leeks in half lengthwise, then rinse, allowing the water to run through the stem layers.

- Use leeks when you want a flavor more delicate than bulb onions: in soups, omelets, sauces, fillings, stews, and marinated salads; roasted; or as a side dish.

- Avoid using the green parts of leeks in puréed dishes, such as tomato soup, because the green will contribute to a muddied color. All of the green leaves, including the tough ones, are suitable for making vegetable stock.

- Leeks are particularly good in puréed soups and cream sauces. As they cook and soften, they "melt" to a smooth texture.

- At Moosewood, we serve the first "baby" leeks of the season whole, about pencil size, steamed and marinated, tied in bundles using a long, green outer leaf as a "ribbon."

yourself traipsing around through snowdrifts trying to find your leeks. On a frigid, scentless winter day, it's a real treat to shovel away the snow, pick up the hay, and smell and feel the earth once again as you harvest leeks.

LETTUCE

Lettuce is the centerpiece of salads at Moosewood. Our salads are celebrations of taste, texture, and visual appeal. Really gorgeous salads can be made with leaves that are wavy, toothed, curly, frilled, or flat and with colors that range from bright lime to dark green, light to deep ruby reds, and rich bronze.

Home gardeners can choose delicate varieties that aren't available in markets because they don't ship well. With seed companies offering so many choices for lettuce, you can choose varieties that are both beautiful and tasty. Lettuce is an easy crop to grow as long as the soil is kept moist and seeds are chosen to suit your climate and season. The ideal weather for lettuce growing is with daytime temperatures below 80°F, nighttimes 40°F minimum. Out of the dozens of lettuces I've tried, the following are all favorites, grouped by category:

Batavian or Crisphead lettuces start life looking like a looseleaf but mature to a fairly dense head. Leaves are crisp like traditional iceberg, but the variety of shapes and colors is more interesting. I've found Batavians to be more heat tolerant than other types of lettuce. Anuenue (Fedco, Johnny's) is my current favorite for a heading summer lettuce. Developed in Hawaii, the leaves are a nice bright green with crisp texture. Sierra (Fedco) has red-tinged leaves that stay sweet in midsummer when other lettuces have become bitter. Reine des Glaces, also known as Ice Queen, has toothed leaves that form a nifty spiral head; it is a bit less tolerant of warm weather than the previous two, but fun to grow for its beautiful appearance.

Butterhead, Bibb, or Boston—the soft, delicate heads of butter lettuces add a nice contrast to salads composed of crunchier leaves or vegetables. Market butterheads seem to easily bruise in transit, a good reason to grow your own. Pirat (Fedco, Seeds of Change) combines the good looks of red-tinged leaves with classic buttery taste and texture to top my list. Other choices: Buttercrunch for heat tolerance, Blushed Butter Oaks (Fedco, Territorial) for its tender, pink and green, oak-like leaves, and Winter Marvel (Cook's, Fedco) for its hardiness in late fall and early winter.

Looseleaf lettuces offer ease in growing and the biggest selection of shape and color, making them essential for a salad greens garden. The plants form more of a loose bunch than a head. I've tried quite a few red leaf lettuces, but Merlot (Fedco) is the deepest burgundy. It works particularly well in custom mixes for cutting lettuces (see below), as well as grown to maturity. Oak leaf types like Red Oak Leaf (Johnny's, Seeds of Change) and Royal Oak Leaf (Cook's) offer interesting leaf shapes for pretty salads, as does Lollo Rossa with its frenetically frizzled, dark red leaves.

Romaine or Cos lettuces are upright plants with crisp leaves and blanched hearts. Romaine is the classic Caesar salad lettuce. Forellenschluss, also known as Freckles, is an Austrian heirloom

I've been enjoying for its cranberry red–speckled leaves and tender texture as well as its good heat tolerance. Little Gem (Cook's, Territorial) has small heads good for sandwiches and allows for closer spacing in the garden. Blushed Butter Cos (Territorial) has attractively savoyed leaves of reds and greens, with good hardiness for early or late planting.

See also "salad greens" on page 72.

STARTING

I really enjoy the first garden salads of the year, so I start my lettuce seeds indoors about 3 to 4 weeks ahead of when I expect to plant outdoors. If, like me, you live in an area where spring can be wet, cold, or late in arriving, this is a good way to relieve early spring restlessness. In general, seeds can be sown outdoors as soon as the ground can be worked, in soil of pH 6.0 to 7.0, $^1/_4$ to $^1/_2$ inch deep (deeper in warmer weather), in rows 18 inches apart. Curb your enthusiasm and resist planting too much, unless you're feeding a big crowd or want to give lettuce to all your friends and neighbors. Tender young thinnings can go into salads. Baby lettuces can be grown in a cut-and-come-again fashion for a long season of harvest. Plant the seeds in a 1-foot-wide band, 3 to 4 feet long. Harvest leaves by cutting them about 1 inch from the ground when they're 4 to 6 inches tall. Plants in good soil with adequate watering should yield two or three cuttings. Looseleaf varieties such as Red or Royal Oak leaf, Merlot, and Lollo Rossa are best for cutting, but I've had success with all other lettuce types as well.

Seeds can be sown throughout the cooler growing season, but lettuce doesn't germinate well in temperatures above 80°F. Lettuces quickly reach maturity in the first warmth of spring. For midsummer plantings, heat-resistant varieties can be sown in small peat pots or soil cells in a cooler, shaded area. Transplant seedlings on a cloudy, calm day and water generously.

Sow seeds for fall-winter types about a month before the first frost or, in hot climates, when cool fall weather arrives. Cover the small plants with a floating row cover before hard freezes. Surprisingly, I have grown lettuce in my Zone 5 garden through an erratic winter with little or no insulating snow cover and no more protection than a fabric row cover. In cold-weather areas, this technique should be tried only with varieties adapted to short-day growing, such as Winter Density, Rouge d'Hiver, or Winter Marvel (Cook's for all three).

Plastic tunnels (page 203) are good season extenders for lettuce crops early in the spring or late in the fall.

✄ Wash whole lettuce leaves in a large pot or basin filled with cool water. Allow them to dry in a colander or between dish towels, or better yet, use a salad spinner. Tear leaves by hand, or use a stainless-steel knife. Iron knives or cleavers will leave a rusty stain on lettuce leaves.

✄ Use the most decorative large leaves of lettuce as beds on platters of other foods or as wrappers for grilled fish fillets, crepes, cheese spreads, and firm dips.

✄ Create a late-spring soup with spinach and lettuce cooked until wilted, then puréed with some of the cooking liquid, scallions, mint, tarragon, and milk or cream.

✄ When I'm in a hurry, the simplest, quickest, and tastiest way of dressing a salad is the Italian way—merely drizzle with olive oil and vinegar. Try extra virgin oil and herbed, fruited, or balsamic vinegar.

✄ Here's a favorite vinaigrette dressing that won't overwhelm the delicate flavors of the greens:

> *1 cup vegetable oil (part or all olive)*
> *$1/3$ cup balsamic vinegar*
> *1 tablespoon Dijon mustard*
> *1 tablespoon chopped fresh tarragon or chervil*
> *1 tablespoon chopped chives or garlic chives*
> *Salt and freshly ground black pepper to taste*

CULTURAL REQUIREMENTS

Lettuce has shallow roots and benefits from a moist (but not soggy), rich soil. Mulching is advantageous in the heat of summer but may attract slugs in damp, cooler weather. Summer plantings can be made where the lettuce will be partially shaded by taller plants such as corn, asparagus, or tomatoes, or trellised beans or cucumbers. Shade netting will also keep lettuce cool. Frequent watering in hot, dry weather is crucial to avoid a stressed and bitter crop.

Lettuces can be interplanted in mixed flower, vegetable, or herb borders where their fringed, savoyed, or color-tipped leaves provide a foreground for taller plants. Follow a late-spring to early-summer harvest with bedding plant annuals or a later-maturing ornamental basil.

HARVEST

Heads of lettuce are best cut in the morning, plunged in cold water, drained, and refrigerated to retain sweeter flavor and crispness. Leaf lettuces can be cut whole or by pulling off the outermost leaves, keeping the growing center intact.

MELONS

Refreshing and fragrantly sweet, melons are a late-summer, early-fall treat here in Ithaca. Though technically a fruit, melons are included here because they are planted annually as are most vegetable crops. The sprawling vines need a lot of room, as they can spread 6 to 10 feet.

Cantaloupe favorites include the distinctively fragrant Charentais, a French heirloom that has ripened well for me in cool seasons, as has Earliqueen (Fedco, Johnny's). The sweetest locally grown melon I've had was Sugar Nut (Cook's, Fedco), which has a smooth texture and mild flavor.

Honeydew is tricky to grow in cool, damp climates: the fruits tend to crack open. I have had good luck with Earlidew (Fedco, Territorial), an early-maturing melon.

Watermelon varieties of a manageable "icebox" size include Yellow Doll and Sugar Baby, which also offer sweet flavor and relatively early ripening for all areas. Yellow Doll has shorter vines than most watermelons, which can ramble several feet. If you want a bigger melon for large-scale get-togethers, try Moon and Stars, an heirloom melon for hot-weather areas. Named for its dark green, almost black skin with yellow dots and crescents, this very sweet melon can reach 20 pounds or more.

STARTING

Gardeners in cool climates should start melon seeds indoors in 3-inch peat pots, 1 month before the last frost. Sow five seeds per pot, thinning to three plants per pot. Seeds need 75°F soil temperatures for good germination. Transplant seedlings after the last frost in rich soil of pH 6.0 to 7.5, supplemented with compost or manure. Plant three seedlings per hill, in hills 3 feet by 6 feet apart, or in rows with each seedling 18 inches apart, 3 feet between rows. In warm climates, seeds can be sown directly in the garden.

CULTURAL REQUIREMENTS

The use of plastic mulches, hot caps, and row covers will help maintain the warm soil that melons need. Soil moisture is more important when fruits are forming than after they have set, when dry conditions are better for ripening. Trellising (page 55) is recommended in damp climates because the fruit is better exposed to sunlight and kept away from moist soil, which can cause rot or disease. Each fruit must be supported in a "sling" made of a section of mesh produce bag, netting, or slightly tattered hosiery.

Cantaloupes are ready when they are aromatic and when pressure applied to the junction of stem and fruit causes the fruit to "slip" or separate. Charentais types do not slip; when they smell ripe and the blossom end is soft, they're ready.

Honeydews are ready to be cut from the vine when the rind begins to turn yellow or when the small leaf at the stem attachment yellows. Allow the fruits to ripen in a warm kitchen for a few days, until they develop a fruity scent.

CULINARY TIPS

- Homegrown melons picked when fully ripe need no further attention or special procedures. They're a sweet, fragrant addition to fruit soups and smoothies.

- Mix Yellow Doll with red watermelon, cantaloupe, and honeydew for a festive fruit salad.

Ripe watermelons will make a deep, hollow sound when thumped; they will have a yellow spot where the fruit rested on the ground and dry, brown tendrils closest to the junction of stem and vine.

PORTABLE TRELLIS

OKRA

Though long considered solely a southern or hot-climate vegetable, okra can be grown well in the North. Cajun Delight is a compact, short-season variety for northern growers. Red Velvet (Seeds of Change), with its red leaves, pods, and stems, serves as an ornamental as well. Okra shares the pretty flowers and interesting leaf shapes of related species hibiscus and hollyhocks.

STARTING

In cool climates, start okra seeds indoors about 1 month before the last frost, in 2- to 3-inch peat pots, two seeds per pot. Soil temperature of 80°F to 90°F is necessary for good germination, so use heat mats or coils. Thin seedlings to one per pot and place in the garden 2 weeks after the last frost, in soil of pH 6.0 to 8.0. Plant dwarf varieties 12 inches apart, taller types 18 inches apart, with 2 feet between rows. Direct seed $1/2$ inch deep when soil temperatures are at least 70°F. Plastic mulches, applied a week or two before transplanting, and fabric row covers will maintain soil warmth in northern gardens. To aid in pollination, remove row covers when the plants flower.

HARVEST

The immature seed pods are ready when they are between 2 and 3 inches in length. Frequent picking is necessary to ensure a long harvest and to avoid older, leathery fruits.

✄ CULINARY TIPS ✄

✄ Okra is indispensable in Creole gumbos and much of the cooking of tropical Africa. The sliced pods make a good addition to soups, stews, and sautés. Whole pods are a unique addition in tempura.

✄ A bit of vinegar added to saucy okra dishes will offset its mucilaginous nature.

✄ Avoid overcooking. Mushy okra is not a pretty sight and has an unpleasant, slimy texture.

✄ Cook okra in stainless-steel or other non-reactive cookware. Aluminum or cast iron will give it an off flavor.

✄ Dip slices of okra in beaten egg and seasoned cornmeal, then fry until tender.

ONIONS

As Julia Child so eloquently stated, "It is hard to imagine civilization without the onion." I guess we're the height of civilization at Moosewood—almost every savory dish on the menu includes onions. Onion growing relates to geography: short-day onions are grown south of 36° latitude, long-day onions north of that line, which bisects California and more or less defines the borders separating Colorado and New Mexico, Oklahoma and Kansas, and Virginia and North Carolina. Long-day onions need to be planted in early spring to make as much growth as possible before days shorten and bulbs begin to form. Short-day onions are fall planted to grow during the shorter days of the year. There are also day-neutral types that can be grown in the north or south.

Baby or pearl onions are quick-maturing, small bulbs that are day neutral. They are elegant served whole with marinated vegetables, or in salads, brochettes, stews, and stir-fries, or pickled. Peel whole baby onions after blanching in boiling water for 1 minute. Purplette (Johnny's, Territorial) expands the onion color palette with pink- to purple-skinned small onions. Sow spring through fall.

Red onions are mildly flavored bulbs that also lend interesting color to salads and sandwiches. Slice into rings for the prettiest effect. Mars (Fedco, Johnny's), a long-day type, produces large bulbs that I've stored well into the winter.

Scallions, green onions, or bunching onions are a specific type that will not produce bulbs, hence there is no concern with day length. Sow in early spring for summer harvest, midsummer for fall or winter harvest, and fall in mild climates for early spring harvest. Any young onion can be cut as a scallion, especially if you need to thin plants that are too close. Evergreen White Bunching is an heirloom that is very hardy and can be overwintered in all zones but the far north, to provide some of the first spring harvests.

Sweet onions are available for different seasons and regions of the country. Short-day types such as Vidalia are grown in the cool winters of the Deep South. Seeds are sown from fall through December for early- to late-spring harvest. Aside from breeding, one reason for Vidalia's lack of pungency relates to soil. The more sulfur in the soil, the more sulfur in the onions to make us "cry"—and parts of Eastern Georgia and the Pacific Northwest have low-sulfur soils. Walla Walla is a classic long-day sweet onion that can be either spring sown in cold climates for fall harvest or late-summer sown for harvest early the following summer. The latter works only in areas with a minimum winter temperature of 10°F. Walla Wallas should be eaten soon after harvest since they are short-term keepers. Candy and Super Star are both hefty-sized, day-neutral white onions that I've successfully stored for 2 to 3 months.

Northern growers should sow seeds indoors from January through February, transplanting in early spring as soon as the soil is workable. In warm climates, sow seeds indoors or out (seeds germinate best at 70°F or higher) in late fall. Sweet onions need to start in cool weather with plenty of moisture and, if possible, low-sulfur soils.

Storage onions are generally more pungent than sweet onions, because the chemical that irritates the eye also preserves the onion. Copra is a standard storage onion that has proven to be one of the best long-term keepers, lasting all winter. Borettana Cipollini (Cook's, Fedco) is an Italian heirloom that makes good-looking braids of gold-skinned, flat onions of medium size. I like to roast them quartered or halved. Seeds for all storage types should be started indoors in January to February for the best-sized onions.

STARTING

Onions can be started from seed or by purchasing seedlings or sets. Sets are small bulbs that will mature to full-sized onions. Seed-grown onions offer a wider range of possible varieties, while sets are limited to the narrow field of what you can purchase. Growing sets has the advantage of saving you time and yielding an earlier harvest.

Sow seeds in the garden (see the preceding list for appropriate times) in a light, fertile soil of pH 5.5 to 7.0, one to two seeds per inch, $1/4$ to $1/2$ inch deep, in rows 12 to 18 inches apart. Thin to eventually stand 3 to 4 inches apart or no less than 4 inches apart for larger sweet types.

Seedlings and sets should be planted in early spring or fall at a 3- to 4-inch spacing, in rows 12 to 18 inches apart. To have a harvest of both scallions and bulbing onions, plant seedlings or sets 2 inches apart, then pull every other onion while it's young and green. The remaining onions can be grown to "bulbhood" for storage or immediate use.

CULTURAL REQUIREMENTS

Onions are shallow rooted and need ample protection from invasive weeds between rows. Mulch at the onset of hot weather to keep soil cool and moist; irrigate if necessary.

HARVEST

Onions are ready for eating at any point. To harvest for storage, check for tops that have yellowed and fallen over. When at least half of the crop has fallen tops, knock down the rest of them (with a hoe or rake) to promote

❧ CULINARY TIPS ❧

❧ Short-term refrigeration of onions will reduce the pungency that provokes tearing.

❧ The easiest way to peel onions is to first cut off the root and stem ends, slice in half lengthwise, and peel off the skin and one or two top layers.

❧ Use a separate cutting board for chopping onions and garlic. It can be deodorized with lemon juice or plain vinegar.

❧ Slow-cooked onions develop a mellow sweetness due to the caramelized vegetable sugars. Cook the onions on low heat in a heavy skillet with oil or butter and a sprinkle of salt. Cook covered for 20 minutes, then uncover and cook for half an hour. Caramelized onions make a great filling for crepes, omelets, stuffed vegetables, and casseroles; a topping for pizzas; a base for onion soup; or a pasta sauce.

❧ Roast whole small onions, or quarters or wedges of larger onions, as another way to caramelize their natural sweetness and intensify flavor. Toss with a little olive oil, a splash of lemon or vinegar, and a dash of salt and pepper, and bake in a 425°F oven on a low-rimmed baking sheet for about 40 minutes, stirring occasionally.

❧ Finely chopped raw onions and minced chiles with some lime juice or vinegar make a fiery condiment for foods needing an extra jolt.

ripening. When the leaf tops brown, pull up the onions and leave them uncut, covered by the tops, to cure in the sun for 3 to 5 days. If the weather is rainy, cure on a covered porch or in a well-ventilated shed or garage. When dry and cured, cut off all but 1 inch of the tops and keep in mesh bags or slatted boxes in cool (ideally 35°F to 40°F), nonfreezing, dry, ventilated spots. Don't store with apples or potatoes: apples give off ethylene gas, which causes onions to sprout, and the moisture from potatoes may encourage mold and sprouting in onions. Smaller onions can be braided at the brown-leaf stage and hung in a cool spot.

PARSNIPS

Parsnips add a sweet, earthy flavor to soups, sautés, roasted vegetables, and stews. We find that this nutritious root vegetable adds a homey, comforting quality to fall and winter dishes.

STARTING

Use fresh seeds every year and start early. Parsnip is a fall vegetable that requires a full growing season of at least 110 days. It's also slow to germinate; try soaking seeds overnight before sowing from early to late spring in a sandy, stone-free loam of pH 6.0 to 8.0. Sow ½ inch deep, in rows 12 inches apart, keeping the seedbed moist. To avoid formation of a crust on the soil, cover with premoistened burlap or lightly strewn straw or grass clippings. Thin plants to eventually stand 3 inches apart.

CULTURAL REQUIREMENTS

A deep-rooted plant, parsnip requires a deeply cultivated soil that's not heavy. The use of manure or fertilizer may result in hairy or divided roots.

HARVEST

Dig parsnips after one or more light frosts: extreme cold improves the flavor by converting more of the carbohydrates to sugar, yielding sweeter roots. Parsnips should be dug carefully; pulling may break the roots from the crown. Roots not dug before the hard freeze can be dug in early spring before growth restarts; these will be even sweeter than fall harvested.

PEAS

For many gardeners, peas are the first vegetable planted each spring. Superbly flavored, fresh garden peas are also high in protein and vitamins A, the B complex, and C. Peas do best with a cool, early start and will not set flower buds in hot weather.

Types of peas include green or shelled peas, petit pois (baby peas), snap peas, snow peas, and soup or dried peas.

Green shelled peas are familiar to all—more often than not, frozen or canned. Freshly picked peas are by weight one-quarter sucrose, which rapidly converts to carbohydrates. This explains why so many peas are gobbled up in the garden before they arrive in the kitchen. Dakota is a very early pea that I plant before any others. It's quick to mature before hot weather arrives, especially in those years in which spring quickly turns to summer. Grow it with or without support. My favorite heirloom pea is Lincoln; grown for its excellent flavor and sweetness, it's a tall-growing variety that will need a fence or trellis.

Petit pois, the authentic tiny French peas, are particularly sweet and delicate. Waverex (Cook's, Territorial) is a medium-tall variety with delightful flavor. Be careful not to let the peas get too big.

Snap peas are a relatively new vegetable. Like snow peas, they have edible pods but taste best when the peas are well-rounded. Most varieties have strings that must be removed—an activity well suited for sitting in a comfortable rocker on a shady porch. Sugar Snap has an excellent sweet flavor and bears long and abundantly in my garden. It can grow as high as 5 to 6 feet and will need a fence or trellis for support. Sugar Sprint (Cook's, Johnny's) is almost as sweet but has the advantage of being stringless, on compact vines 24 inches tall.

Snow peas, picked when the peas have just started to form in the pod, make a sweet, crisp, quickly cooked vegetable, delicious alone or in stir-fried dishes. Oregon Giant is my choice for the sweetest peas with large pods on medium-tall vines. Each spring at Moosewood, we enjoy the young shoots of snow pea vines, a tender, sweet delicacy. Because peas are planted early, when there's a lot of garden space, put in a few rows to be quickly harvested as 5- to 6-inch shoots. For the best quality, cook soon after picking as the vines quickly wilt. Make sure you are harvesting green pea vines and not those of flowering sweet peas—the latter are poisonous.

Soup or dried peas are for gardeners with plenty of space or interest in putting things by for the winter months. Blue Pod Capucijners has the added bonus of being ornamental, with fragrant violet-red and pink flowers on 6-foot-tall vines that I've used to decorate a garden fence. The peas, however, aren't as pretty once they're dried, and they cook to a brownish grey. Oh well.

STARTING

Plant pea seeds in early spring as soon as the soil can be worked. Get a jump on the season by preparing the row on a sunny late-fall day. Soil should be loose and well-drained, with a pH between 6.0 and 7.0. Seeds will rot in heavy, cold, and wet soil. If your native soil is on the heavy side, plant in a raised bed with amended, lighter soil. Use a nitrogen inoculant for all types of peas, as it will help fix nitrogen in the soil by introducing beneficial bacteria. Plant in rows or bands, 18 inches apart for dwarf types and 4 feet apart for taller trellised varieties. Sow seeds $1/2$ to 1 inch deep (plant deeper in warmer, drier soil), 1 to 2 inches apart.

CULTURAL REQUIREMENTS

For bushy pea varieties shorter than 3 feet, insert pieces of brush along the row to help keep the vines off the ground. Varieties taller than 3 feet need a fence or trellis to support the vines. Rotate crops from year to year to avoid soil and plant diseases.

❧ To remove the fibrous strings from snow and snap peas, grasp the stem end and pull down the string running along the pod's straight edge.

❧ Freshly shelled peas are best used in delicately seasoned dishes where their subtle flavor won't be overwhelmed:

- Combine them with the first small white onions, new potatoes, and a little chopped mint.
- Toss with a "baby" pasta such as pastina or orzo, butter, and a bit of grated Parmesan cheese.
- Add to lightly seasoned grain pilafs.

❧ Snap and snow peas give a larger yield of vegetables per foot of garden row and can be used more lavishly than shelled peas. At Moosewood, we use them in marinated salads, pasta sauces, stews, and stir-fries, and sautéed or blanched on their own as a side dish. Blanched snow peas need less than a minute in boiling water; snap peas, being denser, need perhaps 2 minutes. Cut the pods in proportion to the other foods in a dish; for example, long pods would be awkward in a pasta sauce in which the other vegetables are chopped.

❧ Lemon juice and vinegar dull the bright color of green peas, snap peas, and snow peas, so add these just before serving.

❧ Young snow pea shoots simply stir-fried with garlic and soy sauce make a nice side dish. They can also be added at the last minute to vegetable stir-fries.

Sowings for a fall crop can be made in mild cool-summer areas, about 60 days before the first expected frost. Crops will not be as bountiful in the shorter days of fall. Gardeners in frost-free areas can grow peas from fall through winter if temperatures stay above 30°F with average maximum day temperatures below 75°F.

HARVEST

Peas must be harvested often, at least every other day. I've always thought that genetic engineers should create a red-leafed pea plant to make it easier to distinguish the green pods from the leafy vines. As consolation for the hard work, the pea picker *does* get first dibs on all those succulent sweet peas.

PEPPERS

Peppers were cultivated in the New World long before the arrival of Europeans. Sixteenth- and seventeenth-century explorers took hot and sweet peppers back to the rest of the world. Before then, there was no paprika in Hungary nor any fiery chile peppers in the cuisines of Asia.

Pepper plants are a handsome addition to mixed borders of flowers, herbs, and vegetables. The medium-high bushy plants have glossy, deep green foliage, white flowers, and fruit that can be green, gold, red, orange, yellow, chocolate brown, or purple. Peppers require at least 2 months of warm weather after seedlings have been transplanted before the first peppers are ready for harvest. Ideal pepper-growing weather for sweet peppers is with days from 70°F to the upper 80s, nighttime temperatures above 55°F. Most peppers will drop their blossoms if it's too hot or cold. Some varieties, as noted below, are a bit more tolerant of adverse conditions. Chile peppers are more adaptable to temperature extremes; however, they taste hotter when grown in hot weather; they need heat to make heat.

Sweet bell variety Ace (Fedco, Johnny's) is a good choice for enduring difficult weather swings. The peppers are a bit thin walled, but if you've had trouble growing peppers, try Ace. Lipstick (Johnny's), my favorite, is a reliable type that produces tasty red peppers earlier than all others I've tried. Gypsy (Territorial) is also less fussy about ideal weather and has big, yellow-orange fruits. Islander (Johnny's) is an unusual bell with lavender peppers that progress to red in gorgeous stages of yellow, orange, and violet streaks. I've found them to have good flavor at all stages. Nardello (Fedco, Seeds of Change) is an Italian heirloom from the Nardello family. This banana pepper is exceptionally prolific and sweet, best used for frying or raw in salads. Thin walls make it a poor candidate for roasting or stuffing. The "chocolate" of Chocolate peppers refers to their color when fully ripe. These are also good for cold-weather tolerance.

Chiles are prized for their pungent flavor, an essential element of many of the world's cuisines. Capsaicin, the "hot" in peppers, is also valued for its health benefits, ranging from treating muscular aches to lowering blood pressure. Before refrigeration was widely available, foods that included chiles, with their natural bactericide properties, were easier to keep, and eating spicy fare provided a stimulant effect against tropical languor.

The hotness of chile peppers varies widely, from merely perky to volcanic. Wilbur Scoville, an Englishman and devotee of chiles, devised Scoville units, a measure of heat in chiles. Anaheim, familiar for its use in chile rellenos, is a mild pepper ranging from 900 to 2,500 Scovilles. In escalating hotness, we have poblano (1,500 to 4,000), jalapeño (4,000 to 6,000), Thai (80,000), and the super-hot habanero at a walloping 200,000 to 350,000 Scovilles. Dried poblanos (more commonly called ancho peppers) are the classic choice for mole sauces. Jalapeños are likely the most popular hot pepper and the easiest to find as a fresh chile in markets everywhere. Thai chiles can be grown in pots, where the small peppers have ornamental as well as culinary value. Habaneros, also known as Scotch bonnet, are small orange peppers best grown in hot climates.

I've recently grown my own paprika peppers, Boldog Hungarian Spice (Cook's, Fedco, Johnny's). The long, tapered fruit, mature at the deep red stage, can be dried whole in a hot attic room or similar spot away from any moisture. I use a spice grinder to crush one or two peppers at a time for the most rich, deeply flavored paprika—with a hint of heat—that I've ever tasted.

STARTING

Sow pepper seeds indoors, about 8 to 10 weeks before outside temperatures will be consistently warm. Seeds germinate poorly in cool conditions, so soil temperature should be 75°F or higher. When true leaves develop, transplant the seedlings into 2- to 3-inch containers or large soil cells. Plants grown at 70°F day and 60°F night temperatures will be sturdy and not leggy. Set plants in moderately rich soil of pH 5.5 to 7.0 when nights are generally above 50°F and frosts are no longer a threat. Cold temperatures cause bud drop, which may result in no fruit. Space pepper plants 12 inches apart, in rows 24 inches apart. Rich soil that is too high in nitrogen will produce lush, green foliage with few peppers.

Plant hot peppers at the opposite end of the garden from sweet peppers to avoid cross-pollination.

CULTURAL REQUIREMENTS

High yields of fruit can be achieved with the addition of high-phosphorus fertilizer such as rock phosphate. To minimize plant diseases, rotate crops and avoid growing peppers in the same location year after year. Plants heavy with peppers may need to be staked to avoid stem breakage or rot where the peppers touch the ground.

Obtaining sweet, fully ripe peppers may depend upon the use of season extenders (page 201) in cool areas.

Blossoms and young fruit drop when the weather is extremely hot and dry; however, with increased humidity and lower temperatures, plants will set new buds.

HARVEST

Bell peppers can be picked at any stage but are considerably sweeter, thicker, and more flavorful at their ripest. Use a knife or shears to cut the fruit, as the brittle stems break easily. Here in the usually short summers of Ithaca, far too few peppers reach their glorious, fully mature color before the frosts. Harvesting some of the first peppers at the green stage will stimulate more fruit production. After that, be patient and allow the remaining fruit to ripen fully to red, orange, yellow, purple, or chocolate brown.

Harvest chile peppers, green or red, when they are full sized.

❧ Lisa Wickman is our chief advocate for cooking with fresh chile peppers. Some of us are tempted to use the more convenient dried cayenne pepper, but fresh chiles lend a fuller, more complex flavor. Her advice for handling: The seeds and inner membranes of chile peppers are the hottest parts. Make sure to wash your hands thoroughly after handling chiles. Some people wear latex gloves when handling the hottest peppers. Be careful not to touch your eyes.

❧ Small, very hot peppers can be added, whole or halved, to sautés and stir-fries. Toss with the warmed oil before adding other ingredients; the peppers will season the whole dish but can be removed by those choosing not to eat a very hot pepper.

❧ If you've eaten more hot peppers than you can handle, bland starches like rice, potatoes, bread, or tortillas are better at soothing the heat than water, which tends to distribute it around your mouth.

❧ Chiles are traditionally used in the cuisines of the Caribbean, Latin America, Asia, and Africa but can be incorporated into other dishes as well. We find that even a small amount of fresh chile adds a zip that picks up food without making it spicy. Try using less salt and compensating with chiles.

❧ For many years, Dixie Merilahti had a shop across the hall from Moosewood. This is a favorite snack of her invention that we shared together: crusty French bread, sweet butter, and sliced roasted peppers. To roast peppers, bake (page 231) or grill (page 256) and peel. The roasted peppers' lush smoothness and sweet flavor enlivens salads, fillings, sandwiches, and pasta sauces.

❧ The bell pepper's blocky, hollow shape invites stuffing: Cut the peppers in half lengthwise and seed; leave the stems on to help the peppers hold their shape. Stuff the raw peppers with a cooked or prepared filling and place in a baking dish, adding about 1/2 inch of water or tomato juice to the bottom. Bake, tightly covered, at 375°F for about 40 minutes, or until the peppers are tender and the filling is cooked through. We stuff peppers with a variety of fillings that include the following:

- Ricotta and Parmesan cheeses with bread crumbs, fresh basil, and nutmeg
- Corn and pinto beans with garlic, chili pepper, cumin, and coriander
- Mushrooms, dill, and scallions, with cream, cottage, and Cheddar cheeses
- Cooked, drained spinach with leeks, thyme, and Swiss cheese
- Rice pilaf with diced onions, carrots, and parsnips and marjoram, pine nuts, currants, and a pinch of saffron

❧ Have a multicolored sauté using green, red, and gold peppers.

POTATOES

Originally from South America, the potato returned to the New World with Irish immigrants in the early eighteenth century. This most humble of vegetables is now generating a lot of attention as a specialty crop. Even a few square feet can yield a crop of new potatoes or highly prized fingerlings. Whether red, yellow, tan, purple, or blue skinned, with a similar range of flesh colors, potatoes are available in dozens of varieties. Potatoes with moist flesh are best in casseroles, soups, and stews, where their creaminess is an asset. Waxy potatoes are creamy yet firm enough to hold their shape; they excel in salads, roasting, and pan-frying. Dry-fleshed potatoes make the best French fries or chips, simple baked potatoes, and potato pancakes, for which the rule is the less moisture the better.

Early maturing in 65 to 80 days, early potatoes are the first to get to your table; in hot-summer areas they mature while the weather is relatively cool. Yukon Gold is deservedly popular for both the early new potatoes it produces and its good storage potential. It's the first specialty potato to "cross over" to mainstream supermarkets. Yukon Golds are medium dry, with good versatility for all uses. Caribe has dark bluish purple skin, a waxy to dry texture, and very white flesh that makes exceptionally fluffy mashed potatoes. Cranberry Red (All-Red) is a moist potato with red skin and unusual pink flesh. Dark Red Norland is my choice for the first creamy, red-skinned new potatoes, as well as moist potatoes for a main crop.

Fingerlings would be my choice if I were to grow only one potato, because of their wonderful flavor and texture. These waxy potatoes make the best roasted spuds, my preferred potato-cooking method. Late maturing at 90 days, long, thin fingerlings are smaller than most other potatoes. French Fingerling is a red-skinned, high-yielding variety with yellow flesh. La Ratte has a distinctively nutty, almost chestnut-like flavor with yellow skin and flesh. Rose Finn is an attractive heirloom with pink skin, yellow flesh, and high yields. Banana or Russian Banana is one of the most widely available fingerlings, with dense flesh that doesn't fall apart in long-cooked stews.

Mid-season potatoes mature in 80 to 90 days, and there are some wonderful mid-season varieties. All-Blue is the best tasting of the intriguingly colored blue potatoes. With purple skin and deep blue flesh, this moist potato should not be overcooked. Yellow Finn is a high-yielding heirloom golden potato that is versatile and delicious. I find it creamier than Yukon Gold and worth the slightly longer wait. Rose Gold is a beautiful, red-skinned, golden-fleshed, moist potato that also roasts well.

Late potatoes mature in 90 to 130 days; big bakers are the featured players here. Butte is an improved Idaho type with the typical russeted skin and mealy texture. It is reputed to be higher in Vitamin C and protein than other potatoes. It's my favorite dry potato for the best latkes (Jewish-style potato pancakes).

STARTING

Potatoes yield best in a cool growing season, whether spring, summer, fall, or winter. Choose a spot where other nightshade family members (potatoes, tomatoes, eggplant, and peppers) have not been grown for a year or two. Ideal soil is a sandy, not overly fertile, acidic loam with a pH between 4.8 and 6.0. Lime soils and uncomposted manure make soil hospitable to a scab fungus that damages the tubers.

Plant when the soil is relatively dry and workable and the temperature is between 50°F and 60°F. Soil that is cold and wet will rot seed pieces. Buy seed potatoes that are certified disease free; supermarket potatoes may have diseases and are usually treated to prevent sprouting. Once disease is in your soil, it is hard to overcome. Cut seed potatoes into egg-size pieces with one to two eyes each. Allow them to dry in an airy location for 2 to 3 days before planting. Space seed potato pieces with the eyes pointing up, 3 to 4 inches deep, 1 foot apart, in rows 2 to 3 feet apart, depending on soil fertility.

CULTURAL REQUIREMENTS

An acidic mulch of peat moss, pine needles, or pine-leaf mold helps conserve moisture, fight weeds, and prevent potatoes from developing the toxic green spots caused by exposure to light. Cover the tubers with a generous mulch of no less than 10 to 12 inches. Alternatively, hill up soil at the base of the plants when the new shoots are 4 to 5 inches high, leaving only 1 inch exposed. A second hilling when plants are 12 to 15 inches tall is also recommended if you don't apply mulch. Potatoes are 75 percent water by weight, so ample moisture is important for good-sized tubers, but be sure the soil is well drained. Potatoes will not form at temperatures consistently above 85°F.

If potato beetles (page 207) are a problem, the lightest-grade fabric row cover can be used as protection.

HARVEST

Pick small new potatoes before the main crop by careful division. This can be done anytime after the plants flower, or a couple of months from plant-

---

✀ CULINARY TIPS ✀

- ✀ Organically grown potatoes need only be scrubbed in preparation for cooking. But in some dishes the slight sacrifice of nutrition caused by paring away the vitamins contained in the peels may be justified by improved appearance and texture.

- ✀ The eyes and green sections of potatoes are toxic and should be cut off and discarded.

- ✀ Potatoes can appear in any course of the meal, from soup to dessert (*New Recipes from Moosewood Restaurant,* Ten Speed Press, 1987, has a Russian Chocolate Torte with mashed potatoes as a key ingredient).

- ✀ Toss new potatoes with chopped fresh basil and butter or olive oil.

- ✀ Stuff baked potatoes with any of the Herbed Cheese Spreads (page 276).

- ✀ Roast potatoes with one of the marinades for Grilled Vegetables (page 256). Slice, coat

with the marinade, and bake in a 375°F oven, with the pan tightly covered, for 35 minutes. Uncover and bake for another 30 minutes or until tender, stirring often.

- ✀ Sauté small cubes of potatoes with cilantro, dill, marjoram, rosemary, sage, savory, or thyme and use as a filling for crepes or omelets. Or add fresh chile peppers, seeded and diced.

- ✀ For mashed potatoes, use a potato ricer or hand held masher—not a food processor as this does weird things to the starch in potatoes and creates a gluey texture more suitable for wallpaper paste than for dinner.

- ✀ Blend minced or pressed garlic with mashed potatoes. For a nuttier flavor, first sauté the garlic until golden in a small amount of oil or butter.

ing. Gently dig at the base of the plant and remove a few spuds, leaving the rest to mature fully. Crops should be dug when the foliage has yellowed or died back. Potatoes can be left in the ground until hard frosts threaten, but earlier digging prevents damage from burrowing vermin. Dig on a sunny day, allowing the tubers to dry on the ground before storage. Store in a cool, dark location at 35°F to 45°F.

RHUBARB

Rhubarb is an ornamental, long-lived perennial. The unique, tart flavor of the stalks is a delicious addition to dessert pies, sauces, and crisps. It requires cold-winter dormancy that limits its growth to the northern half of the United States.

STARTING

Plant rhubarb in the early spring from root divisions obtained from a nursery or from other gardeners who may be happy to divide a mature, overgrown planting. Set the root 3 to 4 inches deep in fertile, well-drained soil generously supplemented with compost or aged manure. Select a permanent location where it won't be disturbed and where its bright red stalks and large, wavy, green and red leaves will be shown off. Soil should be prepared deeply because rhubarb is a vigorous grower: a single plant can be 4 feet wide and 3 feet high.

CULTURAL REQUIREMENTS

Rhubarb is carefree and easily grown. Plants will bear more abundantly if they're well watered, mulched, and fed.

- ✂ Add diced rhubarb to apple pies, rice and bread puddings, or to fruit crisps for a tart accent.
- ✂ Serve stewed, sweetened rhubarb and sliced strawberries as a topping for yogurt or ice cream.
- ✂ Make a dessert sauce for shortcakes or pound cakes with diced rhubarb, all-fruit berry preserves, apple juice, and sugar or honey to taste.

HARVEST

Refrain from harvesting any stalks the first year. A few can be picked the second year, and by the third year plants are ready for a 2-month picking season. Stalks should be at least 10 inches long and 1 inch thick. Pull the stalk from the base of the plant with a slight twist, separating it from the plant crown. *Rhubarb leaves contain poisonous amounts of oxalic acid and should not be used raw or cooked. The stems are edible only when cooked.*

SALAD GREENS

There is a whole universe of green salads beyond the traditional iceberg lettuce and tomatoes that many of us grew up with. Try some of the greens listed below, singly, in combination, or as intriguing additions to a lettuce-based salad. Many of them can also do double duty as a cooked green vegetable.

STARTING, CULTURAL REQUIREMENTS, AND HARVEST

Amaranth (callaloo) is a hot-weather annual with decorative leaves that can be purple, gold, burgundy, or green brushed with red. The young leaves have a spinach-like quality and can be added to salads or quickly cooked. More mature plants are grown for their seeds, which are used as a nutritious addition to baked goods or cereals. Burgundy (Seeds of Change) and Golden Giant (Seeds of Change) are showy amaranths to grow for young leaves and seeds; Red Leaf Vegetable Amaranth (Johnny's) is a good variety just for greens. Plant amaranth when the weather is warm and all frost danger is past. Sow seeds 1/8 inch deep in a sunny, well-drained location. Burgundy and Golden Giant are pretty enough for flower beds, where they form 6-foot-tall dramatic accents, spaced at least 1 foot apart. At 18 inches tall, Red Leaf Vegetable is more discreet; plant 6 inches apart.

Arugula (rocket, arugula, roquette) has deep green, softly serrated leaves and an unusual toasted sesame–like flavor that is both peppery and nutty. It adds a sharp accent to salads when used in small quantities with other greens. Rustic, wild, or sylvetta arugula is a different species worth growing for its narrow leaves on plants that are slower to bolt than the common type. The flavor is almost identical, perhaps a little sharper. Common arugula dies after it goes to seed, but in my garden rustic arugula has been somewhat perennial. Both, however, broadcast volunteer seedlings here and there if the plants are allowed to go to seed. The flowers, white for common and yellow for rustic, have a mild arugula flavor and make nice edible garnishes well after the leaves are too pungent.

Plant through the early spring and again in late summer. Arugula tastes and grows best in cool weather and can survive light frosts as a seedling. Sow seeds 1/2 inch deep; thin plants to 4 inches apart. For milder flavored greens, harvest the young leaves when they're 3 to 4 inches long, or the whole small plants at 6 inches tall. Older plants, especially ones that have bloomed, will be very pungent and bitter.

If well watered in cool weather, arugula can be grown as a cut-and-come-again crop by harvesting the top growth and leaving 1 to 2 inches at the base for regrowth. Late summer to fall seedings of arugula can be harvested all winter outdoors in mild climates or in a cool greenhouse or cold frame in colder climates.

Chicory, long popular in Europe, adds a bittersweet tang to salads and is particularly nice in mesclun when the tender young growth can be cut as baby greens. Red Dandelion or Italico Rosso (Cook's, Fedco) offers an attractive plant with red-veined, bright green, serrated leaves. Pan de Zucchero (Cook's, Fedco) matures like a romaine lettuce, and as the name suggests (it's Italian for "sugar loaf"), it's sweeter than most chicories. Wait for the first frost to mellow the flavor, and choose the sweeter inner leaves, discarding the outer ones. I've had the best luck with spring sowing for quickly harvested baby greens and late-summer sowing for larger fall-harvested plants. Sow seeds $1/2$ inch deep, 1 inch apart, in rows 18 inches apart. Thin any plants not cut for baby greens to 6 inches apart.

Radicchio is a member of the chicory family, grown for its deep burgundy red and creamy white heads with a distinctive bittersweet flavor. Radicchio's bitterness is mellowed by the cool weather of spring, fall, or mild winters.

Choggia is a type that forms rounded heads. Varieties include Red Preco #1 (Johnny's) and Palla di Fuoco Rossa (Fedco). Treviso types form elongated, conical heads. Cut Treviso back in the fall, and the new growth can be harvested from winter to early spring. Gardeners in cold winter areas can grow Treviso types only with a generous layer of straw or hay mulch to cover the cut-back plants. Treviso varieties include Radicchio di Treviso (Cook's, Fedco) and Indigo (Cook's, Fedco).

Spring-seeded summer crops are viable where night temperatures are cool, below 60°F. Fall crops from mid- to late-summer seedings are more reliably bolt resistant in most parts of the United States. Sow directly in the garden or indoors in peat pots or soil cells, barely covering the seed with soil. Seeding in pots or cells placed in a cool, shady spot will be more successful if the weather is hot and dry. Soil temperatures between 65°F and 70°F are ideal for germination. Space plants 10 inches apart, in rows 18 inches apart, in well-drained, fertile soil. Keep soil moisture consistent; water during any dry periods but not to the point of sogginess.

Choggia types are ready for harvest when the small (6 to 8 inches) heads are firm and no longer growing in size. Treviso types that have overwintered should be harvested before warm weather arrives.

Claytonia (miner's lettuce) bear small, heart-shaped, tender leaves on thin stems, giving this plant a delicacy that belies its tough hardiness. Sow in early spring or late summer for cool-weather crops that can be cut-and-come-again. Seed $1/4$ inch deep, $1/2$ inch apart, in rows 1 foot apart. Thin seedlings to 4 to 6 inches apart.

CRESS

Garden cress may be flat leafed or curly; these greens provide a peppery flavor similar to watercress but require less work. Sow seeds from early spring through fall for outdoor harvest. Plant seeds $1/4$ inch deep as soon as the ground can be worked. Plants are ready to pick in less than 2 weeks, when they're 2 to 5 inches tall. Pots of cress can be grown on sunny windowsills all year long.

Watercress has a perky tanginess that enhances soups, sandwiches, and salads. Seeds should be started indoors in moist soil. Transplant seedlings to large pots of well-limed soil (pH 7.0) or, ideally, to a flowing stream's banks where water depth is about 6 inches. Pots should sit in pans of water that are changed daily.

ENDIVE AND ESCAROLE

Belgian endive is an interesting and unique gourmet salad vegetable: the plants are grown through the summer, then the roots are placed in a cold location to force tender shoots for winter fare. I grew it one year and the endive was crisp and delicious, but it may be debatable whether Belgian endive is worth the trouble.

Sow seeds as for lettuce in mid- to late June and dig up the plants after the first frost. Cut and discard the foliage, leaving 1 inch of crown. Cut the roots back to about 10 inches. Store the roots packed closely together in damp sand, in a covered box with drainage holes, in a dark location with a temperature of 40°F to 50°F. They must be completely dark or the leaves will be very bitter. After about a month, the *chicons* or sprouts can be harvested when they're 4 to 6 inches tall. Two to three cuttings are possible. Totem (Johnny's) is a variety of this not widely available vegetable.

Curly endive or frisée has deeply cut, frilled, crisp leaves that add beauty, character, and a mild bittersweet flavor to salads. Though it's not commonly grown in the United States, I highly recommend frisée for anyone's seed list. Trés Fin Maraîchère (Fedco, Seeds of Change) has the most frizzy leaves of all I've tried.

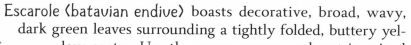

Escarole (batavian endive) boasts decorative, broad, wavy, dark green leaves surrounding a tightly folded, buttery yellow center. Use the young greens or heart in mixed salads. Sauté mature plants Mediterranean-style in olive oil and garlic until wilted, or add shredded greens to brothy soups.

Sow curly endive and escarole seeds in the early spring or late summer for cool-weather growing. Plant seeds directly in the garden, $1/2$ inch deep; thin seedlings to eventually stand 6 to 8 inches apart.

Blanch curly endive and escarole heads a few days before harvest for more tender and sweet greens: tie the outer leaves over the head or cover each with a paper bag, cardboard, or a 6-inch-deep bowl.

Mâche (corn salad, lamb's lettuce) is prized for its very delicate, tender leaves, which have a mild, sweet, almost perfumed quality. The small plants are low-growing and form attractive rosettes that can be an early-season ground cover for later bushier plants like broccoli or tomatoes, because the mâche will be harvested by the time the later plants have filled out.

Sow seeds $1/2$ inch deep, 1 inch apart in fertile soil for cool-weather growing in early spring, late summer, or fall. Do a first thinning to 2 inches apart, harvesting the baby greens for salads, and a later thinning to space plants 4 inches apart. Harvest entire rosettes by cutting at the soil level before warm weather arrives. Let a few plants go to seed if you want volunteers. Mâche has seeded itself here and there in the early fall in my Zone 5 garden, to overwinter and provide welcome, early-spring greens. For a winter crop in mild climates or greenhouses, or to overwinter and get an early-spring start in colder areas, sow mâche in the fall. Vit has proven to be a reliably hardy variety for me.

Mesclun is a salad mixture of young, tender greens and herbs. Originally enjoyed in Southern France and Northern Italy, mesclun's popularity has spread to North American markets and restaurants. Trendiness aside, mesclun salads can be delightfully varied in personality as well as visual appeal. Any of the salad greens in this section, along with baby greens from lettuce, kale, mizuna, pak choi, tatsoi, chard, and tender herb sprigs can be mixed and matched to create colorful, delicious salads. Tart, robust salads made primarily of endive, mustard, arugula, or cress may need only a drizzle of good-tasting oil to be ready for the table. One or two kinds of tender herb sprigs—such as anise hyssop, basil, chervil, chives, dill, lovage, tarragon, or thyme—can be added in moderation so as not to overwhelm the more delicate greens. Garnish with edible flower blooms.

Mesclun seed mixes are available from all seed houses. Or make your own seed mixes from varieties suggested above. Plant short rows of lettuces and greens every couple of weeks for a season-long succession of young, varied salad material.

Sow seeds at the appropriate time for cool-season growth (similar to lettuce) in your climate. Plants should be lightly shaded and frequently watered as spring turns to summer. Harvest greens by snipping off 4- to 6-inch leaves 1 to 2 inches above the soil line. Plants that are watered and fertilized will continue to grow for another harvest in a couple of weeks.

Minutina, a particularly cold-hardy green, forms handsome rosettes of long, narrow, crunchy leaves. I've harvested mildly flavored minutina under a fabric row cover until the heavy snows arrive. Gardeners with a greenhouse or protected cold frame might want to try minutina, claytonia, and arugula as a hardy trio for winter greens. Sow seeds in spring, late summer, or fall, 1/4 inch deep in rows or bands. Thin plants to 4 to 6 inches apart.

Orach adds visual and taste appeal to salads, with its vibrant, red-purple, arrowhead-shaped leaves that have a mild spinach flavor. Unpinched plants can tower up to 6 feet; however, pruning creates bushier plants and more leaf production, and it delays bolting to seed. I usually let a few go to seed; orach has volunteered enough seedlings to provide color here and there. I'm trying Aurora mix (Fedco) this year—it includes gold, magenta, and carmine along with the typical purple. Sow seeds 1/4 inch deep in early spring; thin plants to 12 to 18 inches apart.

Purslane is a somewhat pesky wild green in my garden. Its European relatives, garden and golden purslane, are more desirable, with juicier leaves and upright plants about four times as large. Purslane's claim to fame is its remarkable concentration of omega-3 fatty acids, the highest known among plant sources. Sow seeds 1/4 inch deep and

1 inch apart after all danger of frost. Thin plants to 4 to 5 inches apart. Keep plants pruned to encourage bushy growth, harvesting the mildly acidic leaves. This will also discourage flowering, which lowers quality by toughening the leaves. Plants allowed to go to seed will likely lead to volunteers next season.

Sorrel produces bright green leaves prized for kitchen use in early spring and late fall. A tart soup using the lemony fresh new growth of sorrel is an early-spring favorite at Moosewood.

Because sorrel is perennial, plant it only where it can grow undisturbed. Keep seed heads cut in summer to avoid unwanted seedlings all over the garden and to ensure tender new-leaf growth. Plants form vigorous rosettes with 9- to 12-inch-long leaves.

Sow seeds $1/2$ inch deep in rows $1^1/2$ feet apart. Thin plants to 8 inches apart. Harvest leaves only the first year; after that, whole plants can be cut above the crown. Established sorrel is easily divided to share with friends.

❧ CULINARY TIPS ❧

Amaranth: Use as a hot-weather substitute in recipes calling for spinach.

Arugula: Besides its use in salads, add arugula to sandwiches and dips, pestos, soups, mashed potatoes, and pasta sauces.

Mâche: Use mâche with other, more assertive, greens that contrast with its subtle nature, or feature it alone with a delicate dressing.

Cress: Add small quantities of peppery cresses to dips, omelets, salad dressings, and sauces.

Radicchio: Create a varied salad with the bitter quality of radicchio and the sweetness of ripe pears and sliced fennel bulb. Sprinkle with olive oil and balsamic vinegar.

❧ Sauté chopped or shredded radicchio briefly and toss with pasta, rice, or white beans and freshly grated Parmesan cheese. Or use it as a pizza topping with tomatoes, cheeses, and olives.

❧ Quickly grill or broil quarters of a radicchio head brushed with olive oil, herbs, and garlic for a zesty side dish.

❧ The outer leaves of radicchio make a beautiful, bowl-shaped "container" for salads.

Sorrel: Sorrel adds a zippy touch to salads, soups, sauces, dressings, and herb butters.

SHALLOTS

Milder than its *Allium* family relatives onion and garlic, but sharing qualities of each, shallots are a classy, easily grown vegetable. Each single bulb planted in fall or early spring will provide four to ten new bulbs. Shallots are also available as seeds to be planted indoors with onions in cooler areas or direct seeded in early spring. French shallots are the best-flavored variety. Their distinctive pinkish skins and flesh distinguishes them from other types.

STARTING

Soil requirements and seeding are the same as for onions (pages 58–59). Plant bulbs 1 to 2 inches deep, 6 inches apart, in rows 1 foot apart. Where winter temperatures drop below 0°F, bulbs planted in fall should be generously mulched. Remove the mulch in early spring when the ground is no longer frozen.

CULTURAL REQUIREMENTS

The small bulbs can be easily overwhelmed by weeds. Hand weeding is necessary until the greens are large enough to be well mulched.

HARVEST

When the tops turn yellow, pull up the bulbs and air-dry them in the garden for a few days. Store as for onions (page 60). Shallots can also be wintered over in the garden, with mulching in colder areas. Smaller bulbs can be replanted for next year's harvest.

CULINARY TIPS

- Shallots cook quickly to a soft texture, making them ideal for speedy sauces, sautés, or omelet and crepe fillings.
- Use minced raw shallots in dressings and marinades for a delicate onion flavor.

SPINACH

It's funny how spinach, formerly the bane of childhood dinners, is now a favorite. For those of us who grew up in the fifties, delicately flavored fresh spinach was uncommon; nasty canned or frozen was the norm. We enjoy the fresh green leaves in salads and blended into our Moosewood House Dressing. Dozens of savory dishes are enhanced by its mildly earthy flavor and bright verdancy.

Seeds are available for both smooth- and savoy-leaved types. The savoy varieties are prettier for salad greens, but their crinkled texture requires more careful washing and rinsing. Tyee is a vigorous, heat-tolerant variety that has performed well in my garden for spring and early summer crops as well as overwintering. Olympia (Fedco, Territorial) is my favorite fall-planted variety for spring crops of a very mild-tasting spinach.

STARTING

Spinach likes a cool, fertile soil of pH 6.0 to 7.5 and does not perform well in acidic soils. Sow seeds as early as the soil can be worked, $^1/_2$ inch deep, 1 inch apart, in rows 1 foot to $1^1/_2$ feet apart. Thin plants initially to 3 inches apart, then 6 inches apart. Thinnings can be used in salads or cooked.

Fall crops can be grown in mild-summer areas by sowing seeds from mid-July through August. Seeds germinate poorly in very warm soil, so try refrigerating them between moist paper towels for 5 to 6 days before sowing. Seeds can be sown in September for overwintered plants. A mulch of straw or hay is advisable for northern areas. Southern gardeners can plant spinach through the fall and winter if the temperatures remain above 25°F and daily highs remain below 75°F.

CULTURAL REQUIREMENTS

Keep spinach plants well watered during dry periods. A side dressing of compost or rotted manure will help maintain soil fertility and result in bushier plants.

HARVEST

Plants will bolt to seed in hot weather. Harvest single leaves and small plants at the beginning of the season, followed by whole mature plants later on.

❧ For recipes requiring quantities of cooked spinach, blanch the whole rinsed leaves in a generous amount of rapidly boiling water for 2 to 3 minutes. Drain, squeeze out excess water, and chop. Cooked spinach is condensed and much easier to chop than bulky, raw spinach.

❧ Cook spinach briefly until it's just wilted and still bright green. Overcooked spinach has a strong, bitter taste and an unappealing, drab green color.

❧ Cooked spinach is an excellent addition to soups, sauces, stews, quiches, pizza toppings, pasta, and crepe fillings.

❧ Purée fresh basil and cooked spinach and make a pasta sauce by adding chopped tomatoes, garlic, and olive oil. You can combine the purée with ricotta and Parmesan cheeses for a rich, fragrant filling for lasagna, stuffed vegetables, manicotti, ravioli, or stuffed shells.

❧ Fresh spinach leaves make a deep green bed for other vegetable salads or additions of avocado, croutons, feta cheese, chickpeas, olive oil, and lemon.

❧ Freshly grated nutmeg enhances the flavor of cooked spinach, whether served alone as a side dish or used as an ingredient in other dishes.

❧ Andi Gladstone, our resident link to Japanese cuisine and culture, prepares this delicate spinach side dish: Blanch and chop the spinach as described above. Mix together small amounts of soy sauce, sake (rice wine), freshly grated gingerroot, honey, and sesame seeds that have been toasted in a dry skillet until golden brown and then ground in a spice or coffee grinder. Toss with the chopped spinach.

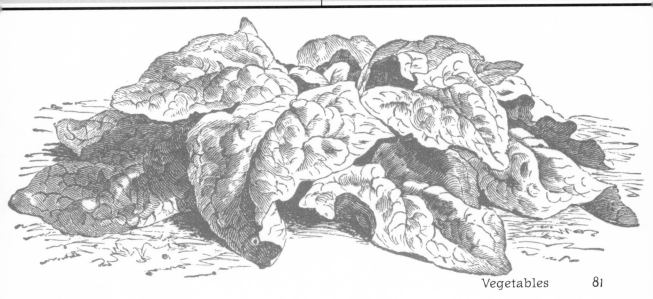

SUMMER SQUASH AND ZUCCHINI

Summer squash plants provide a bountiful harvest of zucchini, yellow straightneck and crookneck, and scallop (pattypan) squash. One hill of three plants can produce at least three dozen fruits in a season. Most squash are yellow; zucchini can be gold, gray, green, or black. Sunburst, a pattypan squash that I'm fond of, has bright yellow skin and tender, buttery texture. Black Beauty zucchini has very dark green skin that contains higher levels of antioxidants than lighter varieties. Costata Romanesco is an Italian heirloom whose grey-green fruits are more flavorful than other zucchini.

STARTING

Direct seed in warm soil (70°F) of pH 6.0 to 8.0. Sow seeds 1 inch deep, 6 seeds per hill, hills 3 feet apart each way. Squash are heavy feeders and need fertile soil; dig in plenty of well-aged manure or compost. Thin seedlings to the three strongest plants per hill.

In short-season areas, start seeds indoors in 3-inch peat pots, 4 weeks before the last frost. Sow three seeds to a pot, thinning to one or two plants. Plant outdoors as above, after danger of frost has passed.

CULTURAL REQUIREMENTS

Young seedlings should be kept weed free. The large, prickly leaves of older plants serve to shade out weed competition. Water during dry periods.

HARVEST

The tenderest, most flavorful squash range from baby-sized (3 to 4 inches) to 8 inches long. Longer ones will be tough and seedy. Pick frequently to encourage production and extend the season. Unpicked squash will quickly grow to an impressive baseball-bat size and retard new fruits. Allowing a few fruits to uninhibitedly grow this big can be done to slow production when the pantry is overflowing, you've exhausted all squash recipes, and the neighbors are trying to give you their surplus.

- Sauté zucchini or summer squash Italian style with garlic, olive oil, tomatoes, and fresh basil or oregano.

- Stuff squash by scooping out the center pulp (use it in stock or other dishes) and filling the shell with one of the following
  - Feta, cottage, and cream cheeses, parsley, dill, and scallions
  - Cooked chickpeas, rice, spinach, garlic, and lemon juice
  - Sautéed onions, walnuts, bread crumbs, Cheddar cheese, and sage
  - Cooked barley, mushrooms, red and green peppers, and marjoram

  Bake, covered, at 350°F for 45 minutes in a pan with about 1/8 inch of water or tomato juice in the bottom.

- Small "baby" squash look best if cut in half lengthwise for marinated salads or stews, or as a side dish. They cook very quickly; remove from the heat when crisp but tender.

- Squash and zucchini are good additions to soups and stews for feeding lots of people. Their delicate flavor harmonizes with most foods, and the abundant yields enable the cook to use them without reserve.

- Squash have lovely, large, bright edible flowers that can be stuffed, batter fried, or sautéed. Use male flowers, located at the end of short stems, because the female flowers yield the fruit. You can recognize female flowers by the small fruit between the flower's base and the vine.

SWEET POTATOES

Whether they're moist, orange, and called yams or somewhat drier, yellow, and referred to as sweet potatoes, we're talking about the same vegetable. (True yams are not to be confused with sweet potatoes; they're a specialty produce from the tropics, starchy and not very sweet.) Gardeners with ample growing space can enjoy sweet potatoes, a luscious, nutritious source of vitamins A, the B complex, and C. Traditionally grown during the long southern summer, sweet potatoes can also be a successful northern crop. I've reaped tasty but modest harvests by warming the soil with black plastic for 2 weeks prior to planting and then using the short-season variety, Georgia Jet. Porto Rico is a mid-season type available in bush form for smaller gardens.

STARTING

A sandy, slightly acid (pH 5.5 to 6.8), low-fertility soil is best for good-sized tubers. Young plants, or *slips*, can be purchased at local nurseries or through mail order. If slips appear particularly dry, soak overnight before planting. Resist trying to start with store-bought sweet potatoes: the potato will be of an unknown, possibly inappropriate variety and perhaps treated not to sprout.

Prepare garden soil into ridge-like rows 6 to 8 inches high, 3 feet apart. When soil temperatures are 70°F and frost danger has passed, plant the slips 1 foot apart along the top of the ridge. Set the slips so that each has 4 inches buried in the soil. Two leaves should remain above the soil line; it's fine if others are buried.

CULTURAL REQUIREMENTS

In cool climates, use heat-retaining plastic mulches (page 201) to warm the soil a week or two before planting; keep it in place throughout the season to maintain warmth. Young plants must be kept well weeded until the vines are robust enough to cover the rows.

❧ CULINARY TIPS ❧

❧ Use sweet instead of white potatoes for a deeper, richer flavor in soups and stews. Or serve simply fried, puréed, or roasted.

❧ We like sweet potatoes in vegetable curries; the sweet smoothness is a good contrast to the spicy, piquant seasoning.

❧ Try an unusual potato salad with

- Cooked sweet potato chunks, lemon or lime juice, vegetable oil, grated fresh gingerroot, parsley, and red onion
- Cooked sweet potato chunks, lemon juice, mayonnaise, apple, celery, and walnuts

Sweet potatoes do not thrive in a continually moist soil. Water only during extended dry periods.

HARVEST

Sweet potatoes can be dug after the first frost blackens the tips of the foliage or, in warmer regions, when the foliage turns yellow. Tubers will be damaged if they sit too long in soil cooler than 55°F. Dig and handle carefully as damaged skins do not store well. Dry in the sun for 3 to 4 hours, then cure in a warm place, 80°F or higher, for 1 to 2 weeks.

Store at 50°F to 60°F in a well-ventilated, dry location. Sugar content improves with storage. Never refrigerate as this encourages rot.

SWISS CHARD

A cousin of the beet, Swiss chard has a similarly earthy, "green" flavor and yields over a long season—from July to frost in my garden. The plant's deep roots condition the soil as well. Chard growing was revolutionized for me by the introduction of the Bright Lights series. This seed mix features chard stems and veins in a dazzling array of red, yellow, orange, gold, white, and purple, with some pastel shades as well. Leaf colors are green or burgundy. I love having edible plants that can do double duty as ornamentals. The plants are ready from the baby stage onward; young thinnings are beautiful salad additions. I start seeds in cell flats so I can indulge myself by arranging the seedlings by color, but chance may be just as rewarding. Of course, starting in flats also gives you a jump on the season. Rhubarb Chard (not to be confused with rhubarb) is an equally ornamental and edible variety with opulent, ruby red stalks and veined, wavy leaves. Fordhook Giant is an old standard, with broad, juicy stems topped by thick, substantial leaves. Perpetual Spinach (Fedco, Territorial) has thinner stems and smooth, very tender leaves with a milder, more spinach-like flavor than other chards. It's reputed to be hardy enough to be perennial in Zone 7 and higher.

STARTING

Chard seeds can be sown early or late in the spring. Soak the heavily husked seeds for 24 hours prior to planting. Plant seeds in soil of pH 6.0 to 7.0, $1/2$ to 1 inch deep, 3 to 4 inches apart, in rows $1^1/2$ feet apart. Thin plants to stand 6 inches apart.

- Tender young chard greens can be used in salads; stalks and medium-sized leaves can be cooked as a green vegetable.
- Cooked Swiss chard can be used where spinach is called for, providing its more robust flavor would not be intrusive.
- Swiss chard leaves can substitute for cabbage in stuffed cabbage recipes.

CULTURAL REQUIREMENTS

Swiss chard can be picked all summer if watered during dry periods. It makes a good hot-weather spinach substitute. Plants can be mulched to overwinter in mild climates and provide early-spring greens.

HARVEST

Snip the outer chard leaves; the new growth will continue to produce greens. Whole plants can be harvested to make room for other plantings.

TOMATOES

What praises can I sing to garden-grown tomatoes that haven't already been sung? Cherished for their aromatic, rich, sweet flavor, fresh tomatoes shine in even the simplest of preparations. Slice and serve with its classic companions fresh basil and golden olive oil, or simply eat them, warm off the vine, like an apple.

You can check with local sources for varieties proven in your area, but with hundreds of unique types available through mail-order seed companies, there's no reason to limit yourself. Differences in soil, temperature, climate, and seed strain affect tomato flavor. A variety that has been rhapsodized about in a seed catalog may be a loser in your garden. Still, they're likely to be better than store-bought, and it's always fun to try new ones. Many of the tomatoes below will only be available at farmers' markets because of their fragility when ripe. Heirloom tomatoes, grown for exceptional flavor, may not match the yields of the modern hybrids.

Most tomatoes fall into one or more of the following categories:

Early/determinate types are so named because their vines cease growing once the terminal buds set fruit. These plants tend to be bushy and can be grown with or without support, although support is always better to prevent rot in climates where the ground is wet. Oregon Spring (Fedco, Johnny's, Territorial) is a specifically cool weather–tolerant tomato that is early and reliable. Taxi (Johnny's, Territorial) is one of the best yellow tomatoes. It's early, sweet, low in acidity, and compact, at 2 feet tall by 2 feet wide.

Indeterminate/main crop are tall, continuous-growing tomato plants. They inevitably need support (see below) for best results. Vines will continue to bear until frost or cold weather. Early Girl is a dependable, luscious beefsteak type reputed to be widely adaptable to climate. Jetstar (Fedco) is popular in my area for its early ripening and resistance to cracking, a problem in wet seasons. Long Keeper (Territorial) is best picked green at season's end to ripen indoors. Though not as spectacular as a midsummer garden tomato, it is far superior to store-bought varieties in the fall and early winter. Store at 55°F to 75°F for up to 3 months, out of direct light, with the tomatoes wrapped in paper and not touching each other (to avoid the spread of any decay).

Heirloom indeterminates from all over the world have had a meteoric rise in popularity in the last decade. Families that had been saving seeds of beloved varieties for generations have been sharing with seed exchanges and collectors. International agricultural programs have helped in the gathering of seed stocks, especially from former Soviet Union countries now in more open contact with the world. I've found the following to be excellent; all are easy to find. Brandywine led the way as the first heirloom to spur the revival of other varieties. It has won a lot of contests for flavor, and the big (up to 1 pound), pink, very juicy fruits exemplify the beefsteak tomato. Cherokee Purple is reputed to have ancestry with the Cherokees of Tennessee. Fruits with purple-brown skin and red interior have a rich, full, sweet flavor. Striped German has beautifully marbled yellow and red fruits that make it a good choice for platters of sliced tomatoes. It's better suited to long growing seasons because the tomatoes mature late. Moskvich is from Siberia, and as you might expect, it's especially hardy, with early tomatoes that have late-season flavor. It provides ripe tomatoes about 2 weeks ahead of the main season plants in my garden. Costoluto Genovese has oddly shaped squat and ribbed large fruits that are versatile for juicing, sauce, or eating fresh. Although not very attractive, the tomatoes have a sweet, complex flavor.

Plum or paste tomatoes are drier and firmer than other types and so best suited for canning or sauces. Amish Paste (Cook's, Fedco) is my choice for a tall-growing indeterminate heirloom that bears abundant, large, flavorful tomatoes for processing as sauce, paste, or ketchup. San Marzano is a delicious Italian heirloom that is just as good for eating in hand as for cooking and drying. Principe Borghese is another Italian heirloom with few seeds and small size that make it a good choice for drying.

Small-fruited tomatoes include cherry and pear salad tomatoes, hanging basket, and container varieties suitable for gardeners with limited space. The following varieties are all indeterminate. My friend and a former Moosewood member Ashley Miller recommended Super Sweet 100, which I've found to be more crack resistant than the popular Sweet 100 variety. Yellow Pear is nice to grow for its unique color and the lower acidity typical of yellow and orange tomatoes. Sun Gold has a remarkably high sugar content with a good tart balance. Attractive, orange-red fruits have won the Moosewood staff's informal contest for best cherry tomato.

In catalogs or seedling packs, you will notice the letters V, F, N, T A, FF, St, and L located next to a variety (for example, Burpee's Supersteak Hybrid VFN). The letters indicate a genetic resistance to or tolerance of Verticillium wilt (V), Fusarium wilt (F), nematodes (N), tobacco mosaic virus (T), *Alternaria alternata*, or crown wilt (A), Race 1 and 2 Fusarium (FF), *Stemphylium*, or gray leaf spot (St), and leafspot or *Septoria* (L). Varieties so marked should not be plagued with the worst diseases, particularly when grown in the same location in continuing seasons.

STARTING

Sow tomato seeds indoors 6 to 8 weeks before the last frost. For good germination, soil temperatures should be 75°F or higher. After true leaves develop, transplant seedlings into individual peat pots or soil cells. Grow in ample light with a soil temperature range of 60°F to 70°F.

Seedlings can be set out when nights are above 50°F and frost danger has passed. Plant outdoors in soil of pH 5.5 to 7.5, 1 to 2 feet apart, in rows 2 to 3 feet apart, depending on the size of the variety. Rotate tomato crops from year to year to avoid diseases. Soil should be supplemented with a shovelful of compost for each plant or with an organic fertilizer.

Young tomato plants can be devastated by cutworms. Before planting, wrap each seedling with a newspaper collar that extends 2 inches above and below the soil level. (These will decompose by the time the plant is no longer vulnerable.)

To set seedlings horizontally in a shallow trench, remove the lower leaves and bury the stem up to the top three to six leaves. Cover with 2 to 3 inches of soil, making sure the top cluster of leaves is above the surface. Additional roots will form along the buried stem. The sun's heat will more readily penetrate to these roots than if the seedlings were planted vertically.

CULTURAL REQUIREMENTS

Tomato vines grow exuberantly with little regard to order or decorum. I never seem to get my plants restrained as easily as I would like. These are your choices:

- Leaving plenty of room around each plant, allowing them space to sprawl on the ground or dry mulch. This is the least efficient method of producing well-ripened, unblemished fruits, but it's good for those in dry climates or with a laissez-faire attitude.
- Using single stakes (details below):
  - With soft twine or yarn, tie vertical stems to 6-foot-tall stakes buried at least 1 foot in the ground.
  - Space plants 18 to 24 inches apart and prune or pinch to a single vertical stem. Single-staked plants will have a more open, manageable growth and earlier-ripening fruits than unpruned plants.
  - Remove suckers (shoots growing from the junction of vertical and leaf stems).
  - Fruits grow between leaf stems.

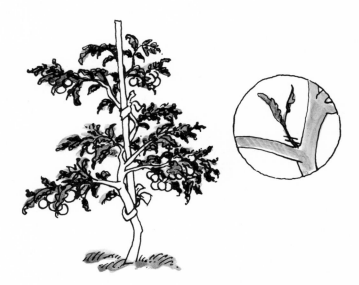

- Spacing plants 3 feet apart and allowing multiple stems to form. Tie the stems to stakes, three or more per plant. Harvests will be later than with single-staked plants but more abundant.
- Trellising (page 55).
- Setting up cages, available at garden stores. These work best with determinate or compact bushy varieties; a tall cage filled with tomatoes and heavy vines can easily topple, even in a moderate wind.

Hotkaps and poly-tunnels (pages 202–203) are useful to protect seedlings from cold late-spring weather. Be sure to remove these when the weather turns warm. Blossoms will not set fruit in excessive heat.

Avoid smoking cigarettes near tomato plants and before handling them to prevent the spread of mosaic virus. (Of course, sensible people avoid smoking cigarettes anywhere.)

With consistent moisture (not soggy soil), the chances of blossom-end rot will be minimized (it first appears as a dark, leathery spot on the side of the tomato opposite the stem). Regular watering, especially with a drip irrigation system or soaker hose, and mulching help maintain consistent soil moisture.

Plants will be neater if pruned to one or two main stems. Suckers—the side shoots that grow between the leaf axil and the main stem—should be removed to maintain open plants with a minimum of unnecessary vegetative growth. About 6 weeks before expected frosts, pinch off the top growing point, leaving two side leaves above the flowers. The plant can then put more energy into ripening the fruit already there, and less into more vegetative growth too late to yield tomatoes. As the fruit ripens, less water is needed.

✄ Broil thick tomato slices with garlic, oregano, and olive oil until the tomatoes are just heated and the garlic is golden.

✄ Prepare tomatoes for stuffing by scooping out the inside, lightly salting, and draining upside down for 15 minutes. Fill with

- Diced cucumbers, peppers, capers, and Herbed Mayonnaise (page 266)
- Diced avocado, minced chilies, cilantro, and Monterey Jack cheese
- Cooked rice marinated with one of the Vinaigrette Dressings (page 262) and diced raw vegetables
- Crumbled feta cheese mixed with cottage cheese, basil, and parsley

✄ My friend and neighbor Ann Pitkin likes to toss hot pasta with chopped uncooked tomatoes, garlic, and olive oil. Serve with grated Parmesan cheese.

✄ An excellent cooked sauce can be made with roughly chopped tomatoes, a clove or two of garlic, two bay leaves, and a touch of basil or oregano. After cooking the tomatoes just long enough to soften, remove the bay leaves and purée until smooth. Cook, uncovered, until reduced to the desired thickness.

✄ At Moosewood, we use chopped fresh tomatoes as a tart-sweet topping for rich, creamy dishes such as cheese rarebit or ravioli with pesto. Chopped basil, oregano, marjoram, chives, or shallots may be added.

✄ We have a different pita sandwich every day. Try the following suggestions with juicy fresh tomatoes and lettuce:

- Sliced mushrooms, grated carrots, and Golden Sesame Dressing (page 264)
- Cooked chickpeas, feta cheese, and Basil-Shallot Vinaigrette (page 263)
- Hard-boiled eggs, chives, celery, and Herbed Mayonnaise (page 266)
- Jarlsberg cheese, minced pickles, and Dill–Red Onion Vinaigrette (page 263)
- North African Roasted Vegetable Salad (page 231)
- Sesame Baked Tofu (page 255), cucumbers, and a Vinaigrette Dressing (page 262)

✄ Make a quick gazpacho by puréeing peeled, seeded tomatoes, onions, garlic, fresh chiles, and sweet peppers with a drizzle of olive oil. Serve at once or chilled.

✄ Freezing whole tomatoes in plastic bags or containers is easier and faster than canning. Once frozen, they can be easily peeled by rubbing off the skin under hot tap water. Thaw only as many as you need.

✄ Fried green tomatoes are a classic fall treat. Dredge the slices in herbed cornmeal and fry in $1/8$ inch of vegetable oil until each side is crisp. Drain and serve immediately.

HARVEST

Pick the ripest tomatoes and store at room temperature for best flavor. Refrigerated tomatoes become mushy and lose their flavor. When frost threatens, green tomatoes can be picked, wrapped in newspaper, and stored in a cool, dark place to ripen gradually.

TURNIPS

The tender, crisp roots of turnips are an essential addition to the soups and stews of fall and winter. Turnips are a cool-weather root vegetable that will be mild and tender if grown in early spring, late summer, or southern winter. But crops will be woody and bitter if temperatures are consistently above 80°F. Purple-Top White Globe is an heirloom variety that I've found to be mild in flavor and appealing in texture.

STARTING

Direct seed in loose, fertile soil with a pH of 6.0 to 8.0, 1/4 to 1/2 inch deep, in rows 12 inches apart. If root maggots and flea beetles are a problem in your area, use a fabric row cover put in place the day of sowing.

CULTURAL REQUIREMENTS

Seedlings should be thinned to stand 3 to 4 inches apart and weeded regularly to avoid spindly roots.

HARVEST

The green turnip tops, an excellent source of vitamin A, will be ready to pick and cook in 30 days, and the roots should be ready for harvest in 35 to 60 days, depending on the variety and growing conditions. Roots are at their best when picked young, 2 to

3 inches in diameter. For storage, turnips should be picked before the ground freezes; store, without the greens, in a root cellar or pit at 32°F to 40°F.

WINTER SQUASH

Winter squash adds a warm, sweet touch to meals in the chilly, dark days of late fall and winter. All types share a sweet, yellow to deep orange flesh, but there are significant differences as follows.

Acorn squash's dark green, ribbed fruit are just the right size for individual servings of half a baked squash. Mature acorn squash are ready straight from the garden, with no curing necessary. Acorns are best eaten within 3 months of harvest.

Buttercup and kabocha are botanically related squash, both sweeter after a few weeks of storage. The Burgess strain of buttercup is the most widely available and one of the sweetest I've tasted. Black Forest is a kabocha type that's a bit drier than the moist buttercups and very sweet.

Butternut is my favorite for cooking in stews or soups because its unridged skin is easier to peel than that of many other squashes. The flavor is superb, especially in the heirloom Waltham strain. Burpee's Butterbush is a good variety, with shorter vines than other butternuts and smaller fruit that is useful for individual servings. Butternuts, the best for long-term storage, are sweeter a few weeks after harvest and will keep for 5 months or more in good conditions.

Delicata/Sweet Dumpling and related types are all good fresh from the garden and need no curing. Delicata is an heirloom squash with rich, sweet, dry-textured flesh and moderately sized fruit that make it my favorite for stuffing. Bush delicata, with shorter vines but similar fruits, was developed here in Ithaca at Cornell. I've been growing it to conserve a bit of garden space and have found the squash to be just as good as the original delicatas. Sweet dumplings are a petite, teacup-sized squash good for individual servings, and with a good eating quality similar to delicata's. Carnival is a bigger version of sweet dumpling and, as one would guess, its skin is more festively colored with various shades of green, orange, and yellow.

Hubbard squash includes the giant, heirloom Blue Hubbards, definitely the ones to grow if you're entering a contest or planning to feed the masses at Thanksgiving. The fruits average 12 to 18 pounds but can grow as big as 30 pounds. Red Kuri, a botanically related squash, is a good variety for pies because the moist flesh purees to a very smooth texture. Kuri, named for the Japanese word for chestnut, has a mildly nutty flavor.

Spaghetti squash's pasta-like strands separate from the cooked pulp. After growing this and tasting the first squash, I thought, why bother? It's not as sweet or flavorful as other squash, nor is it as easy as real pasta.

STARTING

See summer squash (page 82) for starting information. Winter squash have more aggressive vines and should be placed in rows 3 feet apart with 2 feet between individual plants, or three plants to a hill with hills 6 feet apart. Plant winter squash where the up-to-12-foot-long vines have room to ramble without smothering smaller plants.

CULTURAL REQUIREMENTS

Fabric row covers can protect small plants from damaging bugs. As the flowers form, lift the covers to ensure pollination. To save space, small-fruited vining types can be trellised (page 55).

HARVEST

Winter squash is ripe when the fruit has a hard skin and dry stem. Harvest before a killing frost, as this can shorten storage life. Cut with 1 to 2 inches of stem attached and cure in the sun, if possible, for a week to 10 days. Cover well at night if a frost threatens. If the weather is chilly and damp, cure indoors in a warm spot, 80°F or higher.

Store in a cool, dry location, 45°F to 60°F, arranging the squashes so that air circulates between them. Wash off any molds that may appear on the skin. Most varieties will keep for 3 to 4 months.

❧ Butternut or other straight-sided squash are the easiest to peel and use for recipes calling for raw, cubed squash. A good vegetable peeler is easier to use than a knife.

❧ Add cooked winter squash to soups, waffles, muffins, biscuits, and quick and yeasted breads for sweetness and a golden hue.

❧ Winter squash puréed with butter and nutmeg or cinnamon makes a simple, comforting side dish.

❧ Baked halves of winter squash such as delicata, sweet dumpling, or acorn can be dressed up with a filling. Bake seeded halves, cut side up and lightly brushed with oil or butter, in a 400°F oven for 45 minutes to an hour, or until tender. Fill with one of the suggestions below and bake at 350°F to heat through.

- Diced apples, cinnamon, and butter
- Walnuts, dates, lemon juice, and grated lemon peel
- Honey, butter, and raisins
- Cranberries and honey
- Sautéed mushrooms and onions

❧ Baking or roasting winter squash brings out a sweeter and nuttier flavor than steaming or braising. For a quick preparation, cut the squash into rings or chunks. Lightly oil and bake covered at 425°F for 20 minutes, then bake uncovered for 5 minutes.

❧ Cook whole spaghetti squash in water to cover. Simmer for half an hour after the water has boiled, or until tender when pierced with a sharp knife. Drain the squash and allow it to cool. Cut in half, remove and discard the seeds, and scoop the "spaghetti" strands out of the shell. Serve warm with Herb Butter (page 271), pesto, or a sweet red pepper, tomato, or cheese sauce.

❧ Puréed winter squash freezes well.

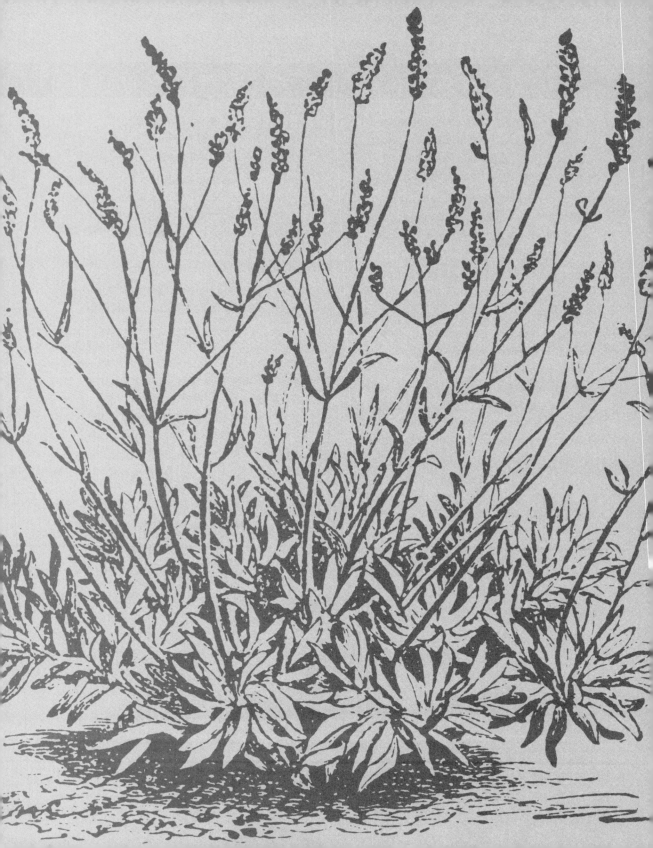

Herbs

THROUGHOUT HISTORY, herbs have been found wherever people have gardened. In the days before mass-produced chemicals and pharmaceuticals, the herb garden supplied nearly everything for cooking, making medicines, and pursuing various crafts such as dyeing and perfume making. I've thought it would be nice to bring back the old custom of strewing herbs across the floor as a primitive air freshener. The prospect of filling the house with the fragrance of mint, artemisia, lemon balm, or hyssop was appealing until I thought about the fact that the earthen floor of a cottage was far easier to sweep clean of trampled leaves and stems than a wall-to-wall carpet. But there remain countless other ways to enjoy the bounty of herbs: in cooking, in potpourri, and as ornamental plants in herb gardens or interspersed in vegetable and flower gardens.

There's confusion regarding the difference between herbs and spices, perhaps because so many of us use the terms interchangeably. Generally, herbs consist of the plant's leafy parts. Spices are primarily of tropical origin: allspice, cinnamon, cloves, ginger, nutmeg, and peppercorns, to name a few examples. Spices are usually derived from seeds, fruits, barks, and roots. (Herbalists complicate matters by referring to seeds, barks, and roots as herbs as well.)

GROWING HERBS

Most herbs are compact and so can easily be tucked into sunny vegetable or flower gardens to fill an empty space or add an interesting note of color, form, or foliage. Some ambitious gardeners plant herb-specific theme gardens composed of plants of similar fragrance, color, origin, use, or value.

Included in the herb listings that follow are a few solely ornamental species that are either very easy to cultivate or have a striking appearance, in bloom or leaf. Kitchen gardens need not be limited to edible plants; cooking and gardening share the ability to be more richly dimensioned when all the senses are treated as part of the experience. The few solely ornamental herbs mentioned represent a small percentage of the hundreds of interesting plants waiting to be explored and enjoyed.

Generally not as fussy as vegetables, herbs thrive in soil less rich than that of a well-tended vegetable garden. Commonly recommended for locations that are moderately dry, lean, or sandy, the herbs basil, lavender, marjoram, oregano, rosemary, sage, and thyme will have a stronger essential oil and taste when grown in such conditions than if grown in rich, moist soil.

Most herbs do best in full sun, with at least 6 hours a day of direct sunlight.

The following listings group together herbs that share certain characteristics. See the individual entries for their botanical names.

HERBS TOLERANT OF PARTIAL SHADE

Angelica	Germander	Lovage	Sweet cicely
Bee balm	Hyssop	Mint	Sweet woodruff
Chervil	Lemon balm	Parsley	

HERBS FOR FRAGRANCE

Basil	Lavender	Rosemary	Scented geranium
Bee balm	Lemon balm	Sage	Thyme
Chamomile	Mint	Santolina	

HERBS TO DRY FOR INDOOR ARRANGEMENTS

Lady's mantle	Lavender	Yarrow	
Lamb's ears	Santolina		

HERBS FOR COLORFUL, FRAGRANT FRESH BOUQUETS
(Using Sprigs, Leaves, or Flowers)

Angelica	Calendula	Lady's mantle	Sage
Basil	Chamomile	Lavender	Santolina
Bee balm	Dill	Lovage	Scented geranium
Borage	Hyssop	Mint	Thyme

HERBS THAT CAN BE GROWN AS HOUSEPLANTS

Basil	Chervil	Mint	Rosemary
Bay	Chives	Oregano	Sage
Calendula	Marjoram	Parsley	Scented geranium

In homes with very sunny, cool (50°F to 70°F) rooms or with grow lights, herbs can be grown in pots. Hot, dry, stuffy rooms invite pests and disease that will reduce harvests. Plants that are brought in from the garden at summer's end should be acclimated gradually to the indoors, beginning 2 to 3 weeks before you start heating your home. Before bringing any plants in, check carefully for insects (page 203) and cut back leggy growth, including blossoms and buds, which will deplete the plant's energy. Pots of chives should be subjected to some freezing weather outdoors to break their dormancy before moving them indoors (page 114). Be careful, however, not to allow them to freeze in a clay or ceramic pot because it will crack.

PRESERVING HERBS

Pick herbs for freezing or drying when the essential oils are at their peak: ideally, when they're on the brink of their flowering cycle, early in the morning after the dew has dried but before the heat of the day.

Strip the leaves from the stems (the house will smell great for hours). Place the leaves on window screens, in mesh produce bags, or in paper bags with small ventilation holes. Or spread the leaves on aluminum foil in an oven set at the lowest temperature. Watch very carefully to avoid overdrying or cooking. I use a warm attic room for drying. Herbs are dry when they're just at the point of crumbling. Cool and then place in containers.

Store jars of dried herbs in a cool, dark spot. It may be convenient to store them near a stove, but you will sacrifice flavor for convenience.

Fresh herbs to be stored in the refrigerator should be loosely wrapped in plastic to avoid drying out or soggy decay. Sprigs of parsley, cilantro, mint, and dill can be kept for a few days in small jars of water if you've picked more than you need.

HERB FLAVORS BEST RETAINED BY FREEZING

Basil*	Cilantro	Parsley	
Chervil	Dill	Tarragon	

HERBS WITH GOOD FLAVOR WHEN DRIED

Basil*	Mint	Sage	
Dill	Oregano	Savory	
Lovage	Rosemary	Thyme	

* The flavor of frozen basil more closely resembles its fresh flavor; dried basil has an appealing, though different than fresh, flavor.

In the discussions that follow, attention is paid to the culinary and landscape use of herbs. Consult the Bibliography (page 287) for resources dealing with a wider range of herb subjects.

Pregnant or nursing women, and people in unstable health, should consult a physician before taking any herbal preparations.

PROPAGATING HERBS

Many perennial herbs can be propagated by simple division. For northern gardeners, a good time to do this is in early spring, when the plants are still dormant. Gardeners with a long, mild fall or winter can divide them in late summer. Use a sharp spade to divide large or overcrowded clumps into smaller sections that can be replanted or given away. Easily divided herbs include bee balm, chives, lemon balm, marjoram, mints, oregano, creeping thymes, tarragon, sweet woodruff, and yarrow.

Cuttings are the best way to propagate woody herbs such as bay, lavender, rosemary, rue, sage, scented geraniums, winter savory, and common thyme. Cut 4- to 6-inch-long growing shoots from about $1/4$ inch below a leaf joint. Do a few at a time because not all will root. Carefully remove all the leaves from the lower half of the stem using a sharp, clean knife or blade. Fill a small pot with moist vermiculite, perlite, or sand. With a pencil, make a hole 1 to 3 inches deep. Insert a cutting and gently firm the damp rooting material. Water and set in a bright spot out of direct sunlight. Keep the cuttings evenly moist but not soggy. If your room is very dry, cover the pots with lightly perforated plastic to retain high humidity. Moisture will condense on the plastic, and if the damp plastic contacts the plant, it can cause rot or mold, so be sure to support the plastic up above the leaves. Use a coated wire hoop, bent pipe cleaner, or three sticks (Popsicle sticks, straws, or wooden plant markers).

POTPOURRI

Regardless of the season, potpourri will bring back the heady fragrance of a warm summer day.

Potpourri is composed of a main ingredient that supplies the dominant scent, usually derived from flowers, aromatic leaves, or roots. To this are added blending scents, fixatives (to "fix" the scent), and possibly essential oils (to intensify a particular scent). Orris root, the ground rhizome of *Iris florentina*, is one of the most widely used fixatives. Essential oils are highly concentrated and should be added a few drops at a time. A general formula for 1 quart of potpourri is 2 cups flowers, 1¼ cups fragrant herbs, ¼ cup spices, 1 tablespoon fixative, and a few drops of essential oil (if desired).

Pick flowers for potpourri early in the day, after the dew has dried. Flowers should be in bud or just beginning to open, but not in full bloom or past their prime. Dry them on a screen in a warm, well-ventilated spot out of direct sunlight until they are just brittle. Use recently dried herbs and freshly ground spices for additional fragrance.

Potpourri ingredients, including fixatives, herbs, and essential oils, are available through Nichols Garden Nursery and Well-Sweep Herb Farm.

Store potpourri in covered, nonmetallic containers to retain the fragrance. (Metal may alter the mixture's scent.) Add colorful, dried flower petals to mixes that will be kept in glass jars or bowls.

Sachets are potpourri mixes sewn into fabric bags to be placed in clothing or linen drawers. Use tissue paper as an inner lining for the bags to prevent small bits of crumbled potpourri from sifting out.

POTPOURRI RECIPES

Combine the potpourri ingredients and store in a covered, nonmetallic container in a cool, dark spot for 1 month to blend the fragrances. Tired potpourri can be revived with a few drops of essential oil or 1 teaspoon of brandy.

ROSE

2 cups rose petals and buds

1 cup rose geranium leaves

1 cup lemon verbena leaves

1 tablespoon ground allspice

1 tablespoon ground orris root

LEMON

1 cup lemon geranium leaves

1 cup lemon basil leaves

1 cup carnation petals

$^1/_4$ cup lemon thyme leaves

$^1/_2$ cup chopped lemon peel

1 tablespoon ground orris root

LAVENDER

2 cups lavender buds

$1^1/_4$ cups sweet woodruff* leaves

$^1/_2$ cup rose petals or buds

2 tablespoons ground nutmeg

2 tablespoons ground cloves

SPICE

1 cup nutmeg geranium leaves

1 cup coconut geranium leaves

$^1/_2$ cup basil leaves

$^1/_2$ cup patchouli leaves

$^1/_2$ cup mint leaves

2 tablespoons ground ginger

2 tablespoons ground cinnamon

1 tablespoon ground orris root

WOODSY

2 cups southernwood leaves

1 cup vetiver root*

$^1/_4$ cup lemon grass

$^1/_4$ cup bee balm leaves

$^1/_4$ cup mint leaves

2 tablespoons rosemary leaves

* Vetiver root and sweet woodruff leaves act as fixatives.

ANGELICA *(Angelica archangelica)*

With handsome, leafy stalks, greenish flower umbels, and an ultimate height of 6 feet or more and width of over 2 feet, angelica has a striking, dramatic presence.

A short-lived perennial, angelica frequently takes 2 or 3 years to flower and dies shortly thereafter. If the rounded flower umbels are cut off early enough, plants should live another year. Or, if you prefer, seeds can be left to self-sow or can be collected and planted shortly after they have ripened. Seeds do not remain viable for long.

GROWING

Native to wet areas, angelica does best in a cool climate, moist, well-drained soil, and full sun to partial shade. Start plants from seeds or purchase seedlings. Set plants 2 to 3 feet from one another or neighboring plants.

CULINARY TIPS

- Angelica leaves and stems have an aromatic, licorice flavor. Add a few young leaves to fruit or leafy salads.
- The tender stems of new growth can be candied for an old-fashioned treat.
- Roots and seeds have been traditionally used in perfumes and liqueurs.

Note: **Angelica should not be ingested by diabetics or pregnant women.**

BASIL *(Ocimum basilicum and other species)*

I had my first taste of fresh basil over 30 years ago at my friend Roseanna Samartano's home in California. Rose had prepared a simple vegetable soup that she'd seasoned with something wonderful that I couldn't quite place. It turned out to be Bronx-grown basil packed in olive oil and salt, which Rose's mother had shipped all the way to Berkeley.

Since then the rest of the country has discovered basil and developed quite a love affair with it. Pesto sauces (of which basil is the key ingredient) are almost a cliché. Still, summer without fresh basil would be dull indeed.

Though sweet, or Italian, basil is the variety most commonly known for cooking purposes, there are other spicy, fragrant, and colorful basils that can be used for cooking, garnishing, making teas and potpourris, and ornamental planting.

Cinnamon basil is strongly fragrant, with attractive, pink-mauve flowers. Grow it alongside a path, and as you brush the leaves they will perfume the air. Dried leaves retain their scent and make good potpourri material.

Holy basil, an ornamental plant, comes in green- or purple-leafed types, both with a sweet, clove-like fragrance. Now grown primarily for potpourri, holy basil was historically used as a sacred herb in the temples of India.

Italian basils include Genovese (from Genoa); its strong fragrance and spicy flavor make it the variety to grow for an authentic Italian pesto. Lettuce leaf basil has large, mild-flavored leaves that make pesto production, drying, and freezing less of a chore. The big leaves also make nifty wrappers for hors d'oeuvres. Mammoth is a widely available basil of this type. Napoletano is another large leaf type but with stronger flavor and attractively frilled leaves.

Lemon basil offers unique lemon flavor that adds a twist to any dish in which sweet basil might be used. The fragrant leaves also enhance herbal tea mixes, potpourri, and iced drinks. Sweet Dani is a popular lemon basil variety that is more vigorous than the unnamed species.

Lime basil combines a distinctive lime flavor with the usual basil flavor.

Purple or dark opal basil varieties include Purple Ruffles, Red Rubin, and Opal. The dark maroon-purple leaves and baby pink flowers make a showy bouquet addition and culinary garnish as well as a good foil for lighter garden plants. My favorite way of using this beautiful basil is in a brilliant ruby red Herb Vinegar (page 260). This strongly flavored basil should be used sparingly in cooking.

Small-leaved basils include Minimum, Spicy Globe, Fino Verde Compatto, and Piccolo. These compact, mound-shaped, 8- to 12-inch plants do well in pots and other containers, and they make an attractive, dense, edible edging for flower or vegetable beds. The leaves are small but have the same flavor and fragrance as sweet basil. Include a pot of mini-basil in a sunny winter window garden.

Thai basil has a more anise-licorice flavor than Italian basil and is the one to grow for authentic Southeast Asian cuisine.

GROWING

Start basil seeds indoors 4 to 6 weeks before the last frost, or sow directly in the garden when the soil is warm and the danger of frost has passed. Lemon basil resents transplanting and should be sown directly in the garden or in peat pots. Thin or plant seedlings to stand 1 foot apart (8 inches for mini-leafed types). Basil likes a hot, sunny, fertile location. The leaves will discolor and be damaged in cold weather, so cover plants if temperatures drop below 40°F. Keep flowers pinched to encourage new growth. Harvest basil before fall frosts or the onset of cold weather.

✖ CULINARY TIPS ✖

✖ Basil is probably the most commonly used herb at Moosewood. We cook with it in some fashion every day, using the fresh leaves in our house dressing and many savory dishes.

✖ Wash and drain the fresh leaves gently; they bruise and blacken easily.

✖ Marinate juicy, ripe beefsteak tomatoes with chopped basil leaves, garlic, and extra virgin olive oil.

✖ Prepare a fast, uncooked tomato sauce with garden-ripe tomatoes, a few cloves of crushed garlic, a small onion, a generous handful of basil, and a little mint and parsley. Purée or process until smooth, toss with hot pasta, and serve immediately with freshly grated Parmesan cheese.

✖ Make a quick "pizza" by cutting a pita bread in half horizontally to yield two "crusts." Top each half with chopped tomatoes, fresh basil, fresh oregano, garlic, mozzarella and Parmesan cheeses, and a drizzle of olive oil. Broil or bake until golden and bubbly.

✖ Toss pasta with a sauce of diced garden vegetables (carrots, zucchini, peppers, fennel, eggplant, or tomatoes) that have been sautéed with fresh basil, a splash of dry white wine, and some cream.

✖ Add basil to cheese fillings for tortellini, lasagna, crepes, omelets, stuffed shells, or manicotti.

✖ Fresh basil's flavor can be preserved only by freezing, canning with olive oil, or incorporating in an herb vinegar. Dried basil is a fine seasoning but has a different taste, subtler and less aromatic than the fresh herb.

✖ Purée or process fresh, stemmed basil leaves with olive oil and freeze in small containers for future use. My Moosewood colleague and dear friend Ned Asta freezes ice cube trays of olive oil–blended basil. When frozen, remove the cubes from the trays and pack in bags. Use to add a "hit" of basil flavor to winter dishes. At Moosewood, we also freeze plastic bags full of stemmed basil leaves when we're too busy for the blending method. Frozen basil will turn blackish when it's thawed, so use it in dishes where appearance will not be a problem.

✖ Chiffonades are very thin shreds or ribbons of herbs or greens used as an elegant garnish and seasoning. To make one out of basil, stack four or five leaves with the stems aligned. Roll the leaves to form a long "cigar," and then, with a sharp knife, cut very thin lengthwise strips. Use right away before the leaves discolor.

BAY LAUREL
(Laurus nobilis)

The bay tree's glossy, deep green leaves and elegant form make it an outstanding ornamental as well as a popular culinary herb.

An evergreen tree native to the Mediterranean, bay is hardy outdoors only to Zone 8. I have a potted bay tree that is many years old. Container- or pot-grown plants need a summer outdoors or a sunny window indoors. Plants can be easily trimmed; train young trees to a single trunk standard or allow them to form a shrubby bush.

The laurel wreaths of classical times were made from bay. Experience a sense of continuity with the ancient Greeks and Romans by presenting a homemade wreath on any occasion, victorious or not.

GROWING

Bay trees are difficult to start from seed. Buy plants from a nursery or root a cutting taken from the new, green growth. Trees can be grown outdoors in partial shade to full sun.

CULINARY TIPS

- All Mediterranean cuisines make generous use of bay leaves. In the New World, Creole and New England cooking rely on bay as a primary seasoning.

- At Moosewood, we use bay leaves in combination with other herbs. Bay is like the bass part in music: perceived, but as a background to other dominant notes. Chowders, stews, vegetable or fish stocks, sauces, and marinades benefit from bay leaves. It's an herb that should be included early in the cooking process because heat draws out the essential oil.

- We also use bay leaves in storage containers for grains and beans; they're reputed to deter cereal moths. Continue the "relationship" by cooking beans or grains with a bay leaf or two.

- Always use whole bay leaves. Even hours of cooking will not soften small pieces of leaf, and they will be hard to find. Thoughtful cooks remove bay leaves before serving a dish to prevent accidental ingestion. However, some people claim that it's good luck to find a bay leaf in your dish. If using the latter method, warn your guests or family to watch for bay leaves.

BEE BALM OR BERGAMOT
(Monarda didyma or Monarda fistulosa)

Drifts of bee balm make a brightly flowered background for sunny borders or partially shaded areas. The 3- to 4-foot-tall plants are topped with unique pompoms of tubular flowers, available in many shades of lavender, pink, white, violet, or red. The midsummer blooms attract butterflies and hummingbirds.

This American native was traditionally used as a tea by the Oswego Indians, and later by the colonists during their boycott of English imported black tea. Its essential oil is the ingredient that gives Earl Grey tea its distinctive taste.

GROWING

You'll find bee balm also identified as bergamot or monarda. Hardy in zones 4 through 9, bee balm is happy in sun or partial shade but will do best in shadier locations in its southern range. To obtain specific colors, buy plants or acquire divisions from friends because seedlings may be variable in color and form. The offspring of one pink bee balm in my garden was a brilliant violet-purple, which I actually preferred to the pink.

Space plants 2 feet apart in a moist location with rich, fertile soil. Bee balm tolerates dryness but may wilt and bloom poorly. Divide vigorous clumps every 2 to 3 years. Colonies tend to form as a "donut" around the bare older center. Cut out wedges of the newer growth to replant, then discard the dead, woody center. Also, be aware that most monarda can be quite invasive, so you may be dividing clumps as early as the first year.

CULINARY TIPS

- Bee balm's vivid flowers and fresh leaves are edible. The leaves have an unusual flavor that I would describe as perfume-mint-oregano. Flower petals make brilliant garnishes or additions to multicolored salads.

- Bee balm is used in the manufacture of perfume. The dried leaves and flowers retain their essential oil, known as bergamot, for fragrant potpourri and herbal tea material.

CALENDULA
(Calendula officinalis)

Single or double daisylike flowers in all shades of cream to deep orange grace the 6- to 24-inch-tall calendula plants. The original species is somewhat floppy and 18 inches to 2 feet tall, with smaller flowers. Named varieties include Pacific Beauty, a standard old-time variety, and Touch of Red, yellow to gold with deep-red petal backs. Many British gardening books refer to calendula as "marigold" or "pot marigold." Calendula should not be confused with the very separate *Tagetes* species that we in the United States know as marigolds. The name *marigold* derives from a medieval association between the Virgin Mary and the golden-rayed flowers of *Calendula officinalis*. *Tagetes* have sharply pungent foliage and flowers and should not be used interchangeably with calendulas.

Historically, calendula was used in Europe for myriad medicinal and culinary purposes. At Moosewood, Myoko Vivino makes a calendula ointment that's a time-honored and -tested remedy for burns and cuts—two mishaps not uncommon in a busy kitchen. It requires no arcane procedures or exotic (eye of newt, and so on) ingredients. Cut two or three calendula plants as they are budding, but before they bloom, when the essential oil is strongest. Either mash the stems and leaves with a mortar and pestle or roll with a heavy rolling pin between sheets of waxed paper until the juices flow. Put 1 cup of this pulverized mash into a 1-quart canning jar, then fill with ethyl alcohol or 100-proof vodka. Let it steep in a dark place, such as a kitchen cupboard, at room temperature. Vigorously shake the jar once a day for 2 weeks, then twice a week. The ointment will be ready in about 100 days from picking the herbs, though you could sneak a little before then in an emergency. Strain and discard the pulp and reserve the fluid, keeping the jar tightly capped. Generously apply with sterile cotton pad to burns and cuts.

GROWING

Calendulas are hardy annuals that can be seeded as soon as the soil is workable. They will self-sow if they're happy in the location. The plants do better in cool weather, so grow them early or late in the season where summers are hot. They can survive light frosts and will do well in coastal California or southern winters.

Space dwarf varieties 8 inches apart, taller types 1 foot apart, all in full sun.

Deadheading, the removal of spent flowers, will considerably lengthen the blooming season.

CULINARY TIPS

Sunny, brightly colored calendula petals are having a renaissance in flower cookery. Fresh petals should be snipped off the flower center: hold the outside edges of the petals with one hand while cutting with the other. Cut so that the somewhat bitter whitish part remains with the discarded flower center. Use 2 to 3 tablespoons of fresh petals (less if dried) for subtle flavor and a golden hue in pilafs, breads, soups, salads, and egg dishes.

Homegrown calendula petals can be substituted for saffron, for a similar color but different flavor.

Note: Pregnant women should avoid ingesting calendula.

CHAMOMILE
(*Matricaria recutita* and *Chamaemelum nobile*)

The word *chamomile* is applied to two separate genera of plants:

One, *Matricaria recutita* (Sweet false or German chamomile), is a 2- to 3-foot-tall annual with feathery, divided foliage and small, apple-scented, daisylike flowers.

The other, *Chamaemelum nobile* (Roman chamomile), is a perennial that grows 8 or 9 inches tall. Its similarly feathery foliage is more strongly scented than that of *M. recutita*, and its flowers can be single or double.

GROWING

Sow seeds for *M. recutita* in fall or spring in a sunny area. Plants will tolerate dry, sandy, and sunny locations. Harvest the flowers when they are fully open, allowing some to remain on the plant to self-sow. This species has been generous with volunteer seedlings in my garden.

C. nobile can be seeded in spring and prefers moist but well-drained soil in sun or partial shade. Roman chamomile makes a feathery ground cover that releases a fruity scent when walked upon. Plants can be mowed to encourage denser growth, but not until they are well established.

Both species do best in the cooler climates of zones 3 to 5 or the temperate areas of the Pacific Northwest and the California coast.

CULINARY TIPS

M. recutita flowers are the ones to grow and dry for chamomile tea. Tisanes (herbal teas) of chamomile have been and remain popular in Europe as a soothing, calming drink that's reputed to alleviate everything from colds to upset stomachs.

Note: **Pregnant women should avoid ingesting chamomile.**

CHERVIL *(Anthriscus cerefolium)*

The fernlike, delicately flavored foliage of this hardy, 2-foot-tall annual is traditionally used in French cuisine. The taste is reminiscent of a mild tarragon combined with parsley. The plant's rounded form and feathery leaves are attractive in flower, herb, or vegetable beds.

GROWING

Chervil does well in cool seasons; it quickly bolts to seed in hot weather. Sow seeds outdoors in the spring, then thin plants to stand 6 inches apart. I've grown chervil between broccoli plants, letting the taller broccoli provide some cooling shade in the hotter months. Allow plants to go to seed. Chervil has generously reseeded itself in my garden from year to year.

❦ CULINARY TIPS ❦

- ✎ Use fresh chervil leaves where their subtle bouquet won't be overwhelmed by more assertive flavors: in creamy dips, sauces, light soups, cheese spreads and fillings, vegetable purées, simple fish dishes, omelets, dressings, mayonnaise, and herb butter.

- ✎ At Moosewood, we use whole sprigs as an elegant, lacy garnish.

- ✎ Toss new potatoes with chopped chervil and mint.

- ✎ Put leafy sprigs into salads of multicolored lettuce leaves and zippy greens such as arugula, endive, and radicchio.

- ✎ Chervil loses most of its flavor when dried; freeze sprigs for winter use.

CHIVES *(Allium schoenoprasum)*

Clumps of chives, with their deep bluish-green, grasslike leaves, make handsome foot-high edgings. In late spring, rosy lavender, purple, or white flowers appear above the foliage, giving a beautiful mounded effect.

GROWING

Chive seeds can be started any time and will germi-nate best if kept in a dark spot with a soil temper-ature between 60°F and 75°F. Get a head start by planting new plants or divisions. Chives are quick-growing, hardy perennials that thrive in good soil. Set plants 6 inches apart in a sunny or lightly shaded spot. Divide clumps every 3 years or so, especially if neighboring plants are being crowded.

To harvest, snip the leaves about 2 inches above the ground—never pull them. Cut off the faded flowers; if allowed to go to seed,

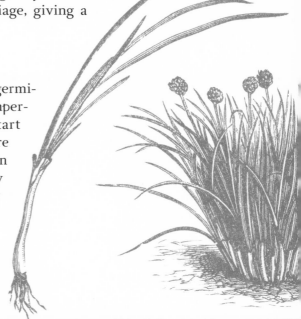

✼ CULINARY TIPS ✼

✿ With a flavor similar to but milder than scal-lions and onions, chives can be used with-out fear of their dominating a dish. Chives should be added at the very last minute to any hot foods; their flavor is diminished by too much heat.

✿ Chives can add a last-minute pick-me-up to dishes that need just a little something to spark the palate.

✿ Creamy, mild dishes such as dips, cheese spreads, white sauces, eggs, herb butters, plain steamed vegetables, grains or noo-dles, and dressings can all be enhanced with a few tablespoons of finely chopped chives.

✿ Use the edible flowers to garnish salads and soups (they float nicely) and to make a pale pink herb vinegar. Taste them first; some blossoms are quite pungent.

✿ Freeze chopped or whole chive leaves; home-dried plants lack flavor.

their progeny will crop up throughout the garden. Clumps may look a bit tired in a hot, dry summer; clip off the yellowed foliage, and plants should revive with new leaves in cooler, moist weather.

For winter windowsill pots of chives, dig up a clump in late summer, place in a plastic pot, and let it remain in the ground for about a month of freezing weather. The plants will then have experienced the brief dormancy they need in order to send up new growth once inside.

CORIANDER (CILANTRO)
(Coriandrum sativam)

Few people are indifferent to the pronounced flavor of fresh coriander leaves, more commonly known as cilantro; there are those who are fans and those who are not. At Moosewood, we use it in a variety of dishes, where its distinctive flavor is ethnically or traditionally appropriate and in newer recipes that cross cultural borders.

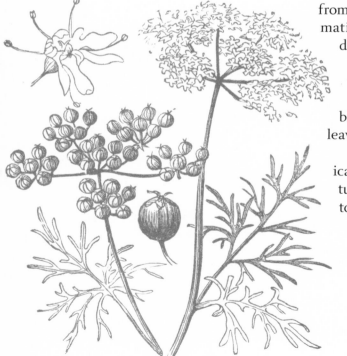

Coriander seeds taste completely different from the leaves. They're more sweetly aromatic and flavor foods as diverse as hot dogs and butter cookies.

An annual, coriander will grow 2 to 3 feet tall in a sunny, fertile spot. The vivid green, divided leaves resemble a smaller, paler version of the flat-leaved, or Italian, parsley.

Although cultivated in Latin America, Asia, and the Middle East for centuries, coriander is a relative newcomer to North American cooking.

GROWING

Direct sow seeds after all frost danger is past, in full sun. Plant often, as even the slow-bolting varieties will go to seed after a few weeks' growth. Thin seedlings to 6 inches apart.

HARVEST

Harvest the fresh leaves before the plant begins to flower. Pick the seed heads when they are dry and brown. In cold or wet weather, plants can be hung upside down indoors, and the seeds will continue to ripen. I allow a few plants to ripen and drop their seeds in the garden for a crop of volunteers in the following season.

❧ CULINARY TIPS ❧

- Add fresh leaves at the end of cooking time for best flavor.

- Spicy salsas with coriander leaf add a distinctive Latin American spark when served with bean dishes, soups, grilled fish or vegetables, chips, guacamole, and casseroles.

- The cuisines of India, the Middle East, China, and Southeast Asia use coriander leaf as a key herbal accent or final garnish. One or two tablespoons of chopped leaf make a cooling, fresh counterpoint to peppery curries, soups, or stir-fries.

- Serve a refreshing cucumber raita with fiery curries: combine one diced cucumber, 2 cups yogurt, $1/4$ teaspoon ground cardamom seeds, and 2 tablespoons chopped fresh coriander leaf.

- Dried leaves lack flavor; freezing is preferred.

- For the richest fragrance, we use freshly ground coriander seeds (a coffee grinder works well).

- Ground coriander seed adds a spicy (though not hot) bouquet to chowder, chili, bean dishes, tomato sauces, marinades, muffins, sweet breads, and cookie batters.

- Add a few whole coriander seeds to mulled cider or wine along with two or three whole cloves or allspice berries and a cinnamon stick.

DILL (*Anethum graveolens*)

If basil is the most frequently used herb at Moosewood, then dill is surely the runner-up. With extremely fine, bluish foliage and chartreuse flower heads, the 2- to 4-foot-tall plants are suitable for the back of the flower border as well as the vegetable garden. The wide, upside-down umbrella–like flower heads of this easily grown annual give cut bouquets unusual form and color. I've enjoyed a planting where the early morning sun shone through plants filigreed with dew.

GROWING

Dill does not transplant happily; sow seeds in good garden soil and full sun in early spring. Thin seedlings to stand 6 inches apart. I've had good luck with dill vigorously reseeding on its own from year to year. Curiously, these volunteer seedlings are taller and more robust than those from purchased seeds. Allow a few plants to stand in the garden until the flower heads have matured and dropped seed.

✺ CULINARY TIPS ✺

✺ Fresh and dried dill leaf are both referred to as dill weed in some recipes.

✺ We use dill weed anywhere its mellow herb flavor will enrich a dish, especially in Jewish, Russian, Greek, Scandinavian, and Eastern European cuisines. Try it with foods for which it has a particular affinity: potato dishes and soups, cucumber salads, eggs, sour cream or yogurt dips, sauces and dressings, hearty fall and winter stews, sautéed mushrooms, cheese spreads or fillings, and green beans; with lemon butter and broiled fish; and in herb vinegars and butters.

✺ Dill seeds have a caraway-like flavor and can be used whole in rye and pumpernickel breads or to top savory pastries. Add ground seeds to soups, stews, and pickled vegetables.

✺ Whole dill flower heads are flavorful, attractive additions to pickling marinades.

✺ Dried dill weed is an acceptable substitute for fresh leaves. Frozen is even better.

FENNEL *(Foeniculum vulgare)*

A tall (4 to 6 feet), striking plant with feathery foliage, fennel, or sweet fennel, is a decidedly ornamental herb. The foliage resembles dill, but its flavor is similar to licorice or anise.

The varieties Bronze, Rubrum, and Copper feature maroon-purple young growth that later matures to bronze. These create a stunning contrast to lighter flowers and green plants. *F. vulgare* should not be confused with the bulb-forming vegetable Florence fennel, or *finocchio* (page 44).

GROWING

Fennel is hardy in zones 5 or 6, but does well as an annual in cooler climates. It has naturalized with abandon in the mild climate of coastal California. Sow seeds in the early spring, thinning small plants to 12 inches apart. Seedlings for the bronze-leafed varieties can be obtained from nurseries specializing in herbs.

Leaves are harvested for culinary use at any time. They do not retain their flavor when dried. Pick the seeds soon after they turn brown, or they will self-sow throughout the garden.

CULINARY TIPS

- Use leaves and tender stems in dressings, marinades, salads, pilafs, stews, and fish dishes.
- Fennel seeds add a nutty, anise flavor to breads, cookies, apple pie, Italian sweet biscuits (biscotti), soups, marinades, and tomato sauces.
- East Indian meals are completed with *paan*, a mixture of fennel or anise that sometimes includes cardamom seeds. It serves as a digestive aid and palate cleanser.

GARLIC *(Allium sativum)*

Universally appreciated for millennia, garlic's place in the pantheon of beloved foods is well established. Images of garlic appear in the Egyptian pyramids, and it's used in almost every cuisine of the world. It's inconceivable to think of cooking without garlic. Although it needn't be in every savory dish, garlic's signature flavor is an important part of the whole in countless recipes. Part of the onion family and technically a vegetable, garlic is used mainly as a seasoning. Its popularity is due to both its culinary value and its many medicinal and nutritive benefits. Garlic has been proven to deter the growth of bacteria and fungi, as well as reduce serum cholesterol levels. It's reputed to support the immune system and enhance circulation. Eating garlic can do no harm, unless you're the only one in a group who has indulged.

Raw garlic is the culprit in breath problems more often than cooked garlic, because the aroma-causing agent in raw garlic enters the bloodstream and is exhaled with each breath. After an especially garlic-filled Bacchanalian feast, the ancient Romans ate raw parsley to cleanse the breath.

Sources that sell garlic for planting offer two distinct kinds, hardneck and softneck.

Hardneck varieties are cold-weather hardy and the best for northern climates. They send up a stiff flower stalk (scape) that will eventually produce small cloves or bulbils. To avoid weakening the underground bulb, remove all of these coiled flower stalks—perhaps sparing one or two to appreciate their elegant, art-nouveau form. If you don't get around to cutting these off, the small bulbils can be planted for spring garlic greens or left to grow for two summers when they'll produce larger bulbs. See below for culinary uses of the scape. Hardnecks produce a few large, easily peeled cloves in one layer surrounding the central stalk. In favorable storage conditions, they'll keep for 3 to 6 months.

German White (Seeds of Change) and German Extra-Hardy (Fedco, Johnny's) are large-bulbed, vigorous garlics with good storage potential and hardiness. Russian Red (Fedco, Johnny's) has smaller cloves but stronger flavor and better storage. Purple Italian Easy Peel (Seeds of Change, Territorial) is a good choice for consumers of vast quantities as it can be quickly peeled, and it has a nice spicy flavor as well. Spanish Roja (Seeds of Change, Territorial) is perhaps my favorite; it's an heirloom prized for especially rich flavor and large bulbs. This variety needs a cold winter to do well.

Softneck varieties are easy to braid because their central stalk isn't stiff like the hardnecks'. They have smaller cloves in overlapping layers, do well in warm climates, tend to be spicier, and have longer storage potential though less hardiness than the hardnecks.

Inchellium Red (Fedco, Seeds of Change, Territorial) has large cloves for a softneck and a mild flavor, especially nice for roasting. New York White (Johnny's) is one of the hardier softnecks for gardeners in colder climates who like to braid their garlic. Transylvanian (Seeds of Change) is a recent import and reputed to keep Count Dracula and his friends at bay. Chinese Pink (Territorial) matures 4 to 6 weeks ahead of most varieties and stores for 4 to 5 months.

Elephant garlic—actually the bulb of a type of leek—has cloves two or three times larger than regular garlic. I don't recommend it because its taste is very bland; you end up using more of it, which negates the size advantage.

GROWING

The onionlike flat leaves of garlic grow 1 to 2 feet tall from cloves planted in fall or winter. Garlic needs a long, cool start, so only in the coldest climates should it be started in the spring. Fall-planted bulbs are usually twice as large as those planted in spring. Plant from right after the first frost up until late fall or 6 weeks before the soil freezes. The larger the garlic cloves planted, the better the potential for heads with large cloves. Small cloves can be closely planted for garlic greens to be harvested in spring. Gardeners who live where winter temperatures regularly drop below 0°F should mulch fall-planted bulbs with 3 to 4 inches of hay or straw.

Space individual cloves 4 to 6 inches apart, with 1 to 2 inches of soil over the top of the cloves. Choose a sunny spot with rich, well-drained soil that is not stony. For the biggest bulbs, keep plants well weeded or mulched. Irrigate, if necessary, to keep the soil moist but not soggy.

✄ When we're talking garlic, we're talking fresh garlic. Avoid the bitter, artificial taste of dried garlic powder, granules, or salt.

✄ To peel garlic cloves, give them a good whack with the side of a sturdy, long knife or cleaver, just hard enough to loosen the skin. Hollow plastic rollers for peeling garlic are also available.

✄ Add small amounts of minced garlic to sauces, stews, or soups that need a boost.

✄ Garlic is a popular seasoning, but for variety and contrast, use it only in one or possibly two dishes at a given meal. Be careful not to overdo garlic in an attempt to give a dish assertive flavor.

✄ Garlic scapes (with the fibrous flower bud removed) and tender spring greens have a gentler flavor than the familiar buds. Use them instead of basil for a garlicky pesto. Alternatively, chop and add toward the end of cooking time for a mild garlic flavor in savory dishes.

✄ Garlic croutons are much-loved at Moosewood as a crisp, savory garnish for soups and salads. Cube leftover bread, toast, and toos with garlic butter. Bake in low heat for a few minutes to crisp.

✄ Garlic's intensity varies, depending upon how it's prepared:

- Whole garlic cloves added to soup, sauce, or stew for long, slow cooking will be mild and gentle.
- Minced or pressed garlic will be strong, as mashing releases its potent oils.
- Roasted garlic has a nutty, sweet flavor quite a bit milder than raw. It makes a rich, creamy, fat-free spread for bread and crackers or a flavorful addition to any savory dish. To roast, remove most of the papery outer skin from three or four heads of garlic. Cut off the top $1/2$ inch of each head, keeping the head intact but slicing off the tips of the uppermost cloves. Lightly rub with oil. Bake uncovered in a small dish, in a 375°F oven, for 45 minutes or more, until the cloves are soft. When cool, squeeze the garlic paste from the heads. If you don't use it all right away, the rest will keep for 1 week refrigerated.
- Whole or half cloves can be used to season cooking oil. Remove the cloves from the hot oil when they are golden; discard. The oil will be garlicky but not overpowering.
- For a subtly flavored salad, rub a wooden salad bowl with a cut clove of garlic (then discard it).
- Garlic should be sautéed carefully; it tastes harsh and bitter if browned or scorched.

HARVEST

To help the bulbs ripen, stop watering once the foliage begins to yellow. Carefully dig the bulbs when 70 percent of the tops are still green. If you wait too long, the skins start to separate from the bulbs and long-term storage is compromised.

Cure bulbs in a dry, shady, ventilated spot for a few days until any clinging dirt can be gently removed. To braid garlic, choose softneck varieties with supple foliage that is not too dry or brittle. Storage is the same as for onions: a cool, airy, dark location, ideally 50°F. Colder temperatures (in a refrigerator, for example) cause the bulbs to sprout; hotter temperatures encourage rot.

GERMANDER *(Teucrium chamaedrys)*

Germander is an excellent visual foil for brightly colored flowers or the gray foliage of lavender, stachys, sage, and other herbs. The shrubby, deep green foliage can be pruned for a hedgelike effect in edging borders or traditional knot gardens. In summer, petite, rosy violet flowers appear atop small spikes on the 1- to 2-foot plants.

GROWING

Purchase small plants from a nursery that specializes in herbs, or propagate by cuttings and division. Plants can be started from seeds but may take more than a month to germinate. Germander is a perennial and will grow in zones 5 to 10 in well-drained, good garden soil. Set plants 1 foot apart.

HYSSOP
(Hyssopus officinalis and *Agastache foeniculum)*

Used as a ritual cleansing herb in biblical times, the sharply aromatic hyssop plant is grown predominantly as an ornamental today. The 1- to 2-foot perennial has spikes of small, blue, pink, or white flowers. Plants can be trimmed to a hedge; however, flower spikes may be cut off in the process.

A dwarf variety, *Hyssopus officinalis* Aristata is a compact plant, no more than 1 foot tall and suitable for low edgings.

Anise hyssop *(Agastache foeniculum)* is a short-lived perennial that features showy, 3-foot-tall, purple flower spikes in summer. It reseeds generously.

GROWING

Both hyssop and anise hyssop are grown from seeds, divisions, or cuttings. Plants do best in full sun to partial shade in well-drained, average soil. Space dwarf hyssop 8 inches apart, *H. officinalis* 1 foot apart, and anise hyssop 1½ feet apart.

✂ CULINARY TIPS ✂

✂ The flowers and leaves of anise hyssop are anise scented and can be used as an edible garnish or herbal tea.

LADY'S MANTLE *(Alchemilla vulgaris)*

A spreading ornamental herb that grows 1 to 2 feet tall, lady's mantle has gray-green, fan-shaped leaves that soften the edges of beds and borders. The "pleated" foliage is valued for its ability to hold sparkling drops of dew or rainwater. Stems of small but abundant yellow-green flowers appear in summer. These can be dried for flower arrangements.

GROWING

Lady's mantle is an easily grown perennial in zones 3 to 9. Plants will spread and possibly self-sow where it's moist (but not soggy) in full sun or partial shade.

LAMB'S EARS *(Stachys byzantina)*

The velvety, remarkably soft foliage of lamb's ears forms a textured carpet of silvery green. Densely growing plants create a tight, weed-resistant ground cover or edging. The foliage's unusual form and color contrast nicely with other garden plants.

Small, purple-flowered spikes appear in summer. They can be dried for winter bouquets but tend to be floppy and unattractive in the garden. A non-flowering variety, Silver Carpet has no flower spikes to detract from the lush, matlike effect.

GROWING

This perennial can be started easily from seed or divisions.

Hardy in zones 4 to 10, *Stachys* prefers a sunny, well-drained, sandy soil. Established plants are drought resistant.

LAVENDER
(*Lavandula angustifolia,* also *L. vera or L. officinalis*)

Prized for the delicious, clean fragrance of the foliage and flowers, lavender adds grace to gardens. It's a native of the Mediterranean, and fields of lavender scent the air and color the hillsides of southern France. Much of the lavender used worldwide for perfumes and cosmetics is grown and processed in Provence.

Varieties of lavender range in height from 1 to 3 feet tall, all with silver-gray foliage and flowers of lavender, pink, or purple. Its mounded, bushy habit makes it perfect for low hedges or aromatic edgings.

Newly opened flower buds make a sedative tea. Years ago, lavender smelling salts were used to revive delicate souls who had fallen into a swoon—something not as common in these tougher times.

- Lavender makes an edible garnish and a violet-colored Herb Vinegar (page 260).
- Steep lavender flower buds in heated milk or cream for 1 hour, strain and discard the buds, and use the milk or cream to make a delicately flavored custard or ice cream. Use 1/4 cup of buds to each pint of dairy product.

GROWING

Lavender is a perennial shrub, hardy to zones 5 to 9 and grown from seed or cuttings. Plants raised from seed will take longer to produce good-sized plants and may not have the desirable characteristics of specific cutting-grown strains.

There are many species of lavender; however, *L. angustifolia* is the most readily available and widely grown. Common named varieties include

- Hidcote: 1 to 2 feet tall, with deep purple flowers and gray leaves
- Munstead: 1 foot tall, with pale lavender flowers and blue-gray leaves
- Jean Davis: 1 to 2 feet tall, with pale pink flowers and green leaves

Lavender is drought resistant and requires a sunny, well-drained spot in light soil. Plants grown in sandy or stony soil will produce flowers with a more potent essential oil than plants grown in rich, moist soil. Good drainage helps lavender survive winter, as will a blanket of pine boughs during times of severe cold.

In the spring, prune off dead growth by trimming back to the new buds. The attractive foliage is evergreen in mild climates and needs pruning solely to maintain a neat appearance. Cut spikes of lavender for dried sachets when the buds are just about to open. Plants may rebloom if the spent flower spikes are pruned off (deadheaded) soon after flowering.

LEMON BALM (*Melissa officinalis*)

The lemon-scented leaves of this 1- to 2-foot perennial are used as a fragrant herb in cooking and for teas. Plant lemon balm at the edge of a path and its refreshing scent will be freely released when the leaves are brushed against or clipped.

The regular species is a bushy, vivid green plant that makes a good backdrop for other colors. Variegated and golden-leaved varieties (*variegata*) are also available.

All varieties have low spikes of inconspicuous white flowers attractive to bees.

GROWING

Start plants from seed or division, or purchase at a nursery. Lemon balm can be grown in zones 4 to 8, in poor to average soil with a sunny or partially shaded location. Space plants 1½ feet apart, where their vigorous growth will not interfere with small or delicate neighbors. Lemon balm has freely reseeded in my garden, almost to the point of being a pest.

CULINARY TIPS

- Add fresh lemon balm leaves to fruit salads or green salads, herb butters, dressings, dips, pilafs, iced tea, conserves, and sorbets for a delicious lemon bouquet.

- Lemon balm loses most of its fragrance when dried but retains its medicinal value as an antiviral and sedative. Freeze some leaves or pot a small plant to keep on a sunny windowsill.

LOVAGE *(Levisticum officinale)*

Considering its many virtues—longevity, celery flavor, and dramatic appearance—it is surprising that lovage is not commonly grown. The leafy growth forms a lush mound of dark green leaves with tall (4 to 6 feet), hollow-ribbed stems topped by flat clusters, or umbels, of minute, yellow-green flowers resembling dill.

Gardeners who have difficulty growing celery (which requires a long, cool season) should try planting lovage.

Lovage leaves, stems, and seeds can be used anywhere celery would be appropriate: in soups, stews, salads, sauces, and stuffings. Lovage has a strong flavor, and a little goes a long way. Young leaves have a milder flavor than older ones. Flower umbels can be used in pickling marinades or as a garnish.

GROWING

Happy growing to Zone 3, lovage needs some winter chilling, which limits its southern range to Zone 8.

Plants do well in fertile, well-drained soil and full sun to partial shade. Start lovage from seed or division, or by purchasing small plants. Space plants 3 feet apart in anticipation of their future size. Seedlings will take a few years to reach full height.

To spur continuous leaf growth, pinch off flowers as they appear.

MARJORAM (*Origanum majorana*)

A useful garden herb, sweet marjoram is a tender perennial best grown as an annual. Bushy plants reach about 1 foot and feature small, oval, gray-green, feltlike leaves and tiny, white or pink flowers.

GROWING

Start seeds indoors in late winter or buy small plants at a nursery. After danger of frost is past, space plants 6 inches apart in a sunny spot with light soil.

Marjoram is well suited to the cuisine of its native Mediterranean region, but we use it anywhere its aromatic, oregano flavor is desired.

Add marjoram to herb butters, soups, stews, bean dishes, vinegars, dressings, and marinades for vegetables or fish. It keeps good company with basil, bay, dill, garlic, parsley, and thyme.

Marjoram's flavor is well preserved by drying; however, it's easy to have fresh leaves on hand as potted plants grow well indoors on a sunny windowsill.

MINT *(Mentha species)*

Deliciously refreshing, mint is one of the most popular and well-known herbs. Vigorous perennials, plants in the *Mentha* family range from a creeping 2 inches to 2 feet tall. Most have square stems, and all have opposite, highly aromatic leaves. Small, white, pink, or lavender flowers appear in summer on slender spikes.

There are many species and named varieties of mint. Here are five of the most useful and popular:

Apple mint *(M. suaveolens)*—The furry round leaves give a light, fruity, mint flavor to cool drinks, fruit salads, sorbets, and tea mixes.

Corsican, or creeping, mint *(M. requienii)*—A low-growing ground cover, this mint's tiny, deep green leaves release a peppermint fragrance when crushed. Not as hardy as other mints, it can be grown to Zone 5.

Orange, or bergamot, mint *(M. piperita citrata)*—The leaves add a citrus fragrance to potpourri and tea mixes and other beverages.

Peppermint *(M. piperita)*—Menthol gives peppermint its distinctive, zingy quality. Best for teas, cool drinks, potpourri, frostings, sorbets, and ice creams.

Spearmint *(M. spicata)*—One of the best mints for culinary purposes. The familiar, gentle spearmint flavor harmonizes with a wide range of seasonings.

GROWING

Specific mint varieties should be obtained from nurseries or friendly gardeners. Seed-grown mint may not be true to type, as varieties frequently cross-pollinate.

Space plants 1 foot apart in full sun to partial shade. Mints are happiest in moist soil, but they survive dry conditions, though growth will be limited. Most mints are hardy to Zone 4.

Mints are wildly invasive perennials and require either isolation from other plants or physical restraint. The latter can be in the form of a moisture-proof barrier of metal or plastic, buried 1 foot down from the surface to keep wandering roots at bay. You can achieve the same result by planting mint in a deep container with drainage holes, then "planting" the container.

Cut mint frequently for more compact, bushy plants with tender new leaves. Mint will grow in pots on a sunny windowsill.

MULLEIN *(Verbascum species)*

With tall spires of furry stalks and foliage, mullein gives beds and borders a storybook or cottage-garden touch. One of my favorite ornamental herbs, it provides height, color, and textural interest. There are several named species, all long-flowering biennials or perennials.

V. bombyciferum (Where *do* they get those names?) is a silvery, particularly woolly-leaved biennial species with 5-foot-tall spires of yellow flowers.

V. olympicum is similar, with smoother foliage and a "candelabra" of spikes with yellow flowers.

V. chaixii is perennial in zones 5 to 10 and bears 3-foot-tall spikes of yellow or white flowers with charmingly contrasting purplish stamens.

GROWING

Mullein is hardy to zones 5 to 9 but can be grown farther north in areas with reliable snow cover or if covered with a generous mound of cut pine boughs.

Preferring poor, sandy, well-drained soil in a sunny location, mullein should be started in peat pots or seeded where it is to grow because it resents transplanting. Mullein will not tolerate wet, soggy soil.

The first-year plants produce a beautiful rosette of leaves; bloom stalks appear the second year. Plants content with the location will self-sow.

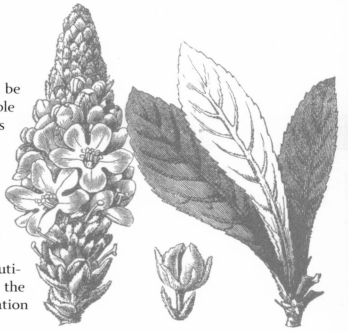

OREGANO *(Origanum heracleoticum)*

Our oregano of choice is the Greek species, noted for its pungent aroma that most people recognize as a key ingredient in pizza sauce. Long before pizza was invented, Greeks were enjoying native oregano, a name that translates as "joy of the mountains."

Even among plant experts, confusion reigns as to just which "oregano" is the best culinary oregano. Some Greek oregano is identified as *O. vulgare hirtum.* In fact, most seeds and plants sold as oregano are nothing of the sort. Though they taste something like oregano, they are frequently a wimpy, pallid variety lacking Greek oregano's bite and aroma. Stick with plants and seeds specifically labeled *O. heracleoticum,* and if it's just labeled *oregano,* taste a leaf or two for that distinctive "pizza sauce" flavor.

O. vulgare Aaream is a golden-leaved, low-growing ornamental. The bright foliage contrasts well with other herbs' various greens and grays.

GROWING

A perennial hardy to Zone 5, Greek oregano forms 1- to 2-foot-tall, vigorous, spreading mounds topped with sprays of small, white flowers. Space plants 1½ feet apart in a sunny spot with well-drained soil. Remove flower spikes to prolong new leaf growth. Oregano dries well, with most of its fragrance preserved.

- ❧ Greek salads combine the sharp, aromatic flavors of feta cheese, chopped fresh oregano, red onion, and kalamata olives with mixed greens, dill sprigs, and tomato and cucumber slices. Serve with lemon wedges and olive oil.

- ❧ Add oregano to Mexican bean dishes for more robust flavor.

- ❧ A simple yet delectable open-faced sandwich can be made with crusty Italian bread and thin slices of fresh mozzarella cheese and tomato topped with chopped fresh oregano and a drizzle of olive oil.

- ❧ Oregano is de rigueur for pizza and most Italian tomato sauces.

- ❧ Add its assertive flavor to marinades for salads, kebobs, and roasted or grilled vegetables and fish.

- ❧ Season vinegars and oils with oregano.

- ❧ Olive oil, garlic, parsley, basil, dill, tomato, eggplant, and zucchini harmonize well with oregano.

PARSLEY *(Petroselinum crispum)*

Parsley is to Moosewood as fairy dust is to Tinkerbell. Few of our savory dishes leave the kitchen without being ritually sprinkled with the chopped green herb, not only for the bright dash of color but also for its clean, mild taste.

A powerhouse of nutrition, parsley contains high concentrations of vitamins A, B complex, C, and E, and the minerals iron, calcium, and potassium.

There are three basic types of parsley: flat-leaf (Italian), curly-leaf, and parsnip-rooted (Hamburg). Curly parsley makes an attractive garnish, but the flat-leaf type has a richer, more substantial flavor and is best used as a culinary herb. "What is this tasteless American parsley?" my Italian friend Luna disdainfully remarked when I suggested she cook with the curly parsley growing in my garden years ago. The roots of Hamburg parsley have a celerylike taste, useful in soups and stews.

The vivid green, divided or frilled leaves make a handsome border or edging plant for vegetable and flower beds.

GROWING

Parsley is a biennial best grown as an annual. The seeds are slow to germinate; soak in warm water for 24 hours to speed the process. Start seeds indoors for a quicker crop or in the garden when the soil has warmed but before hot weather. Keep the seedbed moist (see Carrots, page 30). Seeds do not remain viable for long; use fresh ones each year. Plant 6 to 8 inches apart in fertile, moist soil in a sunny or lightly shaded spot.

Plants can be potted for winter use after a couple of light frosts. They do well in a cool, sunny room.

Parsley may survive mild winters but will send up flower stalks and quickly go to seed with the first warmth of spring.

❧ CULINARY TIPS ❧

❧ Use parsley as a seasoning as well as a garnish. A couple of tablespoons of chopped leaves give a mild, fresh-green taste appropriate to almost any savory dish.

❧ At the end of the cooking time, add some to soups, sauces, or stews that need perking up.

❧ Noodles, potatoes, steamed vegetables, pilafs, and grains benefit from being tossed with chopped parsley.

❧ Mayonnaise, marinades, dips, spreads, dressings, pesto, and cheese fillings that feature a specific, more assertive herb such as basil or garlic will be enhanced by parsley's milder, sweet flavor.

❧ An effective breath sweetener, parsley will help to counter the scents of raw garlic or onions.

❧ Use a few sturdy sprigs of parsley as an edible brush to swab marinades on grilled foods.

❧ Dried parsley has little flavor or appeal. Freeze the leaves for winter use; they will be sweeter when thawed.

ROSEMARY *(Rosmarinus officinalis)*

With its gnarled, twisted growth and gray-green, needlelike leaves, my 10-year-old rosemary plant has the venerable presence of a windswept bonsai. I periodically prune off sprigs for cooking, keeping the plant compact and bushy. It winters in a cool, bright, sunny room and flowers through the cold months.

Rosemary leaves have an aromatic, woodsy fragrance and a piney, resinous taste. This distinctive flavor can be wonderful when used in the right dishes or discreetly. However, I have sampled a few dishes overpowered and ruined by too much rosemary.

Common rosemary *(R. officinalis)* is the best variety for cooking. It grows in an upright, shrubby form and is hardy to 15°F. My 10-year-old plant is a trailing rosemary *(R. officinalis* Prostratus); this variety is hardy to 20°F and mildly flavored. With a picturesque form of trailing, twisting stems, Prostratus looks good in hanging baskets and containers. Arp is the hardiest variety of rosemary, reputed to survive temperatures of -10°F without protection.

Except for the white-flowered Alba, most varieties have blooms in various shades of blue. Rosemary typically blooms during winter.

GROWING

Rosemary is difficult to grow from seed, so buy plants at a nursery or make root cuttings from mature plants. Gardeners in much of the country will have to grow rosemary in containers that can be moved indoors in winter. Indoors or outside, rosemary needs a sandy, well-drained soil and plenty of sun. It should be allowed to dry between waterings but not to the point of wilt. Container-grown plants need more attention to water than those grown in the ground. The essential oils are more fragrant in plants grown in poor, dry soil. Leaves on overwatered plants will brown and may fall off. Keep indoor plants in a cool location away from heat.

❧ The warm, piney essence of rosemary high-lights herb butters, marinades, cheese spreads, dips, soups, stews, grilled or roasted vegetables and fish, crusty bread, rolls, focaccia, crackers, and potpourri mixes. The assertive flavor of rosemary doesn't cook away in long-cooked dishes or those subject to high heat.

❧ Rosemary keeps good company with its Mediterranean cousins: lemon, tomato, and olive oil.

❧ The brittle, dried rosemary leaves do not soften much in cooking; we try to infuse its flavor in oil or liquid. Warm the oil or butter to be used in a dish and add rosemary. Gently heat for a few minutes; strain and discard the leaves. For soups, stews, or other liquid-based dishes, rosemary can be added to a bouquet garni in cheesecloth or a tea/spice ball.

RUE *(Ruta graveolens)*

Rue is grown for its ornamental, lacy, blue-green foliage and provides an unusual counterpoint to other garden colors. This bitter herb of antiquity was once used to ward off evil spirits. Pugnacious qualities may have been attributed to rue because of its pungently fragrant leaves that can be toxic if ingested in quantity. Avoid the fresh leaves and their juice; they provoke dermatitis in many people.

Blue Beauty and Blue Mound are two varieties with richer blue-green foliage than the common species. Variegata has cream-edged leaves.

GROWING

Perennial in zones 4 to 9, rue is a 3-foot-tall evergreen in warmer areas. Start seeds in the winter or buy plants. Plants should be spaced 1½ feet apart in average garden soil in a sunny location.

SAGE *(Salvia officinalis)*

Sage deserves a second chance from people whose sole association with the herb is as a poultry seasoning cliché. Highly aromatic, pebble-textured leaves appear on a shrubby perennial that grows 1 to 2½ feet tall. The gray-green leaves and blue-violet flowers can be an ornamental addition to herb or flower gardens.

Variegated sages, with golden, purple, or tricolored leaves, are available but less hardy than the common species and will reliably winter outdoors only to Zone 7. They make attractive annuals elsewhere.

Sage has been used as a medicinal and culinary herb for hundreds of years. The Latin *salvia* means "to save," testament to its healing properties.

Salvia sclarea, or Clary sage, is a self-sowing biennial that bears impressive 3- to 4-foot spikes of showy, silver-pink flowers and broad, gray-green leaves redolent of pine and sage. The flowers make an elegant garnish, and the leaves can be used in potpourri.

GROWING

Sages do well in dry or average, well-drained soil. *S. officinalis*, perennial in zones 4 to 8, is the best culinary sage. Seeds have a short lifespan, so buy small plants or obtain divisions or cuttings. Space plants 1½ feet apart in full sun.

Evergreen in many climates, common sage can be picked through the winter, even here in Ithaca. In the spring, cut back the woody growth of established plants by half to encourage new, bushy growth.

❧ CULINARY TIPS ❧

- ❧ Fresh sage leaves have a milder, more complex flavor than dried.

- ❧ Sage enhances herb butters, pasta sauces, marinades, cheese dishes, breads, stuffings, beans, omelets, hearty soups and stews, polenta, and potato dishes.

- ❧ An aromatic tea made with sage leaves is a warming, soothing beverage.

SANTOLINA *(Santolina species)*

A shrublike perennial, santolina is a strikingly ornamental herb. The finely cut evergreen foliage is elegantly filigreed, giving the plant a coral-like appearance. Small, yellow button flowers appear in summer.

Traditionally used as an easily pruned herb in knot gardens, santolina is also an excellent specimen for rock gardens or pots. The dried foliage of all species is highly aromatic and can be used in potpourri and decorative arrangements or as a moth repellant.

Santolina chamaecyparissus is silvery leaved with woolly foliage growing to 18 inches. A dwarf variety, Nana is 10 to 12 inches tall.

Santolina virens has deep green, needlelike leaves and grows to 2 feet.

GROWING

Santolina can be started from seed, cuttings, or divisions. It prefers a sunny location in light, sandy soil that doesn't stay wet in winter. Space plants 1 foot apart for a dense, low hedge. Reliably hardy to Zone 6, santolina should be covered with a protective layer of pine boughs in Zone 5.

SAVORY *(Satureja species)*

Savories are good candidates for low-growing edgings and knot or rock gardens. When you brush against the leaves, their aromatic essence is freely released.

Summer savory *(S. hortensis)* is an 18-inch annual bearing small, pale pink or white flowers and gray-green, soft leaves that are more suitable for culinary purposes than the resinous, strong-tasting perennial species.

Winter savory *(S. montana)* is a 1-foot-tall, woody, semi-evergreen perennial with small, deep green leaves and small, white or lilac flowers. This species is best used as a landscape plant.

- We use summer savory in bean dishes, herb breads, marinades, cheese spreads, and split pea, lentil, and other hearty soups. The robust flavor is reminiscent of a combination of sage and thyme.

- Savory retains much of its flavor when dried.

GROWING

Plants can be started by seed, division, or cutting. Ordinary, well-drained soil in a sunny location suits both savories, though summer savory will do well in partial shade. Winter savory is hardy to Zone 5.

SCENTED GERANIUMS
(Pelargonium species)

Scented geraniums offer a multitude of fragrant foliage possibilities. These easily grown plants also come in a wide range of colors, textures, and leaf shapes. The foliage can be smooth, hairy, lobed, ruffled, finely cut, velvety, or pleated.

There are more than fifty different scented-leaved geraniums, with fragrances from "apple cider" to "strawberry." Some require an act of faith or fantasy to appreciate the connection between the name and the perceived fragrance. Here are a few I have enjoyed:

Apple (P. odoratisimum)—small, round, green leaves and white flowers on trailing stems, good for hanging baskets.

Coconut (P. parviflorum)—small, deep green leaves on trailing stems, strong fragrance.

Ginger (P. torento)—ground-ginger fragrance, round, crinkled leaves, and lavender blooms, upright growth.

Lemon (P. crispum)—upright growing, with small, crinkled, green leaves of strong fragrance.

Nutmeg (P. fragrans)—good basket variety with low-growing stems, gray leaves, white blooms, and spicy scent.

Peppermint *(P. tomentosum)*—large, velvety leaves with a pronounced peppermint scent, vigorous trailing stems good for containers or baskets.

Rose *(P. graveolens)*—upright growing, with finely cut, strongly fragrant, green leaves.

GROWING

Hardy only in frost-free areas, scented geraniums are best enjoyed as potted plants to be moved indoors in cold weather. Purchase named varieties from specialty herb growers, or obtain rooted cuttings from other gardeners.

Geraniums do best in a sunny location indoors, but will grow well outdoors with just a few hours' direct sun each day.

Allow plants to dry between thorough waterings. Fertilize only in the spring and summer; winter-fed plants will be leggy and floppy.

❧ CULINARY TIPS ❧

❧ The distinctly flavored fresh leaves can be used to accent bouquets, teas, potpourri, cakes, jams, biscuits, muffins, and custards. Use one large leaf in the bottom of a muffin tin or custard cup, two in the bottom of a cake tin. Add the leaves before the batter or dough.

❧ Make a rose, coconut, or ginger geranium sugar by adding two large, whole fresh leaves to 1 cup of sugar. Store in a closed container for 2 weeks, then sift out the leaves. The sugar can be used for baking or in dessert recipes.

❧ Press scented leaves into butter or cream cheese and wrap with plastic overnight. Remove the leaves the next day and discard. Use the butter or cream cheese as a base for frostings, or serve it with bread, muffins, and other baked goods.

❧ Place some lightly crushed lemon geranium leaves in small finger bowls of warm water for a gracious after-dinner touch.

SWEET CICELY *(Myrrhis odorata)*

A perennial with delicate, fernlike foliage, sweet cicely has a sweet anise flavor. The 3-foot plants are topped with delicate, white flower heads in early summer.

CULINARY TIPS

- ❧ The young leaves, seeds, and roots impart a licorice or anise flavor. We use the chopped leaf in delicate sauces, herb butters, fruit salads, and fruit pies, and tossed with steamed vegetables.

- ❧ The ground seeds can be used in baked goods instead of anise or fennel.

- ❧ Dried leaves lack flavor; freeze sweet cicely for winter use.

GROWING

Sow fresh seeds in the fall or purchase seedlings for spring planting. Plants should stand about $1^1/_2$ feet apart.

Sweet cicely is one of the few herbs that prefers full shade and a rich, moist soil. It is hardy to zones 3 to 10 and will generously self-sow where it is happy. If this becomes a nuisance, cut off the flower heads as soon as they fade.

SWEET WOODRUFF
(Galium odoratum)

A superb ground cover, sweet woodruff can create drifts of low-growing, dark green, pinwheel-shaped leaves in partially shaded or lightly wooded areas. In late spring, dainty, white flowers hover above the foliage. The dried leaves have a delicious scent that reminds me of newly mown grass, pipe tobacco, and vanilla. It makes a wonderful potpourri herb.

CULINARY TIPS

- ❧ A traditional German May wine is made by adding sprigs of sweet woodruff to white wine and letting it steep for a day or overnight.

GROWING

The 6- to 10-inch plants are perennial in zones 3 to 9. Woodruff is difficult to grow from seed. Space plants obtained by purchase, division, or cutting 1 foot apart. The rampant growing habit makes sweet woodruff quite invasive. It's best suited under mature trees where it can freely ramble without trampling smaller-growing species.

TARRAGON *(Artemisia dracunculus)*

One of the classic herbs of French cuisine, tarragon is an integral part of a cook's garden. A perennial, tarragon grows 2 to 3 feet tall, eventually spreading to the same width, its branching stems covered with thin, green leaves.

GROWING

True French tarragon can only be grown from divisions or cuttings. Seed-grown strains are probably Russian tarragon, a poor substitute decidedly

lacking in flavor. To test a plant, nibble a leaf. French tarragon has a bite that numbs the tongue. This quality is not peppery and will be unnoticed when tarragon is used in cooking.

Tarragon is hardy to zones 5 to 9. Place small plants or divisions 2 feet apart in a sunny location with rich, well-drained soil.

Northern gardeners should cover plants after the ground has frozen for better winter survival.

CULINARY TIPS

- The flavor of tarragon has a rich fullness, with a licorice or anise base. To preserve its bouquet, add the fresh herb toward the end of cooking time.

- At Moosewood, we use it in dressings, dips, sauces, butters, marinades, frittatas, vegetable fillings, soups, stews, grains, vinegars, fish dishes, and herb breads.

- Make a tarragon mayonnaise with tarragon vinegar and the chopped herb (page 266).

- Use whole sprigs of tarragon in slow-cooked dishes such as soups or stews. The stem can be pulled out after the leaves fall away from it.

- Tarragon leaves should be frozen to retain their flavor. Though dried leaves are an acceptable substitute, they lack the full-bodied aroma of fresh.

THYME *(Thymus species)*

As a diminutive, spreading ground cover or a low-growing shrub, thyme is a fragrant, ornamental presence. There are a few hundred species of thyme throughout the world. Here's a list of a few easily obtained species we have used for culinary or ornamental purposes:

Caraway thyme *(T. herba-barona)*—a creeping, 2- to 6-inch-tall ground cover and culinary herb with caraway-scented, green leaves and lavender blooms.

Common thyme *(T. vulgaris)*—an attractive culinary herb with petite, gray-green leaves and white or pale lavender flowers on a 10-inch, woody subshrub. Sometimes called English, German, or Winter thyme. French thyme, also referred to as *T. vulgaris*, has narrower, somewhat greyer leaves that are a bit sweeter on less hardy plants.

Lemon thyme *(T. citriodorus)*—a culinary herb with a distinct lemon fragrance and green leaves on a 10-inch-tall, bushy plant. Golden-leaf-edged Aureus or silver-leaf-edged Argenteus types are also highly ornamental.

Red creeping thyme *(T. praecox)*—a slowly spreading ornamental ground cover with prostrate stems and dark green, minute foliage. Coccineus is covered with profuse, tiny, red flowers in summer. *T. praecox* Albus is a white-flowering form. Both make excellent, fragrant, sturdy herbs to place between paving stones or to edge gardens.

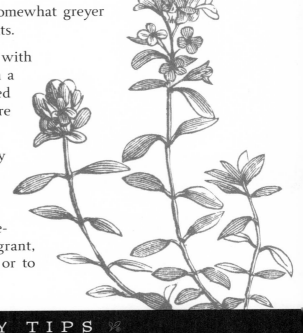

❧ CULINARY TIPS ❧

- ❧ An all-purpose savory herb, thyme is appropriate in many dishes. Its flavor can dominate a dish, so add small amounts at first and more later if necessary.

- ❧ Thyme suffuses its fragrance in slow cooking and can be added early without risking flavor loss.

- ❧ At Moosewood, we use thyme in chowders, stews, sauces, butters, marinades, dressings, stocks, vinegars, seasoned oils, breads, herbed croutons, bean dishes, and stuffings, and combined with nutmeg, bay leaf, and parsley.

- ❧ Thyme has a particular affinity for leeks and onions. Sauté in a heavy skillet with butter or oil, and cook slowly until the onions or leeks are soft and golden. Use the resulting fragrant vegetables as a soup or stew base, pizza topping, casserole addition, or part of a filling for stuffed vegetables.

- ❧ The petite thyme flowers make a dainty, colorful garnish. Float a few in cups of smooth, puréed soup.

- ❧ Use whole thyme sprigs in foods that simmer or sauté for more than a few moments. The stems can be removed after the leaves have fallen off.

- ❧ Thyme leaves can be frozen. The dried herb retains most of the original flavor.

- ❧ Lemon or common thyme is an aromatic addition to potpourri or herbal tea mixes.

Woolly thyme *(T. pseudolanuginosus)*—a prostrate, creeping plant with very tiny, soft, gray-green leaves. It's particularly ornamental where it can languidly drape itself over rocks or cascade down from the top of a wall.

GROWING

Though hardy to zones 4 to 9, common and lemon thymes are short-lived perennials. The creeping species are more durable and long-lived.

Thymes can be started from seeds, cuttings, or divisions. Creeping plants frequently root along their stems as they expand their territory. These "colonies" can be dug up (use a sharp spade and cut out a clump the same way you'd cut a sheet cake) and replanted elsewhere.

All thymes prefer a dryish, well-drained soil in a location where they can bask in the sun. Space plants 1 foot apart.

YARROW *(Achillea species)*

I have a fondness for yarrows; they are truly carefree and sturdy perennials. These drought-resistant, ornamental herbs range from the 2-foot-tall, weedy common wildflower to stately, 5-foot-tall varieties.

Predominantly grown today for its foliage and blooms, yarrow has an ancient history as a medicinal plant. Legend traces its Latin name from Achilles' use of the herb to halt the flow of blood and heal the wounds of his fellow Greek warriors.

Common varieties include

Angel's breath *(A. ptarmica)*—2 feet tall, with profuse, small, white double flowers resembling baby's breath and with fairly mundane foliage.

Coronation gold *(A. filipendulina)*—3-foot-tall, upright stems with grayish green, feathery foliage topped by flat, yellow, 3-inch-wide flower heads. The visual effect has a striking quality of combined vertical and horizontal forms.

Gold plate *(A. filipendulina)*—4 to 5 feet tall, with a form similar to Coronation Gold but with greener foliage and 6-inch flower heads.

Red beauty and white beauty *(A. millefolium)*—2 feet tall, with lacy, finely divided, deep green foliage and red or white flower heads that bloom throughout the summer.

Both the *A. ptarmica* and *A. millefolium* varieties are aggressive spreaders. Take advantage of their pushy habits by using them as ground covers in a location bounded by paving, walls, deep shade, or other barriers to unlimited expansion.

All of the yarrows listed have flowers suitable for cutting and drying.

GROWING

Perennial in zones 3 to 10, yarrow plants can be obtained at most nurseries or started from seed. Plants should be divided every few years to avoid crowding. Yarrows are sun loving and prefer a light soil of average fertility. They will not be happy in wet, heavy soils.

Edible Flowers

ONE YEAR, when my garden was filled with nasturtiums, I brought dozens of blossoms to the Restaurant to use as an edible garnish. The vibrant, colorful flowers were a gorgeous accent. However, most diners had to be informed that they could eat the spicy, watercress-flavored blossoms.

In the last few years, gardening books and magazines, as well as restaurants, have been promoting flower eating as if it were a new idea. In fact, written history cites the eating of blossoms as far back as the ancient Greeks and Romans. When used at the table and as ornamental plantings, most flowering edibles produce enough blooms that you can have your bouquet and eat it too.

A word of caution. Many common garden flowers are poisonous! Poisonous blossoms include autumn crocus, azalea and rhododendron species, buttercup, clematis, daffodil and narcissus, delphinium, dicentra (bleeding heart), foxglove, hyacinth, iris, lantana, larkspur, lily-of-the-valley, lupine, oleander, poinsettia, flowering sweet-pea, and wisteria.

Choose only those flowers listed in this book. Begin with plants or seeds whose true identity is without question. Next, clearly mark your edibles with metal tags or stakes (plastic will fade and wood will rot) until you become familiar with their appearance.

Besides making positive identification, it's important to avoid picking any flowers for culinary use that have been subjected to insecticides or herbicides. To be safe, use only those flowers you've grown yourself or have obtained from a trusted supplier or friend. When in doubt, don't eat.

The following listings include annuals and perennials suited to a range of garden situations. Any of the culinary herb flowers noted in the Culinary Tips in the Herbs chapter (page 97) can be used for culinary purposes, along with the blossoms of squash (page 83) and bean vines (page 17) (scarlet runner bean flowers are the showiest).

Any of the flowers described here can be sprinkled, in moderation, on salads or soups, or simply used to garnish the plate. Check carefully for insects and dirt, but try not to wash flowers. They bruise and tear easily, and a bedraggled flower is not very appetizing. If necessary, soak them in cold water, gently drain, and serve soon after.

BORAGE *(Borago officinalis)*

Blue flowers are my favorite. They're not as common in nature as yellows, reds, and pinks, and so they are highly prized not only for the color but also for the cooling effect they have wherever they appear. Borage's little, sky-blue, star-shaped flowers are not very conspicuous on the plant but make beautiful edible garnishes when viewed up close. They open from nodding, pink buds on the spreading 2- to 3-foot plants. In dramatic contrast, the large, sometimes floppy, gray and green leaves and stems sport bristly hairs.

Partaking of the edible leaves and flowers was traditionally believed to promote well-being and dispel melancholy. Borage is also a good plant for apiculturists because the flowers attract honeybees, which are excellent pollinators for the garden.

CULINARY TIPS

- The blossoms, peeled stems, and tender, fresh young leaves give a cucumber flavor to salads and soups. Try adding a few tablespoons of chopped leaves to chilled potato, tomato, cucumber, or gazpacho soups.

- Blossoms are exceptionally pretty arranged with other edible flowers on a cake with a cream cheese or other white frosting.

- Freeze flowers in ice cubes for tall, cool drinks.

- If you've planted lots of borage, gather a couple of cups of blooms and make a lavender-tinted herb vinegar with a delicate borage flavor.

GROWING

A vigorous, self-sowing annual, borage can be planted in its permanent spot from early spring to early summer. Plants do well even in poor, dry soil but require full sun. When I grew a few in a fertile vegetable bed, the plants were gigantic and crowded all their neighbors. Thin seedlings to stand 12 to 18 inches apart. Because it self-sows so freely, you may be surprised to see where it turns up next year.

CARNATIONS AND CLOVE PINKS *(Dianthus species)*

Annual, biennial, or perennial plants with a delicious, spicy, clove-cinnamon fragrance. Look for varieties that are noted as fragrant—some are not. Recommended: pinks *(Dianthus allwoodii alpinus, D. plumarius, D. gratianopolitanus* Bath's Pink), annual carnation *(D. caryophyllus)*, and fragrance or dwarf fragrance mix. All have low-growing or lax, grassy, gray-green foliage. The perennials form neat tufts for edging, between paving stones, or in rock gardens.

GROWING

Annual carnations should be started indoors early. They take up to 5 months to flower from seed. *Dianthus allwoodii, D. plumarius,* and *D. gratianopolitanus* Bath's Pink are perennial in zones 4 to 10 and can be started from seed or obtained as divisions and plants.

Dianthus needs a sandy, well-drained soil with lime added if conditions are acidic. Plants do best in full sun. Clip off faded flowers for a longer blooming season.

❧ CULINARY TIPS ❧

❧ The clove-flavored petals can be added to custards, muffins, fruit punches and other beverages, and dessert sauces. Whole blooms are excellent garnishes.

CHRYSANTHEMUM
(Chrisanthemum morifolium)

Chrysanthemums, or mums, are appreciated for their profuse, welcome autumn bloom when most other garden flowers are in decline. The garden mums commonly available at nurseries are *C. morifolium* hybrids, ranging from 1-foot-tall dwarf plants to staking varieties reaching 6 feet in height. The familiar, crisp fragrance is reminiscent of autumn and florist shops.

GROWING

Though mums are reputedly hardy to zones 4 to 10, my experience with chrysanthemums has shown them to be short-lived perennials. They can be started from seed or purchased as small plants. Divide clumps every 1 to 2 years for good growth; replant or share with friends and neighbors. Mums like a rich, well-drained soil in full sun. Plants bought at garden centers in the fall have a higher risk of winterkill, because the roots have little time to get established. If you choose to overwinter mums, mulch them heavily. Because of their shallow roots, they're easily damaged by extreme cold.

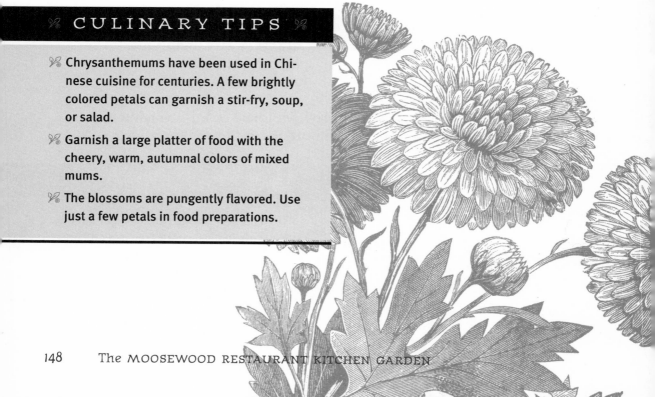

CULINARY TIPS

- Chrysanthemums have been used in Chinese cuisine for centuries. A few brightly colored petals can garnish a stir-fry, soup, or salad.

- Garnish a large platter of food with the cheery, warm, autumnal colors of mixed mums.

- The blossoms are pungently flavored. Use just a few petals in food preparations.

DAYLILIES *(Hemerocallis species)*

One of the most commonly grown perennials, daylilies range from roadside weeds to choice, genetically engineered hybrids. *Hemerocallis fulva*, the orange or tawny daylily, is sometimes mistakenly called *tiger lily* (an entirely separate species). Because the plants are quick spreaders, they should not be used in regular garden beds. Grow orange daylilies where they can naturalize freely. The dense, grasslike clumps or arching, green leaves effectively choke out most weeds. Gardeners with limited space may want to restrict their daylilies to hybrid varieties with more restrained growing habits, or choose locations bound by permanent obstacles (house walls, paving, and so on) for the vigorous wild species.

There are hundreds of named hybrid varieties, their colors running from the warm creams, yellows, peaches, golds, reds, and maroons to the cooler shades of pink, lavender, and purple.

GROWING

Hardy to zones 3 to 9, daylilies tolerate full shade but flower best in partial shade to full sun. Plant divisions (purchased or from other clumps) 1 to 2 feet apart in average, well-drained soil. Divide the hybrid types after 5 to 6 years for best growth.

Individual blossoms last only a day (thus the Latin name, from the Greek, meaning "beautiful for a day"), but plants may flower for a month or more. Though drought tolerant and low maintenance, daylilies bloom best if not allowed to dry out before and during blooming.

CULINARY TIPS

- The largest unopened buds can be quickly steamed or stir-fried for a delicate vegetable with an asparagus-like flavor. These buds are dried by the Chinese and called "golden needles" or "lily buds" in many recipes. They provide a subtle taste and slight thickening effect to hot-and-sour soups and mu shu dishes.

- Opened flowers can be batter dipped and deep-fried, or stuffed and baked. Remove the central pistil and stamens before using for culinary purposes.

- Large, brilliant daylily flowers make elegant garnishes for platters of food. Choose a multicolored variety of blooms.

- Avoid picking buds or blossoms from roadsides; many localities spray herbicides to control weeds.

MARIGOLDS: LEMON OR TANGERINE GEM *(Tagetes signata)*

The Gem series marigolds are the best varieties suitable for culinary use. Flowers and foliage have a fresh, citrus-like taste more pleasing than the pungent quality of other marigolds. I've planted Lemon Gem marigolds in my garden for many years now; the small, cheery blossoms fit in beautifully with other annuals, perennials, and vegetables. Plants form neat, long-blooming, hedgelike mounds, 10 to 12 inches high, with feathery foliage topped by vibrant, single, yellow or orange blossoms. I find them so much nicer than a lot of the big, clunky, larger marigolds. Gems are small enough for containers or to edge borders and beds.

> ## CULINARY TIPS
>
> ✺ Add Gem marigold petals to salads, soups, sauces, marinated vegetables, and pilafs. Whole blossoms are best for garnishes.

GROWING

Seeds can be sown indoors 6 to 8 weeks before the last frost, or outdoors when the soil has warmed and frosts are past. Grow 10 to 12 inches apart in average garden soil in full sun. Marigolds are profuse and long bloomers. Cut spent flowers to encourage the production of more.

NASTURTIUM *(Tropaeolum majus)*

I remember reading about the edibility of nasturtiums long before the current flower cookery vogue. Perhaps this is due to their unique flavor, a peppery-watercress taste with a floral fragrance. Nasturtiums are not just another pretty face in the edible garnish realm; they add a desirable flavor to the foods with which they're combined. The exuberant flowers and handsome foliage are reason enough to plant this easily grown annual that I would never be without. Brilliant red, orange, yellow, peach, maroon, and coral blossoms are some of the most vibrant colors in my garden.

GROWING

Seeds should be planted where they are to be grown when soil is warm and frost danger is past. Nasturtiums are difficult to transplant if the roots are disturbed, but I've had success with starting seeds in peat pots or peat strips that can be planted as is, one plant per pot. Plant in full sun, 8 inches apart, in soil of poor to moderate fertility. (Rich, fertile soil yields bushy plants with few flowers.) Soak the thickly husked seeds overnight in warm water for speedier germination. Whirlybird, my favorite, is a dwarf type that grows 8 to 10 inches tall with upward-facing flowers in a variety of colors. Climbing varieties include Semi-Tall Gleam at 3 feet and Fordhook Favorites at 6 feet. Alaska has the usual warm- to hot-colored flowers, but with handsomely variegated green and white foliage on a 10- to 15-inch plant.

CULINARY TIPS

- Use chopped nasturtium petals for color and peppery flavor in herb butters, cheese spreads, dips, sandwiches, omelets, sauces, salads, and rice pilafs. Whole blossoms make vivacious, elegant garnishes.

- Seedpods picked while still green are frequently pickled and used as a substitute for capers.

PANSIES
(Viola species)

Plantings of pansies and other members of the *Viola* family have an Alice-in-Wonderland quality, their perky "faces" nodding and bobbing in a gentle breeze. Children, especially, are drawn to the richly colored, whimsical blossoms. Some have a delicious fragrance more easily noticed in pots or containers closer to your nose than in plants at ground level. *V. wittrockiana*, commonly called pansies, are the largest of the three listed. Violas *(V. cornuta)* are smaller and come with or without the facelike markings.

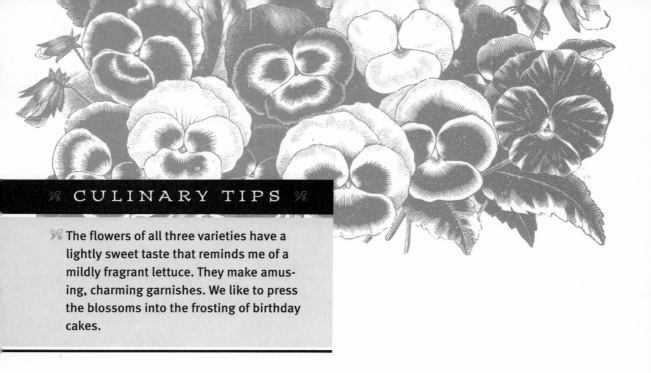

❧ The flowers of all three varieties have a lightly sweet taste that reminds me of a mildly fragrant lettuce. They make amusing, charming garnishes. We like to press the blossoms into the frosting of birthday cakes.

Johnny-jump-ups (*V. tricolor*) are smaller still, with an abundance of yellow, blue, and purple, 1-inch-wide flowers.

GROWING

All three bloom best in the cool weather of spring, moderate summers, or mild winters. I have found the Universal Mix series of violas to be particularly heat resistant.

Flats of pansies, usually available at nurseries and garden centers, give the quickest results. Plants take a few months to start from seed and require cool growing conditions. For spring or winter bloom, start seeds in late summer. Gardeners in cold climates should overwinter small plants in a protected cold frame. Seed sown indoors from early to midwinter will start blooming from late spring to early summer.

Pansies and Johnny-jump-ups are biennials or annuals. Violas are short-lived perennials. All three will self-sow. Johnny-jump-ups are particularly good for naturalizing and will pop up all over the garden, hence their common name.

Grow *Viola* species in full sun to partial shade in a moist, fertile soil. Partial shade is more appropriate in hot climates.

Plants are attractive in containers or at the front of garden beds.

ROSES *(Rosa species)*

Perhaps more than any other flower, the rose embodies a lush, sensual, romantic presence that is perfectly manifested in fragrance and form. It has been employed in perfumes, medicinals, food delicacies, love potions, and as a metaphor by poets through the ages.

Many modern roses have a reputation for fussiness, requiring the gardener's vigilance and a supply of pesticides to thwart pests and diseases. However, if you are an attentive gardener knowledgeable in organic pest and disease control, and you're willing to spend the time on maintenance, these roses can be well worth growing.

Shrub or old-fashioned roses are noted for their relative ease of cultivation compared to some of the newer hybrid varieties. All roses need to be watered and weeded until established, but older shrub roses thrive with only moderate attention.

GROWING

The rugosa rose is one of my favorite shrub types. It is hardy to Zone 2 and disease resistant, and it bears multitudes of single, white, pink, or deep pink blooms in the early summer and beyond. The strongly fragrant blossoms appear on thorny shrubs up to 6 feet tall that are useful for naturalized settings or the back of a border. Rugosa roses have large, vibrant orange-red fruit (hips) from fall through winter. Plants are widely available at nurseries,

❧ CULINARY TIPS ❧

❧ Rose petals have many uses: as garnishes and in jam, syrup, potpourri, sorbet, tea, and vinegar. Clip the flowers above the bitter white heel at the junction of petal and flower center and discard all but the petals. A "confetti" of multicolored rose petals is gorgeous sprinkled on a green salad.

❧ Rose hips can be used for jams, syrups, and herbal teas. They contain 400 times more vitamin C per ounce than oranges. The English used rose-hip syrup as a native vitamin C source during World War II.

or check Resources (page 284). Space shrubs 3 to 4 feet apart (or closer for a tight hedge), in full sun, in a moderately fertile to sandy, well-drained soil.

SUNFLOWER *(Helianthus annuus)*

A field of sunflowers in bloom is an impressive sight, all of the heads facing the same direction, row upon row of dazzling, golden-rayed flowers. The common sunflower, growing up to 10 feet tall, is a wonderful choice for a dramatic plant. Also, birds are attracted to the ripening seeds. For smaller gardens, Sunspot and Zebulon are two dwarf varieties with 10-inch flowers on 2-foot-tall stalks. Breeders keep expanding the sunflower color palette—from pale white through yellow, gold, and orange to deep burgundy.

A superb garden subject is the branching type of sunflower, which continues to bear flowers from late summer until frost on 5- to 6-foot-tall plants. (The common sunflower has one bloom that lasts about 2 weeks.) Autumn Beauty is a recommended branching variety with flowers ranging from yellow to gold and including bronze, crimson, and mahogany, with bicolors as well.

GROWING

The above sunflowers are annuals that should be seeded outdoors where they are to grow, when frost danger has passed. Thin plants to stand 2 feet apart. Plant in full sun or very light shade in average soil.

✄ CULINARY TIPS ✄

✄ The large petals make a showy garnish. Use them as a bed for desserts or vegetable and fruit salads. Their flavor is mild and unobtrusive.

VIOLETS *(Viola odorata)*

Sweetly fragrant, petite lavender, white, and blue flowers are produced by low-growing, 8-inch plants from mid- to late-spring. When not in bloom, the green, heart-shaped foliage makes a handsome ground cover for partially shaded, moist locations.

GROWING

Perennial in zones 6 to 10, sweet violets can be grown from seed, to bloom the following year. Plants can be purchased or obtained as divisions from an established clump.

CULINARY TIPS

❧ The perfume of violets varies with type and growing conditions. However, all are useful as a garnish added to salads or floated in soups, or used in jams and vinegars.

Design

DESIGN CONSIDERATIONS

THERE'S ONE IMPORTANT QUESTION to ask yourself before starting a garden: How much time will I have to devote to this project? For a garden to become an attractive, useful addition to your home, it must be well maintained. Start with a small space that you can care for easily. If possible, locate it in a place that will accommodate future expansion. The temptation for megalomania is great, especially if you plan your garden in the dead of winter, as I do, when the landscape is bleak and barren. Seed and plant catalogs fill the mailbox every day, fueling fantasies of lush, fragrant, dazzling, and abundant Edens. Not surprisingly, most gardeners order far more seeds and plants than they can realistically take care of. I suggest that you make a list of everything you want and then cut it in half. As you are being ruthless, remember a couple of things: your garden may be small but it will be well tended and beautiful, and you'll have time to enjoy all the other pleasures of spring and summer.

In the plans on pages 158 to 180, a wide variety of garden designs are presented, including some that need only minimal time and effort. What your garden will become should be determined by the following factors: climate, site, pattern, plant selection, and maintenance needs.

CLIMATE

Regional differences influence planting schedules, plant selection, and maintenance. In the winter, gardeners in the mild or frost-free climates of the Pacific Coast and Deep South can grow cool-weather vegetables that are grown only in the spring or even just in summer in other parts of the country. Possibilities for winter growing include broccoli, brussels sprouts, cauliflower, cabbage, lettuce, greens for salad or cooking, kale, onions, and spinach. Asparagus and rhubarb need at least minimal winter chilling and cannot be grown in Florida and the Gulf Coast.

Each region has its own climatic character. Arid zones need irrigation; wet areas may require more exacting soil drainage; cool climates benefit from season extenders. These subjects are covered in the Gardening Techniques chapter (page 183).

The USDA hardiness map (http://www.usna.usda.gov/Hardzone) is an important guide to use when selecting perennial plants.

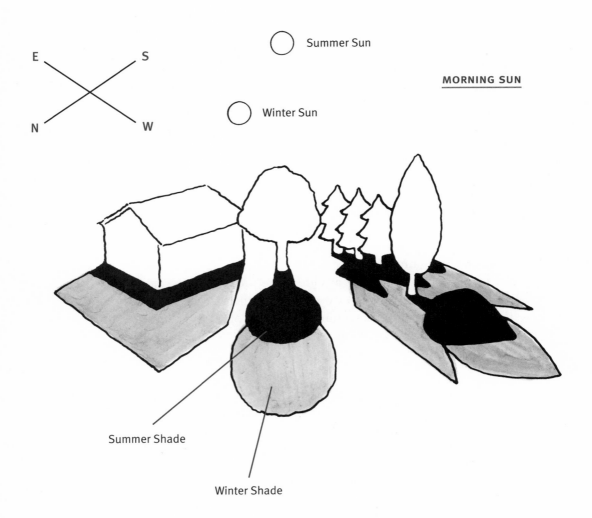

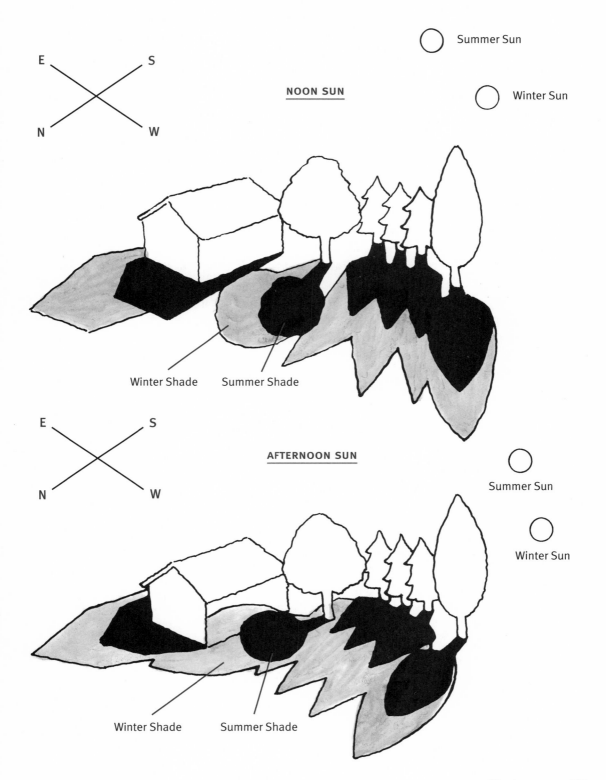

Summer Sun

Winter Sun

E   S

N   W

NOON SUN

Winter Shade   Summer Shade

E   S

N   W

AFTERNOON SUN

Summer Sun

Winter Sun

Winter Shade   Summer Shade

SITE

A kitchen garden should be close to the house. Easy access is a real convenience for the cook, who can dash out to the patio for a sprig of thyme. A touch of grace can be provided by even the smallest doorstep garden: pots of cherry tomatoes, chives, and parsley, with nasturtiums exuberantly climbing up a drainspout. When I was growing up in New York City, all of my neighbors had tomatoes planted in the 2-foot-wide strips between their asphalt driveways. Of course, there was nowhere else to put them, but they grew very nicely as it was a well-drained, sunny spot. Avoid planting near foundation walls treated with pesticides to thwart termites, or below walls painted with lead-based paints.

Sun is a crucial consideration. Most vegetables need at least 6 hours of sun each day. If you live in a northern locale, more than that is necessary for proper ripening. If you're planning a garden during fall or winter, it's good to remember that the sun is much lower in the sky and casts longer shadows than it will in summer. If you don't have much sun, try growing salad greens and herbs. Shade-tolerant ornamentals, such as ferns or hostas, are the only worthwhile possibilities for areas that get no sun at all—under or near heavily foliaged trees and evergreens and in narrow side yards between buildings.

Different sites may contain one or more of the following: varied terrain, attractive views, existing ornamental trees or plantings, a patio or sitting area, and areas to be screened for privacy.

The terrain of your garden site is an integral aspect of the design. Steep or banked sites lend themselves to terracing. Terraced beds can be edged with annual or perennial flowers that cascade down the walls, leaving the center of the bed open for growing herbs and vegetables. Materials to be considered for terrace walls include stone, masonry, old railroad ties, or naturally rot-resistant timbers like cedar, locust, and redwood. Avoid using any chemically treated timbers near food crops.

A patio or seating area surrounded by low plantings is a good choice for any section of a yard or garden with a good view. If you plan to have corn, sunflowers, pole beans, asparagus, or other tall growers, make sure they won't obscure a vista.

Existing trees or specimen plantings also influence the siting of your garden. You may decide to sacrifice proximity in order to save desirable trees or plantings close to the house. Ornamental specimens (flowering shrubs, trees, evergreens, perennial plants or vines) can be interplanted with vegetables and herbs to provide the longest possible season of color and interest. Avoid ornamentals with specific needs that conflict with vegetable growing; for example, rhododendrons and azaleas require highly acidic soil. Vegetables and herbs must be sited in full sun and away from the root zones of large shrubs and trees. A progression from tree to shrub to perennial to vegetable and herb beds could take care of this concern and also create an effective privacy screen (see illustration). For small yards, choose semi-dwarf or dwarf fruit trees or low-growing ornamental trees. Screens can be created with plantings alone or by a "layered" system of plantings with fences, trellises, walls, or arbors. Grape vines, cucumbers, melons, beans, indeterminate tomatoes, and squash can all be trained to grow up a trellised wall or fence, softening the view and creating a lush enclosure. Avoid creating situations where a wall or fence would block the sun from sun-loving plants.

CREATING A LANDSCAPE SCREEN

| Vegetables | Perennial Flowers | Shrubs | Fruit or Ornamental Tree |

PATTERN

Traditionally, a kitchen garden was a simple, rectangular plot in the yard. Today, the integration of ornamental and edible landscaping has opened up possibilities for garden patterns, freeing vegetables and herbs from their conventional boundaries. Regardless of your choice, even though a kitchen garden is utilitarian, it should harmonize aesthetically with the house and landscape.

The stylistic pattern of a garden ideally reflects two things: the personal taste and aesthetics of its creator and the architecture of the house. Where I live, in the hills outside Ithaca, New York, personal taste covers a lot of territory, ranging from tractor tires and toilets filled with geraniums to tasteful English borders lined with statuary.

Asking yourself the following questions may help you decide on a pattern: Does the house have a formal, symmetrical appearance or is it informal and rambling? Would it be softened by curves or enhanced by rectilinear forms? What should its character be to make it a space you enjoy spending time in? Open? Enclosed? Whimsical? Tranquil? Dynamic? The translation of desires to a realized design can be the most creative and personal aspect of the process. The models in this book help to illustrate the variety of patterns possible, from the formal knot garden (page 169) to the dooryard garden entranceway (page 171).

PLANT SELECTION

Now that you've considered how to work with your site and what overall pattern you would like to create, it's time to fill it with various forms, textures, and colors. Of course, the needs of the plants should be your first consideration. For example, some plants (like many of us) do better with specific "buddies." In my garden, I've more or less followed companion planting recommendations (see chart, pages 212–213), but being terribly unscientific, I've never done any controlled experiments to see if it really works. Others, who have, claim that it does work for better growth, pest control, and soil conditioning.

Tall plants should be placed where they will not block the sun from short growers. Short growers such as lettuce, spinach, chives, alpine strawberries, carrots, and many herbs make decorative edging plants. Lowest growers, such as creeping thymes and sweet woodruff, are best appreciated if they're close to a viewing area and planted in sufficient quantity to be noticed.

For accents, rainbow chard, red-leafed lettuce, and flowers like nasturtium and calendula provide a shot of color amidst the predominantly green-foliaged vegetables and herbs. I don't care for the taste of chard, but it looks so glorious with the sun shining through it that I grow it and give it away.

You can create different effects in herb or flower borders through your choice and placement of plants. A border composed of many kinds of plants will have a pointillist quality of varying shapes and colors. Plants arranged in masses, and perhaps repeated or woven through a border, create a tapestry effect of color and form that can be natural and informal or highly staged, like the Victorian-style plantings that spell out names or dates.

In the continuing struggle to accommodate everything I'd like to grow without breaking ground for more beds, I've learned to plant in progression. When planting early-maturing vegetables (peas, spinach, lettuce), leave a little more room between rows than you normally would, for later additions of tomatoes, peppers, basil, squash, or melons. These are all mid- to late-summer maturing and will take over the space left empty by the early bloomers.

I particularly enjoy having fragrant plants near the house or sitting areas. Plants that freely release their fragrance include rosa rugosa, lavender, nicotiana, nasturtium, and thyme. Lilac, mock orange, honeysuckle, and trumpet and Oriental lilies are not specifically kitchen garden material, but all are so powerfully and deliciously scented it would be a shame to leave them out. Detailed information on these, and an infinity of other purely ornamental plants, is beyond the scope of this book but readily available. Many herbs release their scent when brushed against, particularly basil, bee balm, geraniums, lemon balm, mint, rosemary, sage, and thyme. Creeping thyme can be effectively grown between paving stones because it's tough enough to withstand trampling (within reason).

MAINTENANCE

The majority of vegetables, and some herbs, are annuals and have to be replanted every year. Rhubarb, asparagus, many herbs, and fruits of all types are perennials. Place perennials where they will not be disturbed by tillers or other cultivators used to turn and break the soil. If your garden is small and areas are turned annually with a fork and shovel, this may not be so great a concern. Nor is it if the garden is heavily mulched—that is, covered with a thick layer of organic materials to keep the soil loose, moist, and weed free.

When determining the width and type of paths between beds, consider these factors: Will you be using a wheelbarrow, garden cart, lawn mower, garden tractor, or tiller? Is there good maneuverability around the beds? Is the width of the beds such that you can cultivate from the path without stepping into a bed? It's better not to compact the soil or possibly crush some vulnerable, emerging seedling or small plant. Three to four feet is a good width for a bed that is accessible from both sides.

Gardeners who have physical difficulty working at ground level can have walled raised beds built to waist height for easier access.

Low-maintenance perennial herbs are suitable for areas that are too steep or small to mow. They are also an attractive choice for ground covers or mass plantings.

LOW-MAINTENANCE PERENNIAL HERBS

FOR SUNNY LOCATIONS

Chamomile	Lamb's ears	Rosemary	Yarrow
Lady's mantle	Lavender	Thyme	

FOR SHADIER LOCATIONS

Bee balm	Lady's mantle	Sweet cicely	Sweet woodruff

Irrigation is an important consideration for gardeners in drier climates. If you're going to have any kind of system installed in the ground, make sure you consult with a contractor before you finalize your designs.

WALLED PATIO

In this plan, a long and narrow garden is broken up into several different spaces.

An outdoor sitting or dining area easily accessible from the house is enclosed by beds for herbs, flowers, and vegetables, a grape arbor, and a play area for children. Brick raised beds for vegetables or herbs are close at hand, yet out of the reach of small children. (They have the play area to dig in!) Vegetables that could be grown in the limited space of these beds include greens for salad or cooking, bush beans, carrots, cucumbers, eggplant, garlic, herbs, onions, peppers, and tomatoes. The aggressive mints, lemon balm, sweet cicely, and daylilies can fight it out among themselves on one side of the patio.

Past the arbor, paving is flanked with lady's mantle, thyme, and chamomile. These plants soften the edge with their sprawling habits and also make attractive, noncompetitive, shallow-rooted underplanting for the espaliered trees.

A rounded, paved area in the back makes a nice spot for a small bench or garden seat. It's surrounded by relatively low-maintenance perennial herbs selected for the season-long display of their foliage and bloom. (As an aside here: "Low maintenance" is an overused term that should not be taken to mean no weeding, no watering, and so on. It actually means that some plants

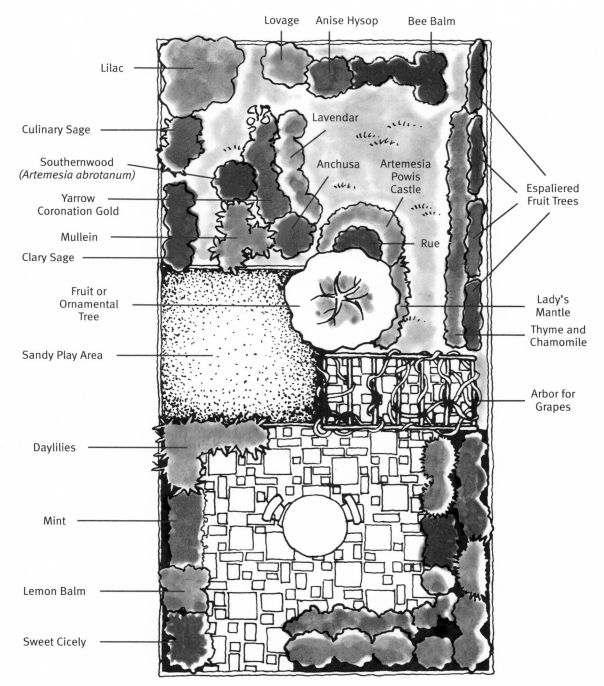

Lovage

Anise Hysop

Bee Balm

Lilac

Lavendar

Culinary Sage

Southernwood
(Artemesia abrotanum)

Anchusa

Artemesia
Powis
Castle

Yarrow
Coronation Gold

Mullein

Clary Sage

Rue

Fruit or
Ornamental
Tree

Espaliered
Fruit Trees

Sandy Play Area

Lady's
Mantle

Thyme and
Chamomile

Arbor for
Grapes

Daylilies

Mint

Lemon Balm

Sweet Cicely

Vegetables in Raised Beds

are tougher and less fussy than others. The only thing that's *really* low maintenance is a good, thick layer of concrete.) There are many perennial plants that could satisfy these requirements; however, I'll limit the selection to herbs discussed in this book.

Some have been chosen for their silver-hued foliage—specifically, yarrow, lavender, mullein, and the artemisias. The gray tones of these plants contrast well with the full spectrum of colors presented in the foliage and blooms of the other plants, and they offer an elegant, cooling effect. Herbs have also been selected for variety of texture and shape of foliage: woolly-leaved mullein; needlelike lavender; finely divided lacy yarrow and artemisias; coarse, bristly sage and anchusa; pleated lady's mantle; and the delicate, minute leaves of thyme, woodruff, and chamomile.

The back wall of the garden is softened by a lilac and a clump of lovage— the latter a tall, tropical-appearing, leafy herb.

Early-spring bulbs and violets would do well planted beneath the central tree, blooming before or at the same time as the tree leafs out.

Espaliered fruit trees are placed against a side wall that will absorb heat and help fruit to ripen. The heavily pruned and shaped trees take up little room and offer a stylized architectural form, especially in the winter landscape. Having chosen lower-maintenance plants, the gardener will have plenty of extra time to devote to pruning and training the espaliered trees! Apples and pears are the most common fruits to espalier. Henry Leuthardt Nurseries (www.HenryLeuthardtNurseries.com) in East Moriches, New York, is a good source of trees available for espalier training. A good text on the subject is *Espaliers and Vines for the Home Gardener* by Harold Perkins (Iowa State University Press, 1979).

SCREENED AND ENCLOSED GARDENS

This plan is designed to create a private space using garden structures, plants, and fruit trees. (See Bibliography, page 287, for books on fruit growing.) A central patio is surrounded by a double row of dwarf fruit trees, a lattice fence, a *Rosa rugosa* hedge, a double row of asparagus, an arbor of grapes and kiwifruit, pines (*Pinus koraiensis*, or Korean pine, for pine nuts!), and blueberry bushes.

The grape arbor is located on the north side of the garden, where it won't shade any plants, while the south side is screened by a *Rosa rugosa* hedge and asparagus (the foliage can be easily 5 feet tall). Mint is located at the corner of the house in its own bed, surrounded by the path. This segregation is necessary as mint is among the most invasive of plants and can bully its neighbors out of existence.

The four central beds are for annual vegetables and perennial alpine strawberries, which make a handsome edging. The edging plants—lettuce, ruby chard, nasturtiums, calendulas, and garlic—are chosen for ornamental qualities such as size, form, and texture. They are all low growing and present a variety of color, leaf shape, and growth habits.

Herbs are located close to the house for easy access. Spring growers leave room, upon their harvest, for later-season replacements: basil follows spinach, radicchio follows cauliflower, eggplant follows pak choi, and peas will be harvested and the vines ready to be removed when tomatoes, peppers, and broccoli have grown large enough to need the space.

Compatible companions include tomatoes and basil, dill and cabbage, melon and nasturtium.

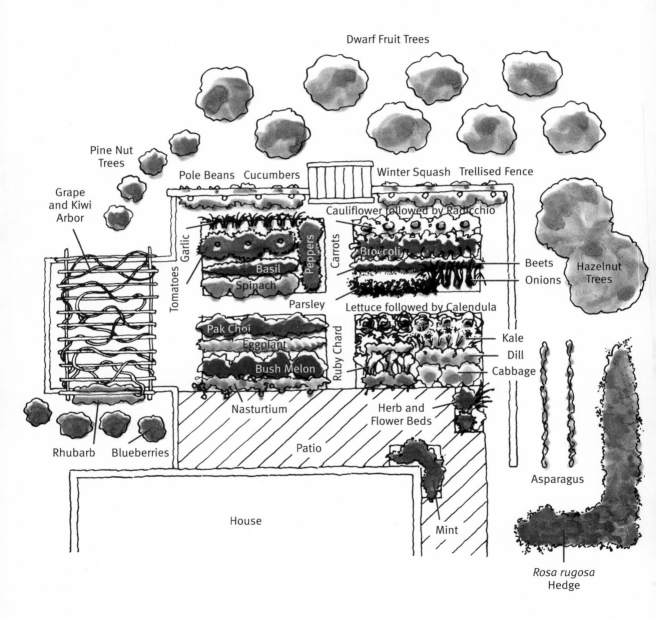

KNOT GARDENS

Knot gardens were very popular in the Elizabethan period of English land-scape design. Herbs used for medicinal, culinary, or simply ornamental pur-poses were arranged in geometric forms that resembled the patterns used in embroidered tapestries.

Plan a knot garden for an area that can be seen from above to best appre-ciate the interweaving of the variously colored and textured plants. The for-mal, symmetrical quality of a knot garden suggests its use as a focal point in the center of a garden or courtyard.

KNOT GARDEN—PERENNIALS

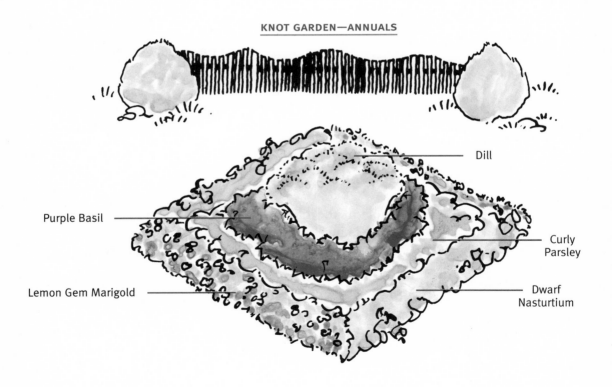

Germander

Rue

Santolina

Lamb's Ears

Lavender

KNOT GARDEN—ANNUALS

Dill

Purple Basil

Curly Parsley

Lemon Gem Marigold

Dwarf Nasturtium

Two knot garden possibilities are presented here, one using perennial herbs, the other annual edible flowers and culinary herbs.

The annual herb-and-flower knot garden will last only a season; however, the design or plant selection can be changed from year to year. The perennial knot garden design is subtle and refined; the annual knot garden design is bright and vivacious, with the hot colors of nasturtium and marigold flowers set off by brilliant purple basil, bright green parsley, and blue-green dill.

To lay out a knot garden, find the center of a square by crossing two strings from the corners to mark an **X**. From this point, you can lay out a cross (+) to determine the axes around which the design is symmetric. To create circles or curves, use a tautly held string measured to the length of the circle radius. Pin one end to the centerpoint and trace the curve onto the ground to use as a guide for planting. Space plants a little closer than usual for a tight, compact design.

To deter weeds, a layer of gravel 4 to 6 inches deep is used as a background for the plants. For a softer effect, try shredded bark. To contain the gravel or bark mulch, edge the garden with a low border of brick, timber, or stone.

The perennial herbs chosen are low-growing plants that will need to be pruned to keep the pattern neat and clear; they also require winter protection in colder regions. It's a good idea to keep some backup plants in another bed to fill in any gaps that may occur. I have selected plants that are fairly dense and offer a variety of texture and color of foliage: incredibly soft, gray, and floppy lamb's ears; small, bright green, pointed germander; rich, unusually blue-green rue; gray-green, coral-like santolina; and silvery, needlelike lavender.

DOORYARD GARDEN

Dooryard gardens can be lush, abundantly landscaped entranceways, filled with plants that have both culinary and ornamental usefulness. Most include herbs, flowers, and a few vegetables.

Many front yards are small squares of lawn edged with plantings. They may be sunnier and more suited to a kitchen garden than, for example, a backyard with mature shade trees.

Plantings of varying heights create interest in a small space; the vertical forms of angelica, mullein, and hollyhock contrast with low, spreading plants such as dianthus, thyme, and lavender. Hardy kiwi vines and cucumbers grow on trellises against the house. Climbing nasturtiums twine up and around a fence by the sidewalk.

Rounded green or ruby lettuce leaves, spiky chive clumps, purple basils, and fine, gray-green lavender leaves, to name a few, provide a textured pattern of various leaf shapes and colors.

Winter interest is maintained by bright orange rose hips adorning the *Rosa rugosa*, crab apples, the tall seed stalks of mullein and hollyhock, the odd yet colorful ornamental cabbages, and the evergreen foliage of the Korean Pine, thyme, lavender, and dianthus.

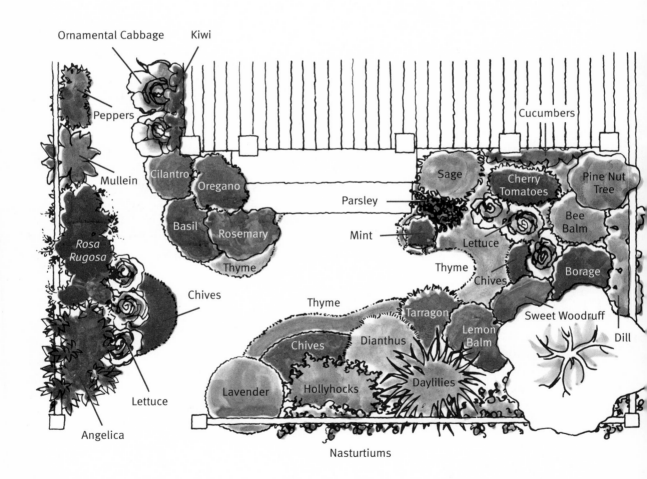

Tender herbs such as rosemary and parsley are grown in pots that will be moved indoors.

All of the vegetables and some herbs—basil, parsley, calendula, borage, dill, cilantro, and nasturtiums—are annuals that must be replanted yearly. The rest of the plants are perennials. This gives the opportunity for a flexible garden that differs from year to year.

LAWN BEDS

This kitchen garden provides a small space for growing a few favorite vegetables and herbs. The site is a front yard, a lawn space with some mature plantings of shrubs and trees. The backyard is too shady for successful vegetable crops, whereas the front receives plenty of sun.

Beds for vegetables and herbs snake their way across the lawn to be in full sun and away from existing plantings—specifically, the sizable shrubs and trees located off the plan to the right. The illustration below shows midsummer plantings. Tall plants are located so as not to shade low growers. Planting succession, ornamental arrangement, and beneficial companions should be considered in the placement of various plants. Herbs are located near the entryway for easy access.

Beds can be maintained from either side, with enough space between them for a lawn mower to pass.

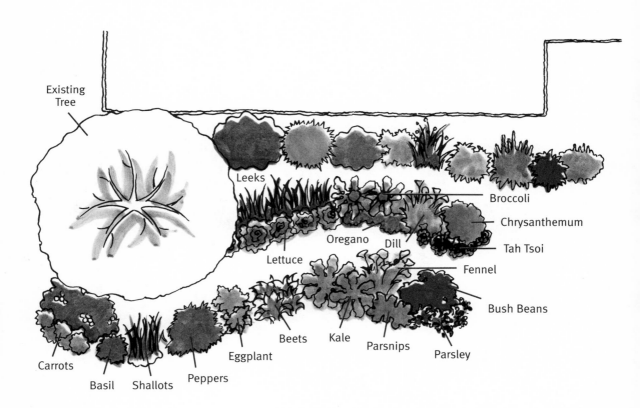

HILLSIDE GARDEN

A garden on a sloping site requires the consideration of specific issues: soil erosion, ease of cultivation, and aesthetic concerns of "fitting in" to a hillside. This design makes use of retaining walls and narrow terraces that follow the contours of the slope, creating beds for planting. These beds are situated and planted so as not to disturb a fine view from the decks on the south and east sides of the house.

The site offers plenty of room for people who have the desire, time, and energy to attend to an array of landscape edibles. Vegetables and herbs, fruit and nut trees, berries, grapevines, and ornamentals all have space in the site plan. This type of plan could be used as a master plan to be developed over a period of years, adding a section year by year.

A professional contractor will be needed to ensure the structural integrity of walls used to retain sizable volumes of earth, which can be dangerously heavy when wet. One bed for vegetables or herbs is located on a terrace that is an integrated, structural part of the outdoor living space of the house. This should be built at the same time the foundation is laid. Terraces involve the initial expense of clearing existing growth, providing drainage if necessary, constructing, and back filling with topsoil, compost, or aged manure. They can be a handsome, useful part of the configuration of house, hillside, and garden.

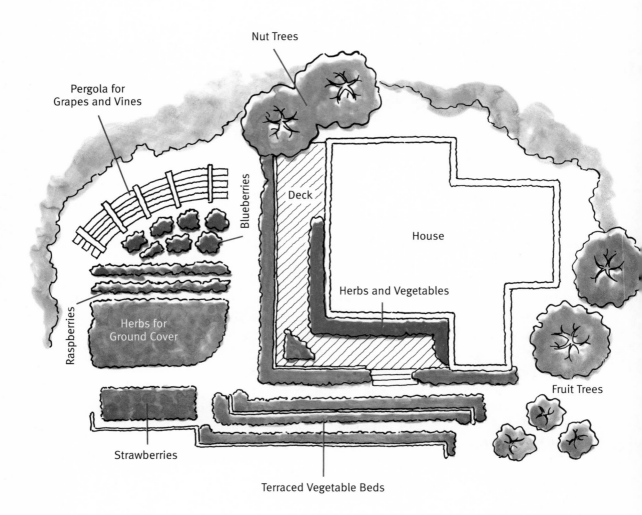

Beds below the house can be planted with space-consuming vegetables such as corn, squash, potatoes, beans, melons, asparagus, cucumbers, or a crop grown in large quantity for winter storage.

Berries and ground covers can be grown directly on the slope because they are tenacious and more or less perennial; their roots will hold the soil in place.

Grape and other vines are grown on a long, curving pergola, a striking landscape feature and a shady spot for a hammock or two.

Fruit trees are located to the side so as not to block the view as they mature.

CONTAINER GARDENING

Container gardening is especially useful where there is no room for an inground garden (as in the following situation) but need not be limited to those conditions. Attractively planted containers can be colorful accents or focal points on decks, patios, stairs, and balconies, near entryways, and at windows.

During the summer, Moosewood Restaurant's outside dining area is bordered by a low wall topped with planters full of brightly colored flowers. The flower boxes create a gracious visual separation between a busy street and the dining terrace. The terrace is shaded by a large canopy, limiting the planting to annual flowers that can withstand shade.

Outdoor spaces with sufficient sun and some protection from strong winds are suitable locations for container-planted vegetables and herbs.

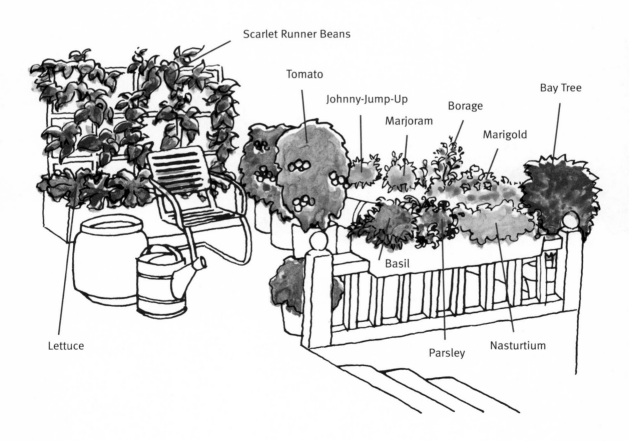

Scarlet Runner Beans

Tomato

Johnny-Jump-Up

Marjoram

Borage

Bay Tree

Marigold

Basil

Lettuce

Parsley

Nasturtium

Containers should be appropriately sized and rot resistant and should have adequate drainage. The range of possibilities extends from pricey, imported terra-cotta to food-service, 5-gallon plastic tubs. A handsome, classic choice is the simple clay pot, available in all sizes. There are also less expensive plastic and fiberglass pots made to simulate terra-cotta. Half-barrels are good for plants that need generous root space, or for mixed planting. Containers that are chosen for the beauty of their form should be matched with a plant that doesn't completely hide the pot with an abundance of flowing vegetation. Conversely, vigorous, fast-growing plants can quickly cover functional but less-attractive containers. Fast growers include tomatoes, lettuce, bush cucumbers, melons, squash, nasturtiums, scented geraniums, parsley, and basil.

Choose varieties that are suited to container planting. Some catalogs key specific flowers, vegetables, and herbs that are compact enough for containers. The following list roughly divides plants into small (6- to 8-inch pots or window boxes), medium (10- to 16-inch pots), and large (24-inch or larger pots, buckets, half-barrels, and troughs).

Vegetables and herbs grown in containers need more than casual maintenance. Plants can dry out quickly in hot weather (especially in clay or terra-cotta) and need to be watered often. Vegetables located close to the wall of a house may be in a substantially hotter microclimate than those a few feet away. This could be advantageous for heat-loving plants such as eggplant or melons, but death to lettuce and other cool-weather greens. A light trellis or pergola is useful to shade places where too much solar heat is trapped. A trellis can also double as a windbreak to lessen the drying-out or knockdown effects of wind.

Frequent waterings and rains can leach out soil nutrients, requiring consistent fertilization of container plants. This should be at a milder strength than for plants in the ground, whose roots are surrounded by absorptive soil.

Gardeners in cold climates should empty ceramic or plastic containers after the first hard frosts to avoid damage from alternate freezing and thawing winter weather.

The placement of large, heavy containers on balconies and roofs should be made with the consideration of what loads the structure can handle. It may be necessary to consult with the building owner or a contractor.

The illustration on page 178 shows a balcony with an assortment of containers. Boxes have been built to fit the top railing of the balcony. Pots of various sizes and shapes are grouped together for a lush display and ease of watering. One end of the balcony has a deep planter in which a double crop of lettuce and trellised beans is growing.

SMALL Edible Flowers

Dwarf carnations or pinks	Dwarf nasturtiums (Whirlybird)	Pansies or violas Mini roses	Violets

SMALL Herbs

Small-leafed basil Dwarf calendula Chives	Marjoram Oregano Parsley	Savory Scented geraniums Thyme	

MEDIUM Edible Flowers

Calendula	Dwarf chrysanthemums		

MEDIUM Herbs

Basil Bay	Lemon balm Gem series marigolds	Mint Rosemary	Sage

MEDIUM Vegetables

Alpine strawberries Asian vegetables— tatsoi, pak choi (mei qing choi), mizuna	Carrots (Minicor, Planet) Chili peppers	Lettuce (grown as a cut-and-come-again crop to a height of 6 inches)	Salad greens—arugula, cress, corn salad Shallots Basket tomatoes (Pixie, Tiny Tim)

LARGE Edible Flowers	LARGE Herbs
Daylilies	Bay

LARGE Vegetables

Cabbage (Early Jersey Wakefield)	Green beans (Provider)	Mint	Tomatoes— determinate or smaller-growing varieties
Bush cucumber (Salad Bush, Spacemaster)	Bush melons (Garden Baby Watermelon)	Peppers	
	Roses	Bush squash (Bush Delicata Winter Squash)	

Gardening Techniques

SOIL

MY FIRST GARDEN was an ill-fated semidisaster located in a spot where coal ashes, which are highly acidic and toxic to plants, had been dumped. It wasn't obvious at first glance that this wasn't an ideal site, although today I know that the scraggly grass growing there should have been a giveaway. It was the only level, nonwooded area available to me, and I was eager to plant. Even with its drawbacks, the plot could have been improved with better drainage and massive amounts of soil amendments.

Soil is more than just dirt. And although improving your soil may be the most labor-intensive, least glamorous part of gardening, it's the most important. Plants derive only 10 percent of nutrients from the soil, but that 10 percent is as crucial as water and air. Whatever attention you give your soil will surely show at harvesttime.

The depth and type of soil in a chosen site give an indication of how much work will be required to create a garden. Dig a 2-foot-square hole to check for soil type, topsoil depth, and drainage.

BASIC TYPE

Soil types can be determined by a simple rule of thumb: Pick up a handful of soil and try to form a ball. If it's loose and gritty without holding any shape, it's sandy. Clay will hold together, mold to the form of your hand, and be sticky when wet. A good loam (the ideal) will hold together when moist but have a nice, crumbly texture, like a pie crust, when it is dry. Some soils are a combination—for example, a sandy loam.

Soils that are too sandy benefit from the addition of organic matter in the form of compost, leaf mold (decayed leaves), peat moss, rotted manure, or trucked-in topsoil.

Heavy clay soils that retain too much water are improved with the addition of organic matter, sand, or grit (finely ground gravel) to provide good drainage. Most vegetables, herbs, and ornamentals need oxygen in the soil, and in soggy soils oxygen is displaced by water. The depth of the topsoil can be seen by changes in color and texture in the dug soil pit. Topsoil should be dark and crumbly, with a generous amount of humus—possibly eons worth of animal, plant, and microorganism residues. It's interesting to note that pre-Columbian American soils averaged 4 percent humus as opposed to 1.5 percent or less now. Clearly, our methods of farming have been depleting the soil at an alarming rate. (See below for a discussion of healthy cultivation practices that help build topsoil.) Thin soils with less than 2 to 3 inches of good topsoil should be enriched with a mix of the soil amendments listed above.

Heavy clay subsoil or bedrock close to the surface may create drainage problems and overly wet soil. Fill the soil-test pit with water and check to see how long it takes to drain. A drainage time of more than 8 hours indicates a need to build raised beds with plenty of soil amended with sand, compost, and organic matter, or to install a permanent drainage system to channel water away from the garden site.

SOIL pH AND NUTRIENT CONTENT

Your soils should be analyzed for pH and the presence of important nutritive elements. Testing for pH is an easy procedure with the purchase of kits; however, soil analysis for nutritive elements is difficult and not recommended for home gardeners. County cooperative extension agents will send your soil sample to the state service for analysis. More often than not, the results return on a computerized printout. It may be necessary to ask your local agent to recommend organic substitutes for the synthetic fertilizers listed.

Readings of pH reflect the acidity or alkalinity of soil. Most soils range from 4.5 to 7.5, with lower numbers acidic, 7.0 neutral, and higher numbers alkaline. Vegetables and herbs do well with a soil pH between 6.0 and 8.0. Specific ideal readings are given for each vegetable; however, most will tolerate a 1-point difference either way. To bring acid soils up to a higher pH, apply ground limestone in the fall at a rate of 5 pounds per 100 square feet. To lower the pH of alkaline soils, ground sulfur can be applied at $1/2$ pound per 100 square feet. Soil additions of organic matter help vegetables tolerate some variation from their ideal pH.

Three crucial nutritive elements for good plant growth are as follows:

Nitrogen (N)—a major constituent of chlorophyll (important for vigorous, sturdy green growth). Deficiencies result in spindly, stunted plants with yellowed leaves. Excess nitrogen causes big, leafy plants with too few flowers or fruits. Fertilizers high in nitrogen include blood meal, cottonseed meal, sea products (fish meal and seaweed), well-rotted manures, compost, and soybean meal. These are organic only if they are processed from appropriate sources.

Phosphorus (P)—necessary for the development of flowers and resistance to disease. Phosphorus deficiency will show with scant flowers and fruit, and small, unhealthy plants with yellow-margined leaves. Bonemeal, compost, sea products, well-rotted manures, and rock phosphate are natural sources of phosphorus.

Potassium or potash (K)—affects root and leaf growth, particularly for underground crops (beets, carrots, and potatoes). It also helps provide drought resistance. Yellow, mottled leaves with brown edges and tips indicate potassium deficiency. Fertilizers rich in potassium include wood ashes (from real wood, not synthetic fireplace logs), compost, greensand, and sea products.

In addition to these three, there are trace elements that plants need in lesser degree for healthy growth: calcium, magnesium, sulfur, iron, manganese, zinc, copper, boron, molybdenum, and chlorine. These should not be lacking in soil where nutrients are regularly renewed. Seaweed is an excellent source of microelements, as it contains minute amounts of a vast array of minerals.

Feeding healthy soil is the best way to avoid unhealthy plants. Soil microorganisms digest nutrients and alter them to a form that is usable by plants. To act effectively, these microorganisms need a regular supply of decomposing organic matter, such as compost, decaying mulches, or well-aged manure. Synthetic fertilizers give plants a quick "shot" that produces vigorous growth, but they do nothing for the long-term health of the soil. In addition, their regular use kills beneficial microorganisms and earthworms, creating nutrient-poor soil that becomes dependent on chemical boosting.

All-purpose, organic fertilizers (with balanced nutrients) are available at garden centers or through mail order. They are particularly valuable for starting new gardens or where a compost supply is not available.

A basic guideline that I follow is to work 1 inch of compost into the top 6 to 8 inches of soil whenever a new crop is planted—spring, summer, or fall. I also supplement with rock phosphate at the rate of 4 pounds per 100 square feet, applied once every 4 to 5 years.

Not all vegetables have the same nutrient needs. Heavy feeders include asparagus, the cabbage family, cucumbers, corn, onions, leafy greens, melons, and squash. Medium feeders are tomatoes and the legumes (peas and beans). Herbs, root crops, potatoes, sweet potatoes, and peppers are light feeders. Heavy feeders yield best if their gluttony is satisfied by the addition of an inch or two of compost, well-aged manure, or an all-purpose, organic fertilizer at the recommended rate, midway through their growing season.

GREEN MANURES AND COVER CROPS

Green manures are crops that are planted and then turned under to decompose and thus enrich the soil. They can be used to increase the fertility of poor soil in gardens where compost or animal manures are not available. Green manures can revitalize "tired" sections of gardens, or improve new areas that will be planted the next season.

As a green manure, legumes are particularly effective for adding nutrients—specifically nitrogen—to the soil. These include the useful vegetables peas and beans, along with clovers, vetch, and lespedeza. Winter rye and oats can be sown in the fall to overwinter and be turned under in the spring. Buckwheat is grown in the summer to break up difficult hardpan subsoils with deep-reaching roots. It should be plowed under soon after the attractive, white flowers open, to avoid reseeding.

COMPOST

One of the best soil additives, compost can be made without great difficulty. It enriches and lightens the soil and increases its ability to retain moisture. The variety of organic matter, in the form of weeds, kitchen waste, leaves, and shredded brush, added to a compost pile widens the range of elements and microorganisms available to plants in the finished compost. This material can be dug into beds, used as a potting soil for container-grown plants, or applied as a mulch.

Summer and fall are excellent times for starting a compost pile. Weeds, grass clippings, shredded or chopped brush, vegetable waste from harvested crops, and sod from newly created beds are all in good supply at this time. Other materials for the compost pile include kitchen waste (vegetable matter and eggshells only; all other waste attracts hungry rodents, dogs, and raccoons). Use manure from chickens, goats, sheep, cows, and horses only. *Never* use cat litter because your pet's feces may contain toxoplasmosis. Add dirt or more dry material to cover the pile if any odors are offensive.

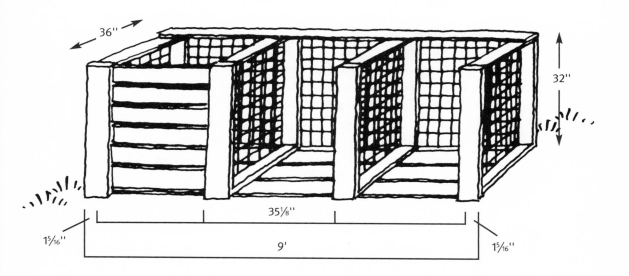

MATERIALS

What	Quantity
2- by 4-inch framing lumber, rot-resistant wood such as cedar, locust, larch, or redwood	3 9-foot lengths (for bottom members and top brace) 5 12-foot lengths (for dividers and grooved strips)
1- by 6-inch common pine	18 3-foot lengths (for front slats)
2- by 2-inch welded, galvanized 36-inch dog wire or wire fencing	21-foot length (for dividers and back section)
5/8-inch galvanized carriage bolts, 4 inches long	12 (to secure dividers to bottom members and top brace)
16-penny galvanized spikes	5 pounds (to fasten the sides of the dividers)
Galvanized poultry-wire staples	250 (to secure wire fencing to dividers and back section)

There are several composting methods, each with its own champions. My compost piles tend to be the slow, lazy type that requires no athletic turning and tossing of the materials. I try to layer the drier grasses and weeds with freshly decomposing kitchen waste, fresh grass clippings, and manure (if possible) to a height of 3 feet or so. It then sits untouched until the next season, 6 months or more later.

Many garden books and articles espouse a faster method (2 weeks to 1 month), but this involves more attention. This quicker compost has these advantages: (1) fast decomposition allows for less leaching of nutrients by rain or snow; (2) it's ready when you need it; (3) actively decaying organic matter contains more beneficial soil microorganisms than slowly decaying compost; and (4) the higher temperatures created destroy many undesirable weed seeds, insect larvae, and disease germs. (They're all such good reasons that I don't know why I haven't been swayed.)

Here's the faster composting method: Materials to be composted should be at least one-third fresh, green matter (weeds, grass, vegetable waste) and no more than two-thirds drier bulk (preferably shredded or chopped leaves, stems, hay, brush). Mix, but don't layer, all the materials in a bin or pile, no smaller than 3 feet by 3 feet for good decomposition. Bins can be made with snow fencing or old wooden pallets. (See page 187 for a compost bin design.) If the bin or pile is not roofed, cover with black plastic to trap and maintain heat and to protect against leaching rains. Turn the pile with a fork on the second day and every 3 days afterward. Keep the compost evenly moist, about the consistency of a damp sponge. Internal temperatures should be between 140°F and 160°F for proper decomposition. Subsequent cooler temperatures of 110°F and crumbly compost indicate a finished product. Gardener's Supply (page 284) has compost thermometers and aerators.

Compact and unobtrusive compost bins or rotating tumblers are available from mail-order sources. They fit in even small backyards.

Newly dug gardens that need a quick boost of nutrients can benefit from a direct composting method. This warm-weather technique requires a soil temperature of 60°F or higher to ensure proper decomposition. Dig an 8- to 10-inch-deep trench where seeds or plants will go. Place 3 to 4 inches of kitchen waste or other compost materials, $1/4$ cup per square foot of high-nitrogen organic fertilizer, and some garden dirt in the trench and chop it coarsely with a shovel. Fill in with garden soil to ground level. Seed or transplant directly above the trench as usual, immediately if desired.

MULCH

Mulch is any material placed on top of soil to inhibit weeds, retain soil moisture, keep soil cool or warm, provide nutrients, or encourage the activity of beneficial microorganisms.

Ruth Stouts' *How to Have a Green Thumb Without an Aching Back* was an early influence in my vegetable-gardening career. Her method of soil building and weed control is a form of mulch mania in which there is no such thing as too much, usually in the form of rotted hay or straw. The goal is to keep a layer of mulch dense enough to block any weed growth. Some hand weeding is necessary around newly emerged seedlings, with the mulch pulled up around them as they mature. Weeds that pop up are covered with more mulch. This technique can build up a rich, deep layer of topsoil as the mulch decomposes. Mulched gardens with soil that is moist and high in organic matter will encourage earthworms. The worms' activity aerates the soil and increases water penetration. Worm "manure" (or *castings*) is remarkably rich in nutrients.

Other mulches can be employed that are locally available through either commercial sources or the gardener's hunting and gathering efforts. These include the following:

- Bark chips
- Buckwheat hulls
- Cocoa bean shells
- Grass clippings
- Leaves
- Rotted manure
- Noncolored newspaper (black ink)
- Pine needles
- Sawdust
- Seaweed
- Woodchips

Bark chips, buckwheat hulls, and cocoa bean shells are attractive but expensive and so best suited for small ornamental beds. They are available at garden centers in 25- or 50-pound bags. Grass clippings and leaves may mat and prevent water penetration. Grass clippings decompose quickly in moist climates. Leaves work well as a winter blanket for annual vegetable beds but may have to be weighted down with brush in windy areas. Pine needles, sawdust, and wood chips may acidify soil if used in quantity, so use them for acid-loving plants: potatoes, rhubarb, blueberries, and ornamentals such as azalea or rhododendron.

Plants mulched with materials that do not decompose quickly—newspaper, sawdust, wood or bark chips, hulls and shells—will need the addition of a nitrogen fertilizer, as the process of decomposition ties up nitrogen, making it unavailable to plants.

There *are* a few disadvantages to mulching. Witchgrass and other weeds that are rhizomatous (spread by underground root stalks) can still manage to put up a good fight, even under mulch. The cool, damp conditions mulch creates can attract legions of slugs during even moderately wet seasons, and soil temperatures may be kept too cool in early spring. I like to mulch beds in late fall and early winter, using rotted hay, straw, or compost. Hay should first be rotted to hasten its decomposition and to destroy any weed seeds. In areas to be planted in the early spring, pull back the mulch a couple of weeks before planting so the soil can warm up. Mulch can be reapplied at the onset of hot, dry weather.

SEED STARTING

Gardeners who can provide the appropriate germination temperatures and conditions start many of their seeds indoors. This is often necessary in short-season areas where warm-weather crops such as tomatoes, peppers, melons, and squash will not produce unless given a head start indoors. Buying seedlings at a nursery may be the best option for those who have neither the time nor space to nurture seedlings for 2 months or more. Seed starting offers its own rewards: primal bonding with your seedlings and the choice of different or unusual varieties not available at nurseries.

Indoor seed starting calls for specific equipment and facilities. You must have a warm location for germination, potting mix, containers with adequate drainage, and fluorescent lights or an extremely sunny area. An indoor exposure where plants thrive in spring and summer may not provide enough light for good, strong seedlings because of the winter sun's weakness.

TEMPERATURE

Most vegetables germinate readily in a soil temperature range of 65°F to 80°F. Peas and early greens like arugula and spinach are best when direct seeded outdoors; they germinate at 50°F. Eggplant, cucumbers, melons, and peppers need temperatures of no less than 80°F. You can also provide consistent warmth with heat mats specifically made for germination or with soil heating cables buried in flats.

POTTING MIX

Potting mixes should be free of weed seeds and disease organisms, provide good moisture retention and drainage, and be of a light texture that allows for the easy pulling apart or cutting of plants with a minimum of root damage. I prefer to use commercial potting soil mixtures because they satisfy all of these requirements. The use of garden soil for all or part of a potting mix requires oven sterilization in pans 3 to 4 inches deep at a temperature of 350°F for an hour or so. This kills weed seeds and prevents the spread of soilborne diseases, but be warned: it creates a nasty smell in your kitchen.

CONTAINERS

Any container that provides good drainage can be used to start seeds: small plastic or fiber packs, plastic dairy containers with holes punched in the bottom, ceramic or plastic pots, wood or plastic flats, peat pots and strips, and plastic soil cell trays. Peat pots are excellent for plants like squash or melons that do not like to have their roots disturbed in transplanting. They can be planted as is: peel away some of the pot here and there to encourage root growth, pop into the ground, and remove any rim sticking up above the soil line. Soil cells are molded trays made up of a number of square or round cells varying in diameter from $1^{1}/_{2}$ to $2^{1}/_{2}$ inches. These trays fit over another tray used as a water reservoir and can be topped with a clear plastic dome to maintain moist soil and high humidity for good germination. Soil cell trays are a very efficient way to start a large quantity of seedlings; they save space, they last for years, and they virtually eliminate the root, leaf, or stem damage associated with other methods, because removing the seedlings is simple: just push them up from the bottom.

SOIL BLOCKS

Soil blocks, or seed-starting cubes, eliminate the need for pots or other containers, making them kind to both the pocketbook and the environment. They can be made at home with commercial soil-block makers, which are widely available through mail-order seed and supply sources. Block makers come in large sizes (2 by 2 inches) for plants that need time to mature before being planted out, or small ($^{11}/_{16}$ by $^{11}/_{16}$ inch) for seedlings that will be transplanted soon after germination.

To make the cubes, simply fill the block maker with thoroughly moistened potting soil, eject the blocks, and plant the seeds. Each block with its seedling can be planted directly, avoiding the messy and traumatic root separation that occurs when seedlings share a container.

SOWING SEEDS

Potting mix should be moist and spongy but not soggy. Use warm water to avoid chilling the seeds. Allow commercial mixes to sit for a couple of hours to fully absorb added water. Scoop potting mix into containers, lightly tapping it down without packing it in.

Seed packages usually give planting information, including optimum planting time, days to harvest, plant size, germination time and percentage rate, seed depth for sowing, and specific light requirements. Seeds with a high germination rate can be sown thinly for economy; those with lower rates can be planted two or three per individual container. Very tiny seeds (such as carrot) can be mixed with sand for easier distribution. Many seeds that are sown on the soil surface and left uncovered need light to germinate. These should be misted and kept moist with a plastic dome or cover of plastic wrap until germination occurs.

Watering is best achieved by siphoning up into the soil through the bottom drainage holes. Place seedling containers in trays of water, promptly removing them as soon as the soil appears to be uniformly moist. Gently probe the soil surface with your fingertip to assess the degree of moisture. Alternatively, purchase growing trays that feature mats of wicking material and water reservoirs to maintain consistent soil moisture. Avoid watering small seedlings from the top. They can be damaged by a strong stream of water and can be made more vulnerable to damping off—a fungus disease that causes the seedlings to keel over at the base of the stem.

LIGHT

Fluorescent lights are an inexpensive, easily obtained source of even, bright light for sturdy seedling growth. More expensive grow lights are not necessary for the short growing period seedlings will be indoors.

Wide temperature fluctuations and a lack of sufficient light intensity may make starting seeds on a windowsill impractical. Weak, pale, leggy plants that flop toward the light are not getting enough of it. Very bright sunrooms or rooms with large expanses of window and an eastern, southern, or western exposure (at least 6 hours) can be effectively used where temperature ranges are not extreme. Southern exposure is usually the longest and so is preferred.

Newly germinated plants can be grown as close as 2 to 3 inches from cool fluorescent lights. As plants grow, maintain a distance of 4 to 6 inches between the tops of the leaves and the light bulbs. Set a timer to ensure that they receive the requisite 16 to 18 hours of light each day.

Most vegetable and herb seedlings can be raised indoors in a room temperature range of 60°F to 75°F. Higher temperatures promote spindly, soft growth, whereas colder temperatures may stunt and delay growth. Feed with a liquid fertilizer such as fish emulsion, especially when using potting mixes that contain no nutrients.

BUYING PLANTS

When purchasing plants or seedlings, look for those that have uniform color and strong stems, with no yellowed or brown leaves, and no considerable insect damage. Compact and well-branched plants will ultimately be stronger and more attractive than tall, lanky ones. Check the undersides of leaves to avoid taking home any unwanted "hitchhikers." Plants in bud handle transplanting better than those already in flower. Hardening off (page 195) is necessary for plants accustomed to greenhouse or indoor conditions.

HEAT AND COLD PREFERENCES OF VEGETABLES

Quite Hardy: *seed or transplant in cool weather, when the soil is workable, 4 to 6 weeks before the last spring frost*

Asian vegetables—daikon, radish, mizuna, pak choi, tatsoi	Cabbage family—broccoli, cabbage, cauliflower, kohlrabi Onion family—leeks, onions, scallions, shallots	Pea family—shelled, snow, sugar snap Potatoes	Salad greens—arugula, mâche, endive, radicchio, sorrel, orach Spinach

Hardy: *seed in cool weather 2 weeks before the last spring frost*

Beets Carrots	Swiss chard	Parsnips	Turnips

Not Hardy: *seed or transplant after the last spring frost (earlier if protected)*

Snap and shell beans Corn	Chinese cabbage	Squash (summer or winter)	Tomatoes

Needing Hot Weather: *seed or transplant 1 week after last spring frost (earlier if protected)*

Cucumbers Eggplant	Lima beans Melons	Peppers Sweet potatoes

Autumn Hardy: *seed in mid- to late summer for fall crops (6 to 8 weeks before frost in northern areas)*

Asian vegetables—Chinese cabbage, daikon radish, mizuna, pak choi, tatsoi Beets	Brussels sprouts (need long season; start in June) Collards and kale	Cabbage family (for southern states and Pacific Coast) Lettuce	Salad greens—arugula, mâche, endive, radicchio, sorrel, orach Spinach Turnips

Succession Crops: *sow throughout the season, where temperatures are appropriate*

Asian vegetables— mizuna, pak choi, tatsoi Snap beans	Beets Cabbage family	Carrots Lettuce	Scallions

TRANSPLANTING

Crowded seedlings can be transplanted into individual containers or thinned when two or more true leaves have developed. The initial leaves that appear at germination are typically two rounded leaves directly opposite each other. True leaves appear after these and are the same as the leaves of the mature plant—for example, the feathered foliage of dill.

When transplanting, hold seedlings by the sturdier leaf and not the fragile stem. Seedlings can be snipped off with scissors to thin. Save the more robust, stocky plants for transplanting.

When garden conditions become amenable (see pages 10 to 95 for appropriate planting times), seedlings should be hardened off—that is, gradually exposed to the elements. Allow seedlings to be exposed to 2 to 3 hours of sun and only moderate wind for the first few days. Follow this with full night-and-day exposure. Keep an eye on the weather; if heavy rains or high winds threaten, they'll have to be moved under a porch roof or another protected location. Small plants in containers can be more easily drowned than those in the ground.

In the best of all possible worlds, seedlings and small plants would be transplanted into the garden on windless, cloudy, or soft, rainy days. If you have no choice but to plant when the weather is particularly hot and dry, cover the new transplants with small berry baskets or tents of burlap or other open-weave fabrics. Water thoroughly.

PLANTING BY THE SIGNS OF THE MOON AND PLANETS

Planting by astrological signs may sound like another bit of New Age folderol. But it's actually one of the wiser things that people have been doing for millennia.

I like doing it to acknowledge the cosmic forces beyond our planet and, more practically, because it gives structure to my gardening schedule. Knowing that the moon is in a propitious sign is an impetus for me to get out and plant. I haven't done any controlled experiments to test the efficacy of this technique, but others have and claim it to be effective. Use astrological signs as a guide, factoring in such constraints as time and weather conditions. The real key to successful gardening is always attentive care, no matter what the signs may be.

Astrological calendars and almanacs, available in bookstores, provide daily information on the signs and phases of the moon. Moon phases go in a sequence of four quarters. The first two occur while the moon is waxing or increasing from new to full. The third and fourth occur while the moon is waning or decreasing from full back to new.

Aboveground annuals are best planted in the waxing moon. The waning moon, especially the third quarter, is best for planting perennials, biennials, and root crops. Cultivate, harvest, till, and destroy weeds and pests in the fourth quarter.

The moon phases through all of the signs in 28 days. Here is a guide to the astrological signs:

- *Aries:* a fire sign, barren and best for cultivating and weeding
- *Taurus:* an earth sign, especially good for planting root crops
- *Gemini:* an air sign, dry and best for harvesting
- *Cancer:* a water sign, particularly fertile and excellent for planting and transplanting aboveground crops
- *Leo:* a fire sign, dry and infertile, good for cultivation
- *Virgo:* an earth sign, but infertile, good for cultivation
- *Libra:* an air sign, especially good for planting ornamentals and flowers
- *Scorpio:* a water sign, very productive for all aboveground plants, especially vines

- *Sagittarius*: a fire sign, good for weeding and cultivation
- *Capricorn*: an earth sign, recommended for planting root crops
- *Aquarius*: an air sign, dry and infertile, good for cultivation
- *Pisces*: a water sign, good for planting or transplanting aboveground crops

When the sun and moon are in the same sign, there is an increase in that sign's effects. Avoid planting when the moon is between signs or void of course—this is not a good time for decisive acts. These periods are noted on astrological calendars.

RAISED BEDS

Historically, kitchen gardens have been located close to houses for convenience, economy of space, and protection from grazing animals. The concept of growing vegetables in a field of long, straight rows derives from large-scale farming and, more recently, commercial agriculture. The near-worldwide depletion of healthy topsoil results from certain commercial agricultural practices. For example, regular plowing and tilling of soils accelerate the decomposition of organic matter into dust and carbon dioxide gas, which then escape into the air. Compaction by machinery or the human foot creates an impervious layer of soil that does not absorb moisture; this impedes the movement of moisture to deeper soil levels and thus encourages runoff and erosion.

Raised beds have many advantages. They drain fast, heat up early in the spring, and can be located in a large or small, convenient, sunny spot with whatever design configuration is pleasing. After the initial rototilling, plowing, or hand turning of the soil, further deep disturbance should be unnecessary. Raised beds that are continually enriched with organic matter and have foot traffic limited to adjacent permanent paths lessen soil depletion, compaction, and erosion.

Limit the width of raised beds to 3 to 4 feet to allow access from either side without stepping in the bed. Topsoil dug from the paths is used to build up the height of the raised beds (see illustration on page 198). Additional topsoil, compost, or rotted manures may be used as well. Wooden planks that evenly distribute a person's weight can be set across a bed for close access.

Mulch paths with straw, hay, shredded tree bark or brush, pine needles, or even newspaper covered with grass clippings. For a patterned, visually striking garden, pave paths with brick, flagstone, precast concrete, cobblestone, or gravel. Raised beds adjacent to paved paths should be edged with a barrier of weather-resistant wood, brick, or concrete to retain the soil.

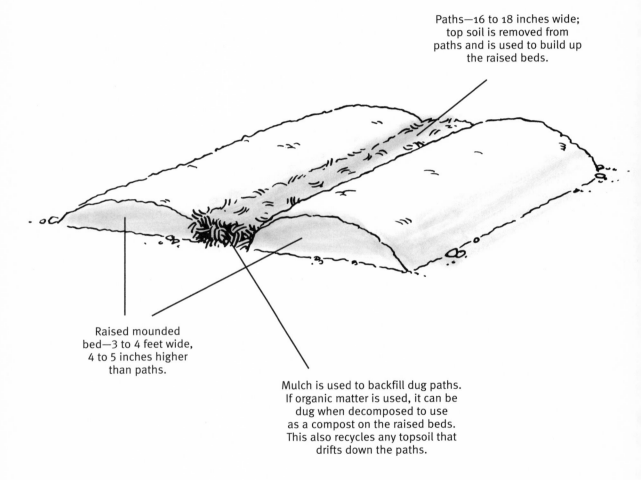

Paths—16 to 18 inches wide; top soil is removed from paths and is used to build up the raised beds.

Raised mounded bed—3 to 4 feet wide, 4 to 5 inches higher than paths.

Mulch is used to backfill dug paths. If organic matter is used, it can be dug when decomposed to use as a compost on the raised beds. This also recycles any topsoil that drifts down the paths.

WEEDING AND CULTIVATION

Gardeners who are attuned to the sensitivities of their plants know what it's like to walk past beds that are filled with weeds. The air hangs heavy with a Darwinian presence of ruthless competition and survival of the fittest. The plants are screaming, "I'm choking! Weed me! Weed me!" This is the time to step in and rescue our little friends from the encroachment of the invading hordes.

Weeding is most crucial at the early growing stages of seedlings. Established plants tend to shade out smaller weeds, which are then more easily pulled or hoed, but you should still be on the lookout.

Hand weeding is most easily accomplished when the soil is moist, after a rain or watering. It's easy to pull weeds out of an established garden with deep, light soil—a genuine reward for the years of soil-building efforts.

Cultivation with a hoe controls weeds and aerates the soil. Work only the top $1/2$ inch of soil, cutting weeds off from their roots without damaging the underlying roots of the "good" plants. I've rarely used a hoe, preferring my hands or small tools. I suppose hoes are more efficient for large gardens and for people who prefer to stand rather than muck around in the dirt.

Organic mulches are also very effective in weed control and soil conditioning (page 189). Rolls of commercially available, biodegradable paper mulch are effective weed barriers. Because the paper "robs" nitrogen from the soil as it decomposes, you'll need to provide extra fertilizer for paper-mulched plants. This is true for newspaper mulches as well. Layers of newspaper can be camouflaged with grass clippings or cut weeds.

New beds can be created without turning the soil or digging, by smothering weeds with paper, newspaper, or cardboard. Weight with stones and disguise as above. Beds will have to sit for one whole growing season for this method to adequately destroy any sod growth or weeds. Black plastic, though unattractive, will accomplish the same job by "burning" the sod in a few weeks of hot weather.

Persistent weeds growing in the nooks and crannies of paved areas or steps can be foiled by an application of boiling water. Avoid using chemical herbicides anywhere. There are some soap-based weed killers that decompose after application. Most effectively used on young weed growth, the naturally occurring fatty acids in soap cause leaves to lose moisture.

CROP ROTATION

Crop rotation balances the give-and-take of plants and the soil. Rotating crops accomplishes three important things:

1. It discourages soil-borne disease organisms and insects that attack specific plants.
2. It prevents the localized depletion of specific soil minerals and nutrients by one vegetable. Alternatively, it can create soils that have been nutritionally improved by a previous crop.
3. It creates deeper, aerated soils by root penetration.

Avoid planting any particular vegetable or any of its family members (listed below) in the same location for 3 consecutive years. It's a good idea to keep a yearly record of your garden layout to consult each year.

Vegetables are botanically classified into the following families:

* *Cabbage family*: broccoli, brussels sprouts, cabbage, cauliflower, kale, mustard, pak choi and similar Asian greens, turnips
* *Carrot family*: carrots, celery, parsley, parsnips
* *Cucurbit family*: cucumbers, summer and winter squash, melons
* *Daisy family*: lettuce
* *Goosefoot family*: beets, spinach, Swiss chard
* *Grass family*: corn
* *Legume family*: beans, peas
* *Nightshade family*: eggplant, bell and chili peppers, potatoes, tomatoes
* *Onion family*: garlic, leeks, onions, shallots

The addition of compost and other organic matter helps to restore nutrients depleted by previous crops. This is important for mini gardens, where crop rotation may be impractical.

IRRIGATION AND WATERING

Regional climate differences create a variety of watering needs, ranging from an occasional soaking to computerized, scheduled irrigation.

A total of 1 inch per week of rainfall should be sufficient for growing most vegetables under temperate conditions. The drying effects of hot, windy weather increase a plant's need for moisture. Poke a finger into the top 2 or 3 inches of soil to gauge the depth of dry soil.

Watering is most efficient when done in the morning, before the sun is strong enough to quickly evaporate moisture. Water thoroughly and repeat the finger test to ensure that absorption has been sufficiently deep.

Sprinklers can be used to cover small or large areas. Take care not to flood the soil: flooding encourages fungi, soil compaction, and suffocation of plant roots. In vegetable and herb beds, sprinklers can encourage fungus diseases and rot.

Soaker hoses are part of an effective watering system for beds and borders. Made of porous or perforated rubber or vinyl, they can be buried just beneath the soil or mulch, or laid upon the ground, for the entire season. Water slowly penetrates into the surrounding soil, usually wetting a swath on either side. Soaker hoses offer advantages over sprinklers: between 50 and 70 percent less water usage (no evaporation to the air), no water damage to blooms and foliage, and less water runoff and erosion.

Soaker hoses work by gravity, so on slopes it's best to zigzag them along parallel contours so that lower areas don't get more water than higher spots. Be sure to mark the course of buried hoses so that they won't be damaged when you're digging in the garden. Rodents, if they are a problem in your area, may chew them, and minerals in your water supply can also clog the pores. At the start of each season, expose the entire length of the hose, then turn on the water to check for adequate water pressure, leaks, or breaks, and anything else that might need repair.

STRETCHING THE SEASON

A variety of devices—both homemade and commercially available—can help you get a head start in spring and extend the growing season into fall and sometimes beyond.

Mulches—Crops that need warm soil for good germination and growth (beans, corn, basil, melons, sweet potatoes, peppers, and tomatoes) benefit from a mulch of plastic sheeting, available in either black plastic or IRT (sometimes called solar mulch). The latter differs from black plastic in that it allows near-infrared light to pass through while visible light is deterred. This is more effective than the black plastic for warming the soil.

Lay sheets of plastic directly on the cool ground 2 weeks before the estimated sowing or planting time. Make small cuts in the plastic here and there to allow for water penetration, bury the edges, and weight down with stones.

Plastic mulches can be left down all season (helpful where summers are cool) but should be picked up before winter to avoid decomposition and eternally shredding bits of plastic in your garden. If you live in a warmer climate, the plastic should come up if the soil gets too hot, as roots can be damaged and beneficial life forms (such as earthworms) will move away.

Biodegradable paper mulches decompose without the problems of plastic, and they are effective at combating weeds but offer less soil warming.

Fabric row covers—These light, porous horticultural fabrics provide protection from frost, animals, and insects, and they create warmer conditions for heat-loving plants. At planting time, drape fabric over seedbeds or seedlings, leaving slack for the plants to push up to their ultimate height. Bury the edges with soil or anchor securely with boards, large stones, or plastic jugs filled with water.

On sunny days, temperatures under row covers can range from 10 to 15 degrees warmer than the outside air. Row covers with the heavier weight fabrics provide frost protection down to about 27°F. Lightweight fabrics are useful for giving insect protection with minimal heat transfer. Airborne insects—such as flea and potato beetles, cabbage loopers, and flies that cause root maggots—are kept off plants. Seedlings are protected from wind, downpours, and hail, yet the covers are porous enough to admit moisture.

Heavyweight fabric covers should be removed when daytime temperatures are consistently above 80°F or when vegetables that require pollination begin to flower.

Unfortunately, synthetic row covers are not biodegradable; however, they usually last three or four seasons. They should be kept out of the sun when not in use, stored dry and relatively clean. I've had good results with covering greens and lettuce in the spring for early harvests and again covering the late fall to early winter crops for harvests that continued 4 weeks longer than with uncovered plants. They are also useful for covering heat-loving seedlings in the early summer, when conditions are not optimum.

Hotkaps—Made of waxed, translucent paper, these little hothouses are slit to allow for ventilation. Seedlings of squash, pumpkins, melons, cucumbers, and other widely spaced, heat-loving crops are more effectively covered with individual hotkaps than with fabric row covers.

Plastic jugs or glass jars—Plastic jugs with the bottoms cut out or inverted glass jars can be used to cover small plants when cold weather threatens. These should be used only at night or on very cloudy days, because in bright daylight the plants would "fry" in the solar-heated, unventilated jars.

Slitted polyethylene tunnels—You can create an environment 6 to 20 degrees warmer than the outside temperature (depending on solar intensity) by installing wire loops covered by slitted plastic sheeting. These are commercially available through many supply or seed houses. Tunnels work well for young plants that require warm conditions: peppers, tomatoes, basil, eggplant, and squash. To encourage pollination and help to avoid blossom drops due to high temperatures, the plastic should be removed when the weather has warmed and before plants begin to flower.

INSECTS AND DISEASES

It's always frustrating to see one's efforts in the garden foiled by various pests. Although there is certainly reason to keep destructive insect populations as low as possible, it's good to realize that some insects are beneficial. Dragonflies, spiders, wasps, yellow jackets, and ladybugs prey upon insects injurious to your garden. Green lacewings, spined soldier bugs, praying mantis, and trichogramma wasps also snack on garden pests and can be ordered from the Resources (page 284).

PREVENTION

- Keep the garden clean, year round, of plant debris that can become a residence for insects.
- Practice companion planting (page 211).
- Grow varieties resistant to insects or diseases prevalent in your region. Your county cooperative extension can help with this.
- Rotate crops to inhibit the population of insects and soil-borne diseases. Pests will not prosper when their favored food is no longer in the neighborhood.
- Use row covers to protect vulnerable plants (page 202).
- If possible, delay planting until the troublesome insect population has peaked. For example, if your spring-planted pak choi is devastated by flea beetles, plant it later in the season.

INSECTICIDE SAFETY

- Even "natural" insecticides require careful handling.
- Follow label instructions for recommended dilution rates, product warnings, and health risks.
- Wear a face mask, long sleeves, and pants. Wash exposed areas after use.
- Don't mix different products.
- Wash equipment carefully after use.
- Dispose of the container at a toxic-materials site.

CHARTS ON INSECTS AND DISEASES, AND PEST CONTROLS

The following charts are an abbreviated guide to common insects and diseases affecting vegetables and herbs. The Bibliography (page 287) lists sources for more extensive information.

I have limited my discussion of controls to simple devices and botanical or biological insecticides. Rotenone, neem, and pyrethrum are botanical insecticides derived from natural plant sources. Biological insecticides include life forms such as predators (ladybugs) and beneficial bacteria (Bt—Bacillus thuringiensis).

Botanical insecticides decompose quickly in the presence of sun and oxygen, and their residues do not contaminate the environment. Use them only as a last resort, however, as they kill beneficial insects as well as pests. Synthetic chemical pesticides became popular because their effects are longer lasting and they require less frequent application. Unfortunately, the residues of these toxic chemicals have been retained in our soils, water supply, and, ultimately, food sources.

COMMON INSECTS AND DISEASES

Vegetable	Disease/Insect
Asian Vegetables (Chinese cabbage, mizuna, pak choi, tatsoi)	*See* cabbage
Asparagus	Asparagus beetles, corn earworm, rust
Beans	Anthracnose, aphids, corn earworms, downy mildew, Japanese beetles, spider mites, rust
Beets	Flea beetles
Broccoli	*See* cabbage
Brussels sprouts	*See* cabbage
Cabbage	Aphids, cabbage worms, club root, cutworms, flea beetles, root maggots
Cauliflower	*See* cabbage
Collards and kale	*See* cabbage
Corn	Corn earworms, Japanese beetles, spider mites
Cucumbers	Anthracnose, aphids, corn earworms, downy mildew, spider mites, striped cucumber beetles, squash bugs
Eggplant	Colorado potato beetles, flea beetles, spider mites, tomato hornworms
Kohlrabi	*See* cabbage
Lettuce and Salad Greens	Aphids, cutworms, slugs and snails
Melons	Anthracnose, aphids, downy mildew, spider mites, squash bugs, striped cucumber beetles
Okra	Aphids, corn earworms, Japanese beetles
Onions	Root maggots
Peas	Aphids, downy mildew
Peppers	Anthracnose, aphids, blossom-end rot, Colorado potato beetles, corn earworms, damping-off, flea beetles, tomato hornworms
Spinach	Aphids, cutworms, slugs and snails
Squash (summer and winter)	Corn earworms, striped cucumber beetles, squash bugs
Swiss Chard	*See* beets
Tomatoes	Aphids, blossom-end rot, Colorado potato beetles, cutworms, flea beetles, tomato hornworms
Turnips	*See* cabbage

CONTROLS

Bacillus thuringiensis (Bt)—This beneficial bacterium is harmless to humans, birds, bees, and many helpful insects but fatal to specific pests, particularly caterpillars. It's dusted or sprayed onto plants, then ingested by the attacking insect, whose digestive system is quickly paralyzed, causing death in 24 hours.

Diatomaceous earth—This powdery substance is composed of the shells of one-celled sea plants known as diatoms. Though it feels like talcum powder to you and me, each tiny grain is sharp enough to injure or kill insects by causing dehydration through cuts. If ingested, the powder damages the pests' respiratory or digestive system. Use with a face mask graded for fine dust protection.

Hot pepper spray—This homemade spray can be whipped up from your own garden to serve as a general insecticide. Blend 1 cup of water with 1 cup of chopped hot peppers and steep for 1 day. Strain and add $\frac{1}{2}$ cup to 1 gallon of water. Do not use on very young seedlings, and avoid getting the spray on your skin or near your eyes. For additional clout, a clove or two of garlic, which is reputed to repel insects, can be blended with the peppers. There are also commercially available hot pepper–wax sprays.

Hand-picked or trapped pests can be destroyed in a container of heavily salted or soapy water.

Insecticidal soap—This liquid solution is derived from the salts of fatty acids by a process similar to that used for all soaps. It can be applied on crops up until harvest; once the soap dries it is no longer harmful. Avoid contact with the spray or concentrated solution.

Pyrethrum—This powder is derived from the flowers of *Chrysanthemum cinerariaefolium*. Pyrethrum and pyrethins (the concentrated active compounds of the flowers) are not toxic to humans but can kill fish. The fast-acting pyrethrums are frequently combined with longer-lasting rotenone.

Rotenone—A powder derived from the roots of several tropical plants, rotenone should be used only when damage is extensive, the insect population is high, and nothing else is working, as its toxicity may harm beneficial insects and fish as well. Avoid inhaling or ingesting it. Wear a face mask when applying it. It lasts in the environment from 3 to 7 days.

Insect	Description	Control
Aphids	Less than $1/8$ inch long; may be red, yellow, green, black, gray, or brown. They suck the juices of stems and leaves and possibly spread disease. Worst of all, a single female aphid can produce *5 billion* baby aphids in a single season. Wide variety of host plants.	• Spray with a strong stream of water • Insecticidal soap • Ladybugs, green lacewings • Pyrethrum • Rotenone
Asparagus Beetles	Black with white spots, $1/4$ inch long. Shiny eggs deposited on stems.	• Pyrethrum • Rotenone
Colorado Potato Beetles	Yellow with black stripes and hard shell, $1/3$ inch long. Orange eggs deposited on undersides of leaves. Eggplant, peppers, potatoes, and tomatoes are common host plants.	• Insecticidal soap • Generous layer of clean mulch will discourage • Row covers • Rotenone • *Bt tenenbrionis* strain • Pyrethrum
Flea Beetles	They hop like a flea. Black, shiny, $1/10$ inch long. Many vegetables susceptible, particularly the cabbage family.	• Row covers applied at time of seeding • Insecticidal soap • Pyrethrum • Rotenone
Japanese Beetles	Shiny, bronze body, $1/2$ inch long with blue and green iridescent wings. Roses, beans, and corn are susceptible.	• Pyrethrum • Rotenone • Soil treatment with milky spore disease to kill overwintering grubs • Commercial traps with scented lures
Striped Cucumber Beetle	Yellow or orange with three black stripes, $1/4$ inch long. Adults eat leaves; larvae eat roots. Affect cucurbits (squash, melon, and cucumber), beans, and peas.	• Row covers (remove at flowering time for pollination) • Trap under boards • Generous layer of mulch • Rotenone

Insect	Description	Control
Squash Bugs	Flat, brown, $1/2$ inch long. Oval, brown eggs laid on the undersides of leaves. Affect cucurbits (squash, cucumber, melon, and pumpkins).	• Trap under boards • Rotenone • Row covers
Cutworms	Soft, 1 to $1^1/_2$ inches long, gray or brown caterpillar. Not seen in the daytime unless you happen to expose them when weeding or hoeing. Seedlings cut off at ground level. Attack all vegetables, particularly young seedlings.	• Insecticidal soap • Expose worms by shallow cultivation around plant • Protect seedlings with paper collars • *Trichogramma* wasps • *Bt* • Apply wood ash
Cabbage Worms (either cabbage looper or imported cabbage worm)	Green caterpillars up to $1^1/_2$ inches long, can destroy crops of the cabbage family.	• *Bt* • Handpick • Row covers • Rotenone • Hot pepper spray • *Trichogramma* wasps
Corn Earworms	White to green, $1^1/_2$-inch-long spined caterpillars. Attack beans, corn, peas, peppers, potatoes, squash, and tomatoes.	• *Bt* • Rotenone
Tomato Hornworms	Smooth, light green caterpillars up to 4 inches long with a "horn" at one end and zigzag stripes. Will strip leaves and eat fruits of eggplant, tomatoes, peppers, and potatoes.	• Handpick • *Trichogramma* wasps, green lacewings • *Bt*
Root Maggots	White, $1/4$-inch-long larvae of flies that hibernate in the soil over winter. Destroy young plants by tunneling into roots. Affect the cabbage family, carrots, onions, and peas, especially in the spring.	• Don't apply manure within 4 to 6 weeks of planting • Diatomaceous earth or wood ash scattered on seedbeds • Use 3-inch tar-paper squares with a slit at the center for seedlings. Lay flat on soil to keep flies from laying eggs at the base of seedlings

Insect	Description	Control
Spider Mites	Tiny, almost invisible spiders that suck plant juices, causing leaves to speckle and curl. Affect indoor plants and vegetables, herbs, and ornamentals in warm, dry seasons.	• Strong spray of water, particularly undersides of leaves • Insecticidal soap • Solution of wheat flour, buttermilk, and water sprayed on plants • Rotenone • Green lacewings, ladybugs
Slugs and Snails	Yellowish or gray, soft, slimy mollusks, $1/2$ to 3 inches long. Snails have a shell. Both feed at night. Can cause extensive damage and kill seedlings.	• Dust with diatomaceous earth, lime, or wood ash. • Lay boards to trap slugs; destroy in the morning when they're full of food and sleepy. • Punch a hole in the side of a coffee can with a lid. Bury the can with the hole at ground level. Fill with a mixture of 1 cup water, 1 teaspoon sugar, and $1/4$ teaspoon baking yeast, to ground level. Remove besotted slugs and refill. • Remove mulch and plant debris. • Cultivate top 2 to 3 inches of soil to expose slugs, then handpick and destroy.

Insect	Description	Control
Whitefly	Small, mothlike, white insects that cluster on leaves and stems. Houseplants are particularly susceptible.	• Insecticidal soap • Pyrethrum • Yellow sticky traps for greenhouses • Hot pepper spray
Anthracnose	A fungus affecting beans, cucumbers, melons, and peppers. Dark, discolored spots appear on leaves, pods, or fruits.	• Rotate crops • Avoid touching the wet foliage • Plant resistant varieties
Blossom-end rot	Dark, pitted, rotting areas at the blossom end (opposite stem) of tomatoes and peppers. Caused by uneven watering and lack of calcium.	• Keep plants evenly watered • Add lime or wood ash to soil
Club root	Roots of the cabbage family are deformed and stunted by a soil fungus. Plants may not form heads; leaves will yellow and drop.	• Rotate crops • Add wood ash and lime
Damping off	A fungus that kills young seedlings. The stem weakens and collapses at the soil line.	• Use sterilized potting soil for seedlings • Do not overwater or overcrowd seedlings
Powdery mildew	White splotches appear on leaves in humid weather due to fungus infection. May cause leaves to shrivel and vegetables to sunscald and ripen poorly. Affects cucurbits (melons, squashes, and cucumbers).	• Dust plants with sulfur
Rust	Red or brown spores appear on leaves due to fungus growth. Leaves eventually yellow and fall off. Affects beans and asparagus.	• Avoid handling or working around the wet foliage of beans or asparagus • Water plants in the early morning and avoid wetting the foliage
Scab	A fungus that causes rough, dark spots on potatoes or brown, sunken areas on cucumbers and squashes.	• Rotate crops • Plant potatoes in acidic soil with a pH of 5.0

COMPANION PLANTING

Not all garden authorities agree on whether or not the proximity of differing species of plants affects their growth and ability to fight off insects and diseases. However, there is some scientific evidence to back up what were once considered flaky claims. Companion planting was first popularized through biodynamic gardening and the 1920s European lectures of Rudolf Steiner. Steiner's teachings promote the connection between farmer and nature and outline specific farming practices to balance "cosmic and earthly forces." Esoteric as this sounds, many of these practices are now common, well-proven organic gardening procedures, such as compost making, crop rotation, planting with the planets, and companion planting.*

Folklore and biodynamic guidelines recommend the plant combinations that follow. There are three main reasons for felicitous companionship:

- Substances released by certain plant roots stimulate mutual growth or protection from diseases and insects.
- Companion plants make complementary nutritional demands upon the soil.
- Intercropped gardens with a variety of scents, colors, and shapes make it more difficult for insects to zero in on their favored plants than do singly cropped spaces. Crops varied within a single row also create interesting visual effects.

A given plant's need for sun, space, and water also must be taken into account, as should the timing of planting. For instance, beans and corn may grow well together, but vigorous bean vines could smother newly emerging corn seedlings.

Ultimately, though, the best companion for any garden is the gardener. Check regularly for soil moisture; insect, disease, or predator damage; and harvest potential.

*For information on biodynamic farming, visit www.biodynamics.com.

BENEFICIAL COMPANIONS

Vegetable	Vegetables (V) or Herbs (H)
Asparagus	V- Tomatoes H- Basil, calendula, parsley
Beans	V- Cabbage family, carrots, corn, cucumbers, eggplant, peas, potatoes, Swiss chard H- Borage, lovage, marigold, nasturtium, oregano, summer savory
Beets	V- Bush beans, cabbage family, lettuce, onions H- Garlic
Cabbage family*	V- Beets, cucumbers, lettuce, onions, potatoes, spinach, Swiss chard H- Chamomile, dill, garlic, hyssop, mint, nasturtium, sage, thyme
Carrots	V- Beans, lettuce, onions, peas, peppers, tomatoes H- Chives, rosemary, sage, thyme
Corn	V- Beans, cucumbers, melons, peas, potatoes, squash H- Marigold, parsley
Cucumbers	V- Beans, cabbage family, corn, lettuce, tomatoes H- Marigold, parsley
Eggplant	V- Beans, peppers H- Marigold, thyme
Lettuce	V- Beets, cabbage family, carrots, onions H- Chives, dill, garlic
Melons	V- Corn, pumpkins, squash H- Marigold, nasturtium, oregano
Onions	V- Beets, cabbage family, carrots, lettuce, peppers, Swiss chard, tomatoes H- Chamomile, dill, summer savory
Peas	V- Beans, carrots, corn, cucumbers, turnips H- Mint
Peppers	V- Carrots, eggplant, onions, tomatoes H- Basil
Potatoes	V- Beans, cabbage family, corn, eggplant, peas H- Marigold
Spinach	V- Cabbage family
Squash	V- Corn, melons, pumpkins H- Borage, marigold, nasturtium, oregano

* Broccoli, brussels sprouts, cabbage, cauliflower, collards, kale, kohlrabi, turnips, Asian greens.

Vegetable	Vegetables (V) or Herbs (H)
Tomatoes	V- Asparagus, beans, carrots, cucumbers, onions, peppers H- Basil, bee balm, borage, calendula, chives, mint, parsley, sage, thyme
Turnips	V- Peas

BENEFICIAL COMPANIONS

Herb	Vegetables
Basil	Peppers, tomatoes
Bee balm	Tomatoes
Borage	Beans, squash, tomatoes
Calendula	Asparagus, tomatoes
Chamomile	Cabbage, onions
Chives	Carrots, lettuce, roses, tomatoes
Dill	Cabbage, lettuce, onions
Garlic	Beets, cabbage, lettuce, roses
Hyssop	Cabbage
Lovage	Beans
Marigold	Beans, corn, cucumbers, eggplant, melons, potatoes, roses, squash
Mint	Cabbage, tomatoes
Oregano	Beans
Parsley	Asparagus, corn, tomatoes
Rosemary	Beans, cabbage
Sage	Cabbage, carrots, tomatoes
Summer Savory	Beans, onions
Thyme	Carrots, cabbage, eggplant, tomatoes

Poor companions may be detrimental to the growth of some neighbors. Happily, this is a short list. Keeping these plants a couple of rows apart shouldn't be too difficult.

POOR COMPANY

Vegetable	Vegetables or Herbs
Beans	Chives, garlic, leeks, onions, shallots
Beets	Pole beans
Cabbage family	Kohlrabi, pole beans, tomatoes
Carrots	Dill
Corn	Tomatoes
Cucumbers	Potatoes, sage
Onions	Beans, peas, sage
Peas	Chives, garlic, leeks, onions, shallots
Potatoes	Cucumbers, squash, tomatoes
Tomatoes	Corn, dill, kohlrabi, potatoes

Recipes

YOU CHOSE the perfect spot for your garden: sunny, well drained, framing a nice view down the valley. Regionally appropriate seeds were selected and started when the moon was in a most propitious stage. Your raised beds were tilled with the richest soil, and the plants were all perfect companions, both biodynamically and aesthetically. Thinned, nurtured, watered, and fed with compost and sea nutrients, the seedlings grew, protected from frosts, hail, and insects. Now harvest is at hand; the vegetables will be picked at the peak of perfection. You can't help but succeed now, especially if you use the cooking techniques that follow.

VEGETABLE BASICS

Properly cooked, flavorful, and attractively presented vegetables are the happy ending to this story. Proper cooking chiefly requires attention in order to avoid a common, but always preventable, error: overdone, soggy, and tasteless vegetables. Pace tasks so you can focus your attention where it's needed, and begin the actual cooking with all the ingredients ready for use—peeled, chopped, minced—as the recipe calls for. At Moosewood Restaurant, we work at a brisk pace, but I still have time to admire a long cutting board filled with the assorted colors and shapes of vegetables, and time to be refreshed by the clean fragrance of minced herbs.

Vegetables can be loosely grouped into three general categories based on their cooking times:

Hard Carrots, cauliflower, celery, green beans, onions, potatoes, sweet potatoes, turnips, winter squash

Medium hard Asparagus, broccoli, brussels sprouts, cabbage, eggplant, fennel, leeks, mushrooms, okra, parsnips, peppers, shallots, summer squash, zucchini

Soft Greens, peas, snow peas, scallions, spinach, tomatoes

Cutting foods uniformly ensures that they'll cook in about the same amount of time. We like to vary vegetable shapes and sizes from dish to dish. Soups work well with smaller-cut or diced vegetables (one large hunk of potato could almost fill a cup). Stews are often heartier, with chunkier shapes. Stir-fried dishes look attractive and cook more uniformly when foods are cut similarly. Long, slender strips of vegetables are visually suited to (and tend to clump less in) dishes featuring thin noodles.

We tend to cut vegetables by hand for dishes in which appearance is important—for example, in salads, soups, and stews. We use a food processor to grate some vegetables that won't be "on display" but hidden in fillings or casseroles. Hand cutting yields more pleasing, somewhat uneven food pieces, as opposed to the manufactured "perfection" of processor-sliced foods.

COOKED VEGETABLES FOR SALADS

Marinated, cooked vegetables are a standard menu item at Moosewood. They can be prepared ahead of time to intensify in flavor as they marinate and to free your attention for other last-minute dishes.

Salads reflect the seasons: early greens, lettuce, and asparagus in spring; scallions, new potatoes, baby carrots, and peas in early summer. The abundance of midsummer brings green beans, eggplant, peppers, zucchini, and juicy tomatoes; in the fall, endive, cabbage, broccoli and cauliflower, radicchio, and fennel are enjoyed.

Here are a few pointers:

- Be sure to remove vegetables from the heat when they're still slightly crunchy.
- Immediately plunge cooked vegetables into ice water to halt the cooking process and preserve good color. Drain well.
- Add the marinade well before serving so the seasonings can be more fully absorbed. When using green vegetables (beans, broccoli,

peppers, and peas—shelled, snap, and snow), withhold the lemon juice and vinegar until right before serving time, as the acidity will dull their color to an unappetizing khaki green.

- Salads that taste just right soon after a dressing is added may need more seasonings later, after the flavors have been absorbed. This is especially true for grain and pasta salads.
- Marinated salads are best served warm or at room temperature in cool weather, chilled in hot weather. Vegetables à la Grecque (page 234) is an interesting way of cooking foods in their marinade.

The attractive appearance of a meal is appreciated before anything is even tasted. Before I garnish a meal I've prepared, I take a walk through the garden to gather decorative edibles—sprigs of herbs and blossoms or flower petals—keeping in mind color and textural contrasts and complementary tastes. A green gazpacho is nicely set off by a garnish of bright red nasturtium; Johnny-jump-ups or violet blossoms add color to a simple salad of butter lettuces. A spring pasta salad with the varying shades of green spinach, peas, chives, asparagus, and herbed mayonnaise might need nothing but a sprig of herb to enhance the subtle harmony.

HERB BASICS

Herbs are an integral part of the Moosewood cooking style. Fresh herbs add a fuller richness to any food. It's hard to imagine pasta primavera without fresh basil, a Russian vegetable strudel without fresh dill, a vegetable ragout without fresh tarragon, or a spicy salsa without fresh cilantro. We also use many dried herbs.

Some uncommon herbs—such as chervil, the scented thymes, lemon or cinnamon basil, and sorrel—are available fresh only in season. Other popular fresh herbs, such as dill, cilantro, basil, and parsley, can be found year-round at large supermarkets or greengrocers.

Using herbs effectively requires learning what combinations of foods and seasonings work well together. New cooks, excited by a garden or shelf full of herbs and spices, may naively assume that more is better. The disappointing results are often analogous to mixing together every color on the paint pallette and coming up with drab brown. The fresh taste of garden produce should not be overwhelmed by competing flavors.

Exercise a light hand with herbs, adding more if desired at the completion of a dish. Cooking with just one or two herbs in a given preparation and following recipes are excellent ways to learn the basics. With knowledge of herbs, innovative cooks can successfully improvise new dishes that are variations of their standard repertoire. The following culinary guidelines will help you make the most of herbs:

- Pick herbs as close to cooking time as possible for maximum flavor. Leave behind enough foliage for the plant to sustain itself.
- Chop or mince herbs to release their essential oils. Food processors are effective for large quantities or for blending herbs into a sauce or dressing. Some herbs should be coarsely chopped before processing to avoid stringiness.
- If a recipe calls for dried herbs and you want to convert to fresh, the general rule for leafy herbs, such as dill or basil, is to use three to four times the quantity called for dried. Fresh sage and thyme or the needlelike leaves of rosemary are dry and potent, so you may need only about twice as much fresh as dried.
- Herbs that are better added at the beginning of cooking for heightened flavor include: bay, garlic, lovage, oregano, rosemary, sage, savory, thyme, and seeds (mustard, caraway, coriander, dill, fennel, cumin).
- Fresh herbs with essential oils that are less potent when heated should be added toward the end of cooking: basil, chervil, chives, cilantro, dill weed, fennel leaf, lemon balm, marjoram, mint, parsley, and tarragon.
- Some recipes call for a bouquet garni—a bundle of seasonings—when a delicate flavor or clean visual effect is desired. It's added during cooking and removed before serving. Fill a cheesecloth bag or a tea ball with herb sprigs, peppercorns, cloves, allspice berries, or other seasonings and add to a simmering sauce, stew, or soup. Remove before serving or as the recipe indicates.
- Allow an hour or more for the essence of herbs to infuse uncooked dressings, sauces, butters, and spreads.

If, despite all of our warnings, you are still guilty of overseasoning, before you compost the dinner, try one of these remedies:

- Prepare more of the original ingredients, minus any herbes or spices, cook them to the same stage as the overseasoned food, and then add them to the original pot to dilute the seasoning. Invite some neighbors to share the unexpected abundance.

- Add bland foods that thin out or add bulk to a dish. Try milk, cream, potatoes, rice, pasta, cooked beans, bread crumbs, or grated mild cheese.
- Toss a couple of peeled raw potato chunks into an overseasoned soup or stew and remove them before serving. They may absorb some of the extra seasoning.

COOKING TECHNIQUES

The heating process can take many forms: blanching, boiling and simmering, deep-frying, grilling, roasting, sautéing, steaming, and stir-frying. When you cook vegetables by any technique that uses medium to high heat, remove them from the heat when they are a little crunchier than desired. Their retained heat will continue the cooking process.

Blanching—Blanching, or briefly boiling, takes the raw edge off vegetables to be used in salads or as crudités, and it can be a preliminary to freezing, roasting, or grilling vegetables.

The key is to provide a generous quantity of boiling water that will not quickly cool down when the vegetables are added. Use a slotted spoon or a mesh skimmer to remove the cooked vegetables from the water.

Foods such as bean sprouts, mushrooms, snow peas, and finely cut julienned (matchstick) vegetables may be completely cooked by blanching.

Boiling and simmering—Boiling liquids have quickly moving bubbles that break on the surface. In simmering, the bubbling occurs at a more relaxed pace.

Boil vegetables in generous quantities of water. This can be a quick-cooking technique, as the water doesn't cool down much with the addition of foods. Some nutrients are absorbed by the cooking liquid, which can often be used as a stock.

Cook sauces and stews at a gentle simmer, as there is less danger of sticking or burning and more time for flavors to mingle and blend.

Deep-frying—Submerge foods in very hot oil and cook briefly. Deep-fried foods have a crisp succulence that is universally appealing. The goal of perfect frying is to seal the food's exterior without overcooking it before the inside is done.

It's important that the oil reach a temperature between 350°F and 375°F. A deep-fry or candy thermometer is a good investment. If you don't have a thermometer, you can test the temperature by dropping in a 1-inch cube of bread. It should turn golden brown in 45 to 60 seconds. Oil that's not hot enough will result in slow cooking and excessive oil absorption. Even a high oil temperature will be lowered by attempting to cook too much at one time.

Deep-frying works well for batter-dipped or dough-wrapped foods. Hard, dense vegetables used as filling should be cut into thin slices so their cooking time matches the time it takes their batter or wrapper to cook.

Grilling—Cooking foods on a rack or mesh a few inches above a charcoal, gas-fueled, or similar heat source. This technique is best used for the following vegetables: asparagus, corn on the cob, eggplant, mushrooms, onions, peppers, tomatoes, zucchini, and summer squash, as well as blanched white and sweet potatoes, carrots, and winter squash. (For instructions and recipes, see page 256.)

Roasting—Oven cooking of food frequently includes a marinade or basting liquid to increase flavor and prevent drying out. Roasting brings out vegetable sugars and seals in juices while creating a crisp, crunchy outer layer. It is the most time-consuming method, but it can be energy efficient if you roast vegetables while the oven is already in use. Dense, hard vegetables like potatoes or carrots that are blanched first will roast more quickly. Root vegetables are particularly good roasted, because their innate sweetness intensifies.

Sautéing—Vegetables and seasonings are cooked uncovered, in oil or butter, on a fairly high heat. Sautéing is a good method for sealing a crisp outer surface on a quickly cooked vegetable, or to deepen the flavor with a light browning before further cooking. Sautéing is a technique we use all the time with aromatic vegetables, such as onions, carrots, celery, peppers, and garlic, that will then simmer for a longer time with other ingredients.

Steaming—Foods are cooked over—but not submerged in—boiling or simmering water or stock. Properly cooked steamed vegetables are crisp and tender with good color. Use a stainless-steel steaming basket or rack that can be inserted into a pot, or a special two-piece steaming pot. Keep the water level lower than the bottom of the steamer to avoid sogginess. Allow the water to come to a boil, and steam the vegetables covered for heat efficiency and better color.

Leftover noodles, rice, and other grains can be reheated in a steamer.

Save the steaming liquid from mildly flavored vegetables for a nutritious stock. Stocks from strongly flavored vegetables—such as asparagus, cabbage-family members, bitter greens, and pepper stocks—are useful only for soups that feature these ingredients; they would probably be overwhelming in anything else.

Steaming is an effective cooking method for all vegetables, with the possible exception of potatoes and sweet potatoes. Dense, hard vegetables are usually better cooked by boiling in liquid to cover.

Stir-frying—Continuously toss and stir foods in a small amount of oil over a relatively high heat. The high temperatures seal in juices, and the quick cooking helps preserve vitamins and nutrients. Perfectly stir-fried foods are tender yet still crisp.

Stir-frying works best in a wok, where the ample surface area heats food quickly and thoroughly, and the steep, rounded sides facilitate stirring and tossing. A heavy, deep skillet can also be used.

Because this is a fast-moving procedure that requires your full attention, it's important to have all the ingredients near the stove, lined up in the order in which they're to be cooked. Cooked vegetables that are crisp and juicy can be achieved by adding little or no liquid during the cooking process. Although stir-frying is good for all vegetables, hard, dense ones, such as potatoes, green beans, carrots, and cauliflower, should either be cut small for faster cooking without extra liquid or initially blanched.

🌿 Soups

VEGETABLE STOCK

Soups and sauces cooked with vegetable stock are noticeably more flavorful than those made with water. At Moosewood, we make stock every day for soups and stews using this basic recipe, sometimes adding some of the optional vegetables or herbs when we have them left over or close at hand.

2 large potatoes, thickly sliced

2 to 3 onions, quartered

3 to 4 carrots, thickly sliced

1 celery stalk, chopped

1 apple or pear, quartered

1 or 2 bay leaves

6 peppercorns

10 cups (2¹/₂ quarts) water

OPTIONAL VEGETABLES OR HERBS

Garlic cloves

Leeks, including the tough green leaves

Mushrooms, whole or stems

Parsley, including stems

Parsnips

Scallions

Sweet potatoes

Tomatoes (in small amounts only or the stock may be too acidic)

Winter squash

Zucchini or summer squash

Scrub the unpeeled vegetables and cut into chunks. Place in a stockpot with bay leaves and peppercorns; cover with water. Bring to a boil, then simmer for an hour or more.

Strain the stock through a colander or cloth, pressing out the liquid from the vegetables. (The remaining solid vegetables make good compost material or can be discarded.)

The stock will keep refrigerated for 3 to 4 days, or may be frozen in 1- to 6-cup quantities.

Note: Vegetables should be rinsed, but there is no need to peel them. Avoid such strongly flavored vegetables as broccoli, cabbage, cauliflower, eggplant, peppers, and turnips. Natural food stores and well-stocked supermarkets carry a good selection of organic vegetable stocks in 1-quart boxes that can be used when time is short; flavors we've enjoyed include mock chicken and roasted vegetable.

Variation: For stock with an Asian flavor, add 4 or 5 quarter-sized slices of fresh gingerroot and water from soaking dried shiitake mushrooms.

🌿 Yields 2 quarts

GAZPACHO VERDE

This refreshing, deeply green, and healthful soup is best served chilled.

Bring the water to a boil. Add the spinach, arugula, and the three scallions. Cook until the spinach just begins to wilt, not more than 1 minute or so. Drain.

In a food processor or blender, purée until smooth the cooked greens with the parsley, dill, cucumber, olive oil, garlic, lime juice, stock, salt, and pepper.

Stir the one finely chopped scallion and the diced cucumber into the puréed soup. Chill and serve with one of the recommended garnishes.

🌿 Serves 4 to 6

GAZPACHO

8 cups water

2 large bunches of fresh spinach (about 8 ounces) with large stems removed, well rinsed and drained

1 cup loosely packed arugula leaves

3 scallions, white and green parts, roughly chopped

$1/4$ cup loosely packed fresh parsley leaves

$1/4$ cup loosely packed fresh dill leaves

1 cucumber, roughly chopped

2 tablespoons extra virgin olive oil

1 or 2 garlic cloves, minced or pressed

3 tablespoons fresh lime juice

3 cups vegetable stock (page 224)

$1/2$ teaspoon salt

Freshly ground black pepper to taste

1 scallion, white and green parts, finely chopped

$1/2$ cucumber, seeded if mature, finely diced

GARNISH (USE ONE)

Thin lime slices

Nasturtium or chive blossoms

Cherry tomato halves

Croutons

PORTUGUESE KALE SOUP

This hearty, colorful soup is perfect for fall and winter meals. The sun-dried tomatoes add a nice piquancy and chewy texture. If you don't have parsnips, just add some more carrots.

½ cup dried white beans (navy, pea, or Great Northern)

2½ cups water or vegetable stock (page 224)

2 whole garlic cloves, peeled

2 bay leaves

3 tablespoons olive oil

½ teaspoon ground fennel seeds

1 garlic clove, minced or pressed

1½ cups chopped onion

1 potato, chopped (about 1 cup)

1 small carrot, chopped (about ½ cup)

1 small parsnip, chopped (about ½ cup)

1½ cups chopped fresh or canned tomatoes

6 cups vegetable stock (page 224)

2 bay leaves

1 tablespoon chopped fresh oregano (1 teaspoon dried)

12 dry-packed sun-dried tomatoes (about ½ cup), soaked in boiling water to cover

4 cups loosely packed, chopped kale

Pinch of saffron (optional)

Salt and freshly ground black pepper

Cook the beans in the water or stock with the whole garlic and two bay leaves. The beans should be tender in 1 to 1½ hours.

While the beans are cooking, prepare the other ingredients.

Heat the olive oil in a soup pot, add the ground fennel and minced garlic, and sauté for a minute. Add the onion and sauté for 2 minutes. Add the potato, carrot, and parsnip and sauté for another minute before adding the tomatoes, stock, two bay leaves, and oregano. Simmer for 10 minutes.

Drain the soaked sun-dried tomatoes and chop coarsely. Add to the soup pot with the kale and the drained, cooked beans.

Simmer for about 10 minutes, until the vegetables are tender and the flavors have mingled. Add the saffron and salt and pepper to taste.

❧ Serves 4 to 6

TWO LITTLE CARROT SALADS

We like to serve raw carrot salads as light accompaniments to rich dishes, or as part of multifaceted combination plates with a variety of salads. They're quick to prepare and colorful on the plate.

Whisk together all of the ingredients of the Minted or Herbed Carrot Salad—except the carrots. Toss in the carrots. Serve right away, or chill until serving time.

Note: Freshly grated nutmeg is always more fragrant than commercially ground.

🌿 Serves 4

MINTED CARROT SALAD

$1/2$ teaspoon salt

$1/2$ cup plain yogurt

1 tablespoon chopped fresh mint

1 tablespoon fresh lemon or lime juice

2 teaspoons maple syrup

$1/8$ teaspoon freshly grated nutmeg

2 cups grated carrots

HERBED CARROT SALAD

$1/2$ teaspoon salt

1 tablespoon extra virgin olive oil

1 tablespoon raspberry vinegar

2 tablespoons snipped or chopped chives

1 tablespoon chopped fresh chervil or tarragon (1 teaspoon dried)

$1/4$ teaspoon ground black pepper

2 cups grated carrots

CORN SALSA

Grilling fresh corn caramelizes the natural sugars to give more dimension and adds a smoky flavor too. I enjoy this as a salad with lettuce or, with the larger amount of lime and jalapeño, as a topping for filled tortillas like burritos or simple bean dishes.

1 red bell pepper

4 ears of sweet corn, silk and husks removed

1 to 2 jalapeño peppers

2 tablespoons olive oil

1 to 2 tablespoons fresh lime juice

1 garlic clove, minced or pressed

2 tablespoons chopped cilantro

1 tomato, chopped

$1/2$ teaspoon salt

Hot sauce to taste

Preheat the grill. If using charcoal, the coals should be at the grey-ash stage. For gas grills, set to medium-high. Brush the bell pepper, corn, and jalapeño with 1 tablespoon of the olive oil and grill. The bell pepper will take about 4 to 5 minutes per side, or 16 to 20 minutes until it's softened and charred. The corn takes about 5 minutes total, turning it frequently until the kernels are browned but not charred. The jalapeño takes about 10 minutes, turning it frequently until it's softened and charred.

Place the bell pepper and jalapeño in a closed paper bag for 10 minutes to facilitate peeling. Let the corn cool for a few minutes, then use a sharp knife to cut the kernels off in four or five long cuts down the cob. Rub the charred skin off the cooled peppers. Chop the bell pepper and dice the jalapeño. Combine the corn, peppers, remaining 1 tablespoon of olive oil, lime juice, garlic, cilantro, tomato, and salt in a bowl. Because jalapeños vary in their hotness, taste and add hot sauce if desired.

Variation: If grilling is not an option, try broiling the corn. Cut it off the cobs and mix the kernels on a baking sheet with 1 tablespoon of oil. Broil 3 inches from the flame for about 10 minutes, stirring three times until the corn is lightly browned. This will work with frozen corn as well, using $2^1/2$ cups of kernels. Roast the unoiled peppers over medium heat on the gas burners of your range, as you would for grilling, or in a 400°F oven, 15 minutes for jalapeño, 40 minutes for large bells. Proceed as above.

🌿 Yields 2 generous cups

ARUGULA SALAD

Baby arugula, picked when the leaves are no more than 3 inches long, makes a wonderful salad green. Here, its natural pepperiness is mellowed by buttery pine nuts and smoked mozzarella. I like the smoky flavor, but creamy fresh mozzarella is just as good. Most commercial sun-dried tomatoes are salty, as is the mozzarella, so you may not need any additional salt.

In a heatproof bowl, soak the sun-dried tomatoes in boiling water to cover for 15 minutes.

Meanwhile, prepare the other ingredients. In a large bowl, place the arugula, pine nuts, and mozzarella. In a cup, mix together the oil, lemon juice, garlic, and black pepper.

Drain and chop the soaked sun-dried tomatoes and add to the bowl. Pour on the dressing and toss.

🌿 Serves 2

6 sun-dried tomatoes (dry packed, not in oil)

4 cups arugula (about 5 ounces)

$1/4$ cup pine nuts, toasted in a 350°F oven for 3 to 4 minutes

$1/2$ cup cubed smoked mozzarella cheese

1 tablespoon extra virgin olive oil

2 teaspoons fresh lemon juice

1 small garlic clove, minced or pressed (optional)

Freshly ground black pepper to taste

FRISÉE SALAD WITH ROASTED APPLES

One of my favorite fall salads, this combination of sweet, rich, and mildly bitter is very satisfying—and good-looking too. Everything can be prepared ahead of time for last-minute assembly.

2 large, peeled and cored apples; each cut into 12 wedges (about 4 cups)

2 teaspoons vegetable oil

$^1/_2$ cup pecan halves or pieces

MAPLE CIDER DRESSING

2 tablespoons pure maple syrup

1 tablespoon Dijon mustard

2 tablespoons cider vinegar

1 teaspoon fresh thyme or lemon thyme ($^1/_4$ teaspoon dried)

$^1/_4$ cup vegetable oil

$^1/_4$ teaspoon salt

Freshly ground black pepper to taste

2 small heads frisée (curly endive), rinsed and drained (about 7 packed cups)

3 ounces sharp or extra sharp cheddar

Preheat the oven to 400°F.

Toss the apples with the 2 teaspoons oil in a low-rimmed baking dish or sheet large enough to spread them into a single layer. Bake uncovered for about 30 minutes, stirring two or three times, until the apples are tender but still hold their shape. Remove the apples from the hot pan to cool for 20 minutes or more.

Reduce the heat to 350°F and toast the pecans for 5 to 8 minutes, until fragrant. Set aside to cool. In a small bowl, whisk together the dressing ingredients. Pull apart the frisée into bite-sized pieces and place it in a large bowl. Top with the roasted apples and toasted nuts. Use a swivel-headed vegetable peeler to shave the cheddar into strips—I do it right into the bowl. Pour on the dressing, toss gently, and serve.

Note: If you're in a hurry, raw apples or pears work well too. Crispin apples are my favorite, or use another firm apple with a balance of sweet and tart. Baby greens are fine to use when frisée is hard to find. If you have more apples, make extra roasted apples because they're nice with maple syrup on pancakes or waffles, or on their own over ice cream or yogurt.

🌿 Serves 4 as a main dish, 6 as a starter

NORTH AFRICAN ROASTED VEGETABLE SALAD

Roasted eggplant, peppers, and tomatoes have a sweet juiciness. The simple marinade is highlighted by the aromatic flavors of garlic, olive oil, and rosemary. We like to serve this as part of a combination plate with hummus, stuffed grape leaves, and pita bread. On its own, it can be an appetizer, dip, or sandwich filling with pita bread.

Preheat the oven to 400°F.

Prick the eggplant five times with a fork.

On an unoiled baking sheet, roast the peppers for 35 minutes and the eggplant for 35 to 50 minutes, turning the vegetables every 10 minutes or so. About 25 minutes into the cooking time, add the tomatoes and bake for about 10 minutes, or until softened. The eggplant and peppers are done when they're tender and look somewhat collapsed.

While they're still hot, place the peppers in a paper bag and seal. (This will facilitate peeling later.) Allow the other vegetables to cool.

Scoop the mushy eggplant pulp from the skin and chop any long strands of pulp. After 10 minutes in the paper bag, the peppers' skin should rub off easily. Chop the roasted peppers into 1/2-inch pieces. Peel the tomatoes if desired, and cut in half to remove the seeds and juice (reserve for other uses). Chop the pulp into 1/2-inch pieces.

Mix the roasted vegetables with all the remaining ingredients. If the salad is to be served within 2 to 3 hours, use the greater amount of rosemary. Because the intensity of rosemary increases with time, a teaspoon or less will be plenty if the salad is refrigerated overnight before serving.

🦋 Serves 6 to 8 as an appetizer, side dish, or pita-bread filling

1 large eggplant, about 8 inches long (not the slender Asian type)

2 bell peppers, 1 red and 1 green if possible

2 firm, not overripe, tomatoes

2 tablespoons olive oil

2 tablespoons fresh lemon juice

2 garlic cloves, minced or pressed

1 1/2 tablespoons minced onion

2 tablespoons chopped fresh parsley

1 to 1 1/2 teaspoons chopped fresh rosemary (1/2 to 3/4 teaspoon dried)

Salt and freshly ground black pepper or cayenne pepper to taste

VIETNAMESE RICE NOODLE AND VEGETABLE SALAD

This was inspired by a dish I had in a San Francisco Vietnamese restaurant: a soup-salad that impressed me with the clean, unencumbered taste of its fresh herbs and greens. We make our version as a refreshing summer salad. Serve with Spring Rolls (page 243) for a savory crispness that harmonizes well with the slippery, soft noodles.

SWEET AND SOUR DRESSING

1 cup vegetable stock (page 224)

¼ cup soy sauce

¼ cup plus 2 tablespoons fresh lime juice

3 tablespoons brown sugar

Pinch of cayenne pepper *or* a few drops of Tabasco sauce

1 tablespoon chopped fresh cilantro

2 garlic cloves, minced or pressed

⅓ cup loosely packed, torn fresh basil leaves

½ cup loosely packed, torn fresh mint leaves

1½ cups grated or shredded carrots

1 cucumber, cut into matchsticks (see note)

4 to 6 leaves of a crisp leaf lettuce (romaine, buttercrunch), torn or cut into shreds

½ cup chopped scallions

¾ pound rice noodles (sticks about ⅛ inch wide or the vermicelli type)

3 quarts boiling water

6 cooked shrimps per person (optional)

Fresh hot pepper slivers (optional)

Lime wedges (optional)

Make the dressing by combining the stock, soy sauce, lime juice, brown sugar, and cayenne, Tabasco sauce, or hot pepper. If serving spring rolls as a garnish, divide the dressing into two equal portions and make a dip for the spring rolls by adding the cilantro and garlic to one portion. If not serving spring rolls, add the cilantro and garlic to the dressing.

Divide the basil, mint, carrots, cucumber, lettuce, and scallions equally into four to six individual, shallow, wide pasta or soup bowls.

Put the rice noodles in a pot and cover with the boiling water. Boil for a couple of minutes until tender, then drain.

Portion out the noodles into the bowls. Pour the sweet-and-sour dressing over all, then toss with chopsticks. Garnish with shrimp, hot peppers, and lime and serve at once.

Note: If you are using a store-bought, waxed cucumber, peel it and remove the large seeds before cutting into matchsticks.

❧ Serves 4 to 6

SUMMER TOMATO AND BREAD SALAD

Simple and refreshing, this is one of our favorite salads for high summer, when toma-
toes are juicy and ripe. You won't have to dip your bread to soak up the flavorful
juices—it's already in there. The opal basil vinegar adds a brilliant, ruby color and
enhances the basil flavor.

Combine all the ingredients except the bread cubes and marinate at room temperature for 30 minutes.

At serving time, toss in the bread cubes.

Note: You can make this a substantial one-dish meal with the addition of fresh mozzarella cheese cubes, artichoke hearts (canned or frozen), and roasted red peppers.

🌿 Serves 6 or more

4 fresh tomatoes, cut into $1/2$-inch slices, then $1/2$-inch cubes (about 3 $1/2$ cups)

1 cucumber, peeled and seeded, cut into $1/2$-inch cubes (about 1 $1/2$ cups)

2 tablespoons chopped fresh basil

2 tablespoons chopped fresh parsley

1 tablespoon chopped fresh oregano

$1/3$ cup chopped red onions or scallions

2 garlic cloves, minced or pressed

$1/4$ cup olive oil (extra virgin is nice)

2 tablespoons opal basil vinegar (page 260) or red-wine vinegar

Salt and freshly ground black pepper to taste

2 heaping cups stale Italian, French, or sourdough bread, cut into 1 $1/2$-inch cubes and lightly toasted until golden

VEGETABLES À LA GRECQUE

Simmered in an herbed broth, these vegetables fully absorb the seasonings for a richly flavored dish.

MARINADE

4 cups vegetable stock (page 224)

³/₄ cup olive oil (part or all extra virgin)

1 cup dry white wine

1 tablespoon tarragon vinegar

¹/₂ cup fresh lemon juice

3 garlic cloves, coarsely chopped

¹/₄ cup fresh parsley leaves

1 sprig fresh thyme (¹/₂ teaspoon dried)

1¹/₂ tablespoons chopped fresh dill
   (1¹/₂ teaspoons dried)

1 teaspoon salt

12 peppercorns

VEGETABLES

1 carrot, cut into sticks 2 inches long by
   ¹/₄ inch square

1 leek, white part only, cut into sticks
   2 inches long by ¹/₂ inch square

1 red pepper, cut into ¹/₄-inch-thick
   strips

1 yellow squash, cut into sticks 2 inches
   long by ¹/₄ inch square

¹/₄ pound green beans, stem ends cut
   off

1 fennel *(finocchio)* bulb, cut into
   ¹/₄-inch-thick slices

Combine all the marinade ingredients in a stainless-steel or enameled saucepan. Heat the marinade and let it gently simmer, partially covered, for ³/₄ hour to 1 hour. Strain and discard all the solid ingredients. Return the marinade to the cooking pot.

Bring the marinade to a gentle boil again. Cook each vegetable separately in the simmering liquid until just tender, then remove with a strainer or slotted spoon and place in a deep dish or bowl.

Pour marinade over the vegetables, just to cover. Serve right away, or after 3 or 4 hours for a more intense flavor. To serve, remove the vegetables from the marinade and artfully arrange on a serving platter. Serve at room temperature or chilled for a hot-weather salad.

🍃 Serves 4 to 6

Other Dishes 🌿

JOHN'S PIZZA

It wasn't that long ago that a pizza without tomato sauce was an oddity; these days, it's the opposite for me. In this tomatoless pizza, escarole's mildly bitter taste and the sharpness of the olives are mellowed by the creamy richness of the cheeses and the sweetness of golden onions. My partner, John Campione, first cooked this as a home-made calzone, and then we made it as a pizza using a prepared crust when we were in a hurry for dinner. I like both versions, but there's something to be said about the topping's flavor being more of a presence on the pizza than in the crustier calzone.

Warm 1 tablespoon of the oil in a heavy cast-iron or nonstick pan large enough to hold all of the escarole. Add the onions and salt and cook on high heat, stirring often, for 3 to 4 minutes. Reduce the heat to medium-low and cook, stirring occasionally, for 15 minutes or until the onions are softened and golden. If they're in danger of sticking, cover the pan, but uncover if they're getting soupy.

While the onions cook, prepare the other ingredients. Combine the olives and ricotta in a bowl. Preheat the oven to 425°F.

Add the cooked onions to the ricotta and olives. Wipe out the pan and warm the remaining tablespoon of oil. Add the garlic and escarole, and sauté on high heat for a couple of minutes, stirring the whole time to quickly wilt the escarole without overcooking it. If there's liquid in the pan, drain the escarole, pressing out any excess juices. Add to the onions, ricotta, and olives, and stir well. Stir in black pepper to taste.

Place the pizza crust on a low-rimmed baking sheet. Spread the filling to within an inch of the crust edge. Sprinkle the grated cheeses on top.

2 tablespoons extra virgin olive oil
2 cups chopped onions
¼ teaspoon salt
2 large garlic cloves, minced or pressed
1 head escarole, rinsed, drained, and coarsely chopped (about 4½ packed cups)
⅓ cup chopped pitted olives (kalamata, amfissa, niçoise, or gaeta are nice)
½ cup ricotta cheese
Freshly ground black pepper
1 pre-baked, 15-inch pizza crust, such as Boboli
1 cup grated mozzarella cheese
½ cup grated Parmesan cheese

(continued)

Bake for 12 to 14 minutes, until the crust is lightly browned and the topping is thoroughly melted. Allow to cool a few minutes before serving.

🦋 *Serves 4 as part of a larger meal*

POTATO KNISHES

My earliest summertime memories are of Coney Island. Our family would pack up the car and make the drive across the city from the Bronx to Brooklyn, to a rented "bunga-low" where we spent the summer with lots of extended family. It was a great place for a kid; the beach and the famous boardwalk were just a block away. Anyone in my fam-ily can tell you that my favorite treat on the boardwalk was a potato knish. This is my answer to Marcel Proust's madeleine. In terms of flavor, there's really just the potatoes and onions; but when I taste it, I can smell the sea and tar, the sun makes me squint, the sand is hot, kids are laughing, the ocean is a machia ("a pleasure," in Yiddish).

3 tablespoons vegetable oil

4 cups chopped yellow onions (see note)

$^1/_2$ teaspoon salt

8 cups peeled, 1-inch-diced Yukon Gold potatoes (about $2^1/_2$ pounds unpeeled)

1 teaspoon salt

$^1/_2$ teaspoon freshly ground black pepper

1 large egg, lightly beaten

$^1/_2$ to $^3/_4$ cup vegetable oil

1 pound (12 by 17-inch) phyllo pastry sheets (see note)

Warm the oil in a large skillet. Add the onions and the $^1/_2$ teaspoon of salt, and sauté on high heat for a couple of minutes. Reduce the heat to low and cook for 40 minutes, stirring occasionally, until golden brown and soft. Put the potatoes in a pot with enough water to cover and a sprinkle of salt. Bring to a boil. Lower to a simmer and cook until soft, about 10 minutes. Drain the pota-toes. In a bowl, combine the potatoes with the cooked onions and any onion-flavored oil left in the pan. Mash the potatoes with a hand masher (a food processor will give the potatoes an unpleas-ant, gluey texture). Add the teaspoon of salt and the pepper, taste, and add more if desired. Stir in the egg.

Preheat the oven to 375°F and lightly oil two baking sheets.

Place the filling, $^1/_2$ cup oil, and a pastry brush near a dry, spacious work surface. Unfold the phyllo. Lift two sheets of phyllo from the stack and place them with short sides closest to you. Brush the top sheet lightly with oil. Fold the sheets in half lengthwise and brush the strip with oil. Spread $^1/_2$ cup of the filling near the bottom edge. Fold the lower right corner up and over diagonally until the bottom edge is flush with the left side and you have a triangle at the end. Brush once with oil, and then keep folding the triangle up, as you would a flag, to make a triangular pastry. Brush both sides of the knish lightly with oil and place on one of the prepared baking sheets. Repeat to use all of the filling.

Bake for 20 minutes, or until golden and puffed. Serve warm, with applesauce, sweet-and-sour red cabbage, or a cucumber salad.

Note: Use conventional yellow onions, not sweet or Spanish onions which don't have a strong enough flavor. Unoiled phyllo becomes brittle when exposed to air, so it's best to work in a draft-free spot and to keep a damp towel on the not-yet-used phyllo. An inexpensive, new, 2-inch paintbrush works great as a phyllo pastry brush.

🌿 Yields 10 to 12 knishes

BAKED SQUASH

Here's a sweetly "dressed up" holiday dish. If you're serving it as part of a big, multi-course meal, one quarter of a squash for each diner may be sufficient.

Preheat the oven to 400°F.

Toast the nuts on a baking sheet in the oven for 4 to 5 minutes, until lightly browned. Cut the squash in half lengthwise and remove the seeds. Salt the inside of each half and place in a lightly oiled baking dish. Coarsely chop the toasted nuts. Combine the butter, apricots, orange juice concentrate, and chopped nuts in a small bowl. Spoon an equal amount of this mixture into the squash cavities. Bake covered for 50 to 60 minutes or until the squash is tender. Serve warm.

$^1/_2$ cup whole almonds or pecan or walnut halves

2 winter squash (delicata, acorn, or carnival squash)

2 tablespoons butter, melted

$^1/_2$ cup chopped dried apricots

$^1/_4$ cup undiluted frozen orange juice concentrate

🌿 Serves 4 to 8

FRITTATA

Frittatas are a popular, frequent feature on Moosewood's lunch menus. Home cooks can use this basic recipe with a host of variations to create an appealing main dish for brunch, lunch, or a simple dinner. Give leftover cooked vegetables a new lease on life in a frittata. The recipe is very forgiving of the quantity of cooked vegetables—a bit more or less won't matter. In fact, you could make just a cheese and herb frittata, but it's a more balanced dish with the vegetables.

6 large eggs

1/2 cup milk

4 ounces softened Neufchatel or cream cheese

1/2 teaspoon salt

1/4 teaspoon ground black pepper

2 tablespoons chopped fresh herbs

1/3 cup chopped scallions (optional)

2 cups cooked vegetables (see variations)

1 cup lightly packed, grated cheese (see suggestions)

Preheat the oven to 350°F.

In a blender or food processor, whirl the eggs, milk, Neufchatel, salt, pepper, and herbs until smooth. Stir in the scallions. Lightly oil or butter an oven proof, 10-inch skillet or a baking dish. Place the vegetables on the bottom, cover with the egg mixture, and top with grated cheese. Bake until the top is set and lightly browned, 35 to 45 minutes.

Variations: Peperonata (page 241), basil, Parmesan and mozzarella cheeses

Steamed broccoli or cauliflower florets, dill, sharp and smoked cheddar

Sautéed mushrooms and leeks, 1/2 teaspoon fresh thyme and 1 tablespoon fresh tarragon, a mixture of Fontina and Gruyère cheeses

Sautéed kale and garlic, oregano and Italian parsley, feta and mozzarella cheeses

Roasted Potatoes (page 70), dill and rosemary, dilled Havarti cheese

🦋 Serves 4

PROVENÇAL BEANS

I enjoy making this recipe when I've harvested shell beans (flageolet, cannellini, edamame, baby lima, or cranberry), a summertime treat. Shell beans are picked at a maturity midway between green snap beans (when the bean is just beginning to form) and fully mature dried beans (when most moisture has evaporated). It's usually a quick job to remove the beans from the shells by inserting your thumbnail along the "string" and popping open the shell. Shell beans are best simmered with some seasonings. Serve with a crusty bread to dip into the juices.

Warm the oil in a pan that has a tight lid. Add the garlic, shallots, fennel bulb, and salt. Sauté uncovered on high heat for a couple of minutes before adding the ground fennel, thyme, and rosemary. Continue to cook on medium heat for 5 minutes, stirring occasionally. Add the wine and simmer for a couple of minutes. Add the beans and tomatoes and bring to a boil. Lower the heat to a simmer, cover, and cook for 15 minutes or until the beans are tender. Add the parsley, lemon juice, salt, if needed, and pepper.

Note: This recipe works any time of year with canned beans. Although these are fully cooked when you add them, simmer canned beans for 15 minutes too, so that they'll absorb the seasonings. Canned beans tend to be well salted, so taste before adding more salt. When it comes to the seasonings, I like an assertive rosemary flavor; use the smaller amount if you want it more in the background. If you can make the recipe ahead of time, the flavors marry nicely; the beans keep for 4 or 5 days in the refrigerator.

🌿 Serves 4

2 tablespoons olive oil

2 large garlic cloves, minced or pressed

³/₄ cup chopped shallots

2 cups chopped fennel bulb (1 bulb)

¹/₂ teaspoon salt

1 teaspoon ground fennel seeds

1 teaspoon fresh thyme

1 to 2 teaspoons fresh rosemary (see note)

1 cup dry white wine

3 cups fresh shell beans or 2 (15-ounce) cans, drained and rinsed (see note)

2 cups chopped tomatoes

2 tablespoons chopped parsley

1 tablespoon fresh lemon juice

Salt and freshly ground black pepper to taste

SUMMER ROLLS

My version of this Southeast Asian classic borrows from California cuisine in the use of avocados. Thai basil gives a wonderful fragrance and flavor but can be replaced with the more readily available cilantro, a combination of mint and cilantro, or Italian basil. Sesame Baked Tofu (page 255) or a commercial, Asian-style baked tofu works well in this recipe.

¹/₄ pound rice stick noodles

1 cup baby greens, or shredded romaine
  or napa cabbage

¹/₂ cup grated carrots

¹/₄ cup chopped Thai basil

¹/₂ cup chopped scallions

1 cup cubed, baked seasoned tofu
  (¹/₂-inch cubes)

1 teaspoon fresh lime juice

Pinch of salt

1 avocado, cubed and tossed with
  2 teaspoons fresh lime juice

DIPPING SAUCE

2 tablespoons soy sauce

2 tablespoons water

2 teaspoons fresh lime juice

1 teaspoon brown sugar

Splash of hot sauce

Rice paper wrappers

Cook the rice noodles in a generous amount of salted, boiling water for about 5 minutes, until al dente. Drain, rinse with cold water, and drain again. With a sharp knife or kitchen scissors, cut the noodles here and there into shorter lengths to facilitate mixing with the other ingredients. Place in a large bowl.

Add the greens, carrots, basil, scallions, tofu, and the 1 teaspoon lime juice to the noodles and toss. Add salt to taste. Put the avocados tossed with lime in a separate bowl. Combine all the dipping sauce ingredients in a small, wide bowl.

To assemble the rolls: Dampen a large, clean dish cloth and lay it flat on a work surface. Fill a large bowl with hot water. Holding a rice paper disc by the edge, gently lower one side of it into the hot water—it will soften as it absorbs water. Slowly turn the disc in the water just until it has completely softened. Carefully place the disc on the damp towel and flatten it out. Soften a few more and lay them side by side without overlap (so they won't stick together).

Just below the center of each disc (above the 6 o'clock position), place about 1 tablespoon of the avocado and ¹/₃ cup of the filling. Fold the two side edges over the filling to form a rectangular shape with curved ends. Tightly roll up from the bottom to make a neat roll. Place seam side down on a platter. Repeat until the filling is gone. Serve at once, or cover the rolls with plastic wrap and chill. For best quality, serve within 5 hours.

Note: Both the rice stick noodles and the rice paper wrappers can be found with other Asian specialties in well-stocked supermarkets or in Asian groceries. Rice sticks, resembling vermicelli, are the thinnest rice pasta, and many brands are available. Rice paper wrappers are thin discs, about 8 or 9 inches across, that come in 12-ounce packages. Most brands are from Vietnam or Thailand.

🦋 Yields 12 rolls

PEPERONATA

Some of the simplest dishes are the best. Slow-cooked, multicolored bell peppers with onions are meltingly soft, sweet, and scrumptious. This peperonata can be used as a side dish; a pasta or pizza topping; or an omelet, crepe, or frittata filling; or you can just spread it on crusty bread. The optional tomatoes make a saucier dish for pasta or a base for stew.

In a heavy or nonstick pan large enough to hold all the ingredients, warm the oil. If necessary, use two pans. Add the peppers and sauté on high heat for 3 minutes. Add the onions, garlic, and salt, and continue to cook on high heat for 3 minutes to lightly caramelize and brown the vegetables. Lower the heat to medium and cook uncovered, stirring often, for 25 minutes. If the vegetables look too dry or are in danger of scorching, reduce the heat to low or cover the pan. Add the vinegar and the tomatoes, and cook uncovered for an additional 10 minutes until the peppers are quite soft. Remove from the heat. Taste for salt and pepper.

Peperonata will keep refrigerated for 1 week.

🦋 Yields 4 generous cups

2 tablespoons extra virgin olive oil
8 cups sliced bell peppers (4 or 5 large peppers), choose a mix of colors
3 cups sliced onions
1 teaspoon salt, plus additional to taste
1 tablespoon pressed or minced garlic
1½ cups chopped tomatoes (optional)
1 tablespoon balsamic vinegar
Freshly ground black pepper to taste

SUMMER GARDEN FAJITAS

This is a quickly executed sauté that helps you use up those popular and prolific vegetables of the summer garden. Serve with rice and a salad, or guacamole and chips.

2 tablespoons vegetable oil

2 fresh jalapeños, seeded and diced

2 cups sliced onions

3 cups sliced bell peppers, a mix of colors

1/2 teaspoon salt

3 garlic cloves, minced or pressed

2 teaspoons ground cumin

4 cups zucchini or summer squash, cut into sticks (3 inches long, 1/2 inch wide)

2 cups chopped plum tomatoes

Hot sauce to taste

3 cups shredded lettuce

1/2 cup sour cream

1 cup grated Monterey Jack or soy cheese

4 to 6 large (8- to 10-inch) flour tortillas

Heat the oil in a large, heavy skillet on medium to high heat, and sauté the jalapeño, onions, bell peppers, and salt for about 5 minutes, until lightly browned. Add the garlic and cumin, lower the heat to medium, and continue to cook for 4 to 5 minutes. Add the zucchini and tomatoes and cook for 5 to 10 minutes, stirring often and increasing the heat if the vegetables look too wet, until everything is tender. Add hot sauce and more salt to taste. Set aside.

In another large unoiled skillet, briefly heat the tortillas on each side, just until they puff up a bit. Place each warm tortilla on a dinner plate and, on its bottom half, pile some lettuce, about 3/4 cup of the sautéed vegetables, a dollop of sour cream, and some cheese. Roll up.

Fastidious diners will prefer a knife and fork to the risky pick-up-and-eat method.

Note: If your jalapeños are mild, for added heat do not remove the seeds. If you use regular tomatoes and they are juicy with a lot of seeds, slice off the stem end and squeeze out the seeds and watery juice before chopping.

Variation: Eggplant, cut in the same manner as the zucchini, could be used to replace half or all of the zukes; add the eggplant with the onions and peppers.

❧ Serves 4 to 6

SPRING ROLLS

This popular appetizer uses spring roll wrappers which are more delicate than egg roll wrappers. I recommend Oriental Mascot brand: they're 8 inches square, made of wheat, and available frozen in Asian food stores. Serve with Vietnamese Rice Noodle and Vegetable Salad (page 232), or as an appetizer.

Prepare the vegetables and have all the ingredients close to the stove. You'll be quickly stir-frying the vegetables until just barely wilted.

Heat 1 tablespoon of vegetable oil in a very hot wok or large skillet, add the ginger and garlic, and stir-fry for a moment. Add the vegetables to the wok in sequence, stir-frying continuously. Start with the pak choi or cabbage, followed in a minute by the peppers, then 30 seconds later the carrots, and 30 seconds later the scallions and mung bean sprouts. Add the soy sauce. Remove from the heat.

Scoop the vegetables into a strainer or colander and set aside to drain. Wipe the wok clean and add the oil for deep-frying. Use 1¹/₂ cups for cooking the spring rolls one at a time, or 4 cups of oil for two at a time. Heat the oil slowly to about 375°F while you assemble the spring rolls.

On a clean work surface, place the spring roll wrappers so that their corners form a diamond shape. Spoon 2 to 3 tablespoons of filling onto the lower third of a wrapper. Lift the bottom corner up and over the filling. Fold in the side corners, making them even with the bottom rolled section. Continue rolling upward and seal the top corner and remaining edges with the beaten egg.

Deep-fry in the hot oil for 5 minutes each, until the rolls are crispy and golden. (See page 222 for deep-frying instructions.)

❧ Yields 8 spring rolls

1¹/₂ cups shredded pak choi or Chinese cabbage

1 red or green bell pepper, shredded (about 1 cup)

1 large carrot, shredded (about 1 cup)

³/₄ cup chopped scallions

2 cups mung bean sprouts

1 tablespoon vegetable oil

1 tablespoon grated fresh gingerroot

2 garlic cloves, minced or pressed

2 tablespoons soy sauce

1¹/₂ to 4 cups vegetable oil for deep frying

8 spring roll wrappers

1 egg, beaten

CRISP-FRIED TOFU
AND GREENS

Here, tofu is paired with stir-fried greens in a classic sauce. Tofu that has been frozen and thawed better absorbs the seasonings of a marinade. When you plan this dish, allow for thawing time: 24 hours in the refrigerator or 8 hours at room temperature.

2 16-ounce cakes firm or extra firm tofu (not silken), frozen overnight and thawed

MARINADE

1/3 cup soy sauce

1/4 cup rice vinegar

1 tablespoon finely grated fresh gingerroot

2 garlic cloves, minced or pressed

Pinch of cayenne pepper

3 tablespoons soy sauce

1/4 cup rice wine or dry sherry or sake

2 teaspoons rice vinegar

2 teaspoons honey or brown sugar

1/2 cup water or vegetable stock (page 224)

1 teaspoon cornstarch

1/2 cup cornmeal or cornstarch

Vegetable oil for frying

3 tablespoons vegetable oil

3 garlic cloves, minced or pressed

1 cup thinly sliced onions

6 cups coarsely chopped pak choi, tatsoi, Swiss chard, kale, or Chinese cabbage (you may use only one variety or a mixture), or 9 cups spinach or 9 cups mustard greens

Chopped scallions or mung bean sprouts, for garnish

To prepare the thawed tofu, gently squeeze out as much liquid as possible without tearing or breaking the cakes. Cut the tofu blocks, first crosswise into four 1/2-inch-thick slices, then diagonally to make four triangles per layer, sixteen triangles total.

To make the marinade, combine all the ingredients and mix well. Arrange the tofu triangles one layer deep in a dish, cover with the marinade, and let sit for at least 30 minutes to absorb the flavors.

Meanwhile, combine the soy sauce, rice wine, vinegar, and honey in a small bowl. In a separate bowl, stir together the water and 1 teaspoon of cornstarch.

Dredge the marinated tofu pieces in the cornmeal. In a skillet on medium-high heat, fry the coated tofu in 1/8 to 1/4 inch of oil. Fry for 3 to 4 minutes on each side until golden. Drain and keep warm in a 200°F oven.

Add any leftover marinade to the sauce mix.

Heat the 3 tablespoons of vegetable oil in a wok or large skillet. Stir-fry the garlic and onion until the onion is fairly tender, about 3 to 4 minutes. Add the greens and continue stir-frying on fairly high heat until just wilted but not mushy. Add the sauce mix and the cornstarch mix, and stir-fry for a moment or two, or until the sauce has thickened slightly. Add the reserved fried tofu.

Garnish with chopped scallions or mung bean sprouts.

Note: For coating the tofu before frying, cornstarch is the more traditonal coating, but cornmeal gives a crunchier texture.

🦋 Serves 4 to 6

VEGETABLE "PASTA"

For this recipe, vegetables are cut into long, thin strips to resemble spaghetti. This is a pretty side dish, or toss it with fettuccine or linguini, or use it to make a "nest" for broiled or grilled fish. Use two of any vegetable if they're small.

Cut each vegetable into lengthwise slices, 4 to 5 inches long, $1/8$ to $1/4$ inch thick. Then cut the slices into sticks, about $1/8$ to $1/4$ inch square by 4 to 5 inches long.

In a large pot, bring 16 cups of water to a boil (see page 221). Blanch each vegetable separately: a couple of minutes for the carrot, celery, and parsnip, and a minute for the zucchini, leek, and pepper. They should be crisp but tender.

Remove each vegetable with a strainer or slotted spoon and place on a covered platter to keep warm. If you're cooking a large quantity, keep the vegetables warm until serving time in a 200°F oven.

Top with a simple Herb Butter (page 271), Shallot-Herb Butter Sauce (page 259), Red Pepper Sauce (page 258), or a light tomato sauce, or toss with pasta, butter, and grated Parmesan cheese.

🦋 Serves 4

1 large carrot
1 celery stalk
1 large parsnip
1 zucchini
1 red or green bell pepper
1 large leek, split in half and rinsed carefully, tough greens removed

RED, WHITE, AND GREEN PHYLLO PIZZAS

Rich with a variety of herbs, vegetables, and cheeses, phyllo pizzas are a popular lunch entrée at Moosewood. Using packaged phyllo pastry saves the time of preparing a yeast dough for the crust. We make large sheets of this pizza with a variety of toppings. Feel free to make just one kind. Doing all three at once is an ambitious effort for special occasions or when you have kitchen helpers.

RED TOPPING

1/2 cup loosely packed, dry-packed sun-dried tomatoes

2 fresh tomatoes, sliced

1/4 cup chopped fresh oregano leaves (2 tablespoons dried)

2 garlic cloves, minced or pressed

1 tablespoon olive oil

1 cup grated mozzarella cheese

1/2 cup grated Parmesan cheese

WHITE TOPPING

2 tablespoons olive oil

2 Spanish onions, thinly sliced (about 2 1/2 cups)

3 garlic cloves, minced or pressed

1 teaspoon fresh thyme leaves

1/2 cup cream cheese

1/2 cup grated smoked mozzarella or smoked Swiss cheese

1/2 cup grated cheddar cheese

To make the red topping, soak the sun-dried tomatoes in 1 cup of warm water. Set aside for at least 20 minutes. Drain and chop coarsely. In a separate bowl, gently toss the fresh tomato slices with the oregano, garlic, and olive oil. Have the cheeses ready for assembly.

To make the white topping, in a heavy skillet on low heat, heat the 2 tablespoons of oil and gently cook the onions, garlic, and thyme until lightly browned, about 20 minutes. Cut the cream cheese into small bits, add to the cooked onions, and stir until smooth. Reserve the grated cheese for assembly.

To make the green topping, blanch the spinach in boiling water until just wilted, about 2 to 3 minutes. Drain, press out the excess water, chop, and mix with the remaining green topping ingredients.

Preheat the oven to 400°F. To assemble the pizzas, either use all three toppings on a 12-by-18 baking sheet or each topping separately on a 9- or 10-inch pie plate.

Lightly brush the baking pan with oil. Lay two sheets of phyllo so they just reach the edge without hanging over. Fold the overhang back into the pan. Brush with oil. Cover any gaps with the next two sheets of phyllo dough, then brush with oil. Repeat this process until you have a "base" of phyllo about twelve sheets deep. (It doesn't matter if some sections are thicker where there's an overlap.) When spooning on the topping, leave a $^1/_2$-inch-wide outer margin of pastry uncovered.

If using a baking sheet, fill each third of the surface with one of the toppings, yielding an Italian flag: red, white, and green from left to right.

Red: Sprinkle the drained, chopped sun-dried tomatoes over the pastry. Top with half of the mozzarella and Parmesan, then the fresh-tomato mixture, followed by the remaining cheese.

White: Spoon the onion and garlic mixture onto the pastry and top with the grated cheese.

Green: Spoon the spinach mixture onto the pastry.

Bake for 20 to 30 minutes, until the pastry is lightly browned and the toppings are bubbly and melted.

🦋 Yields one 12-by-18 sheet pizza or
three 9- or 10-inch pies

GREEN TOPPING

10 ounces fresh spinach, stemmed, rinsed, and drained

$^1/_4$ cup chopped scallions

$^1/_4$ cup chopped fresh parsley

$^1/_4$ cup chopped fresh basil

1 cup grated feta cheese

$^1/_2$ cup cottage cheese

CRUST FOR A 12-BY-18 BAKING SHEET

$^1/_2$ cup vegetable oil or olive oil, or a combination of the two

1 (1-pound) box phyllo sheets

CRUST FOR A 9- OR 10-INCH PIE

3 tablespoons vegetable oil or olive oil, or a combination of the two

$^1/_3$ of a 1-pound box of phyllo pastry

MAMA FLORA'S BAKED LEEKS

Flora Marranca is a former, but not forgotten, cook at Moosewood. She and her husband, Jonathan Kline, have a wonderful country garden. This is a delicious, saucy side dish of her invention.

3 good-sized leeks, 1 to 2 inches in diameter (use more if the leeks are too small to yield about 1 pound after the tough upper greens are removed)

2 tablespoons vegetable oil (olive oil is nice)

8 sprigs fresh dill, about 4 inches long (1 tablespoon dried)

3 garlic cloves, halved

2 teaspoons miso

1 teaspoon soy sauce

$^1/_2$ cup water

Preheat the oven to 350°F.

Cut and split the leeks in half and carefully rinse to remove any dirt lodged between the layers. Choose a baking dish that will accommodate the leeks in two layers, about 10 by 16 inches. Put 2 tablespoons of oil into the dish and coat the leeks, using your hands or a pastry brush. Tuck in the dill and garlic cloves here and there.

Whisk together the miso, soy sauce, and water in a small bowl to make a smooth sauce. Pour over the leeks.

Bake covered for 25 minutes. Uncover, stir to prevent sticking and scorching, then bake uncovered for an additional 20 minutes. Add small quantities of water if the leeks are in danger of drying out; they should be lightly sauced.

Variations: In place of the leeks, use 2- to 3-inch-long, thin slices of carrots, fennel, onions, parsnips, potatoes, or turnips, or a combination.

🍂 Serves 4

FETTUCINE WITH CHÈVRE, SPINACH, AND HERBS

This recipe is a collaboration between me and my late partner, David Deutsch. At our house, the Double Dave Goat Ranch and Gardens, David H. grew the vegetables and herbs, while David D. tended the goats.

Boil 1¹/₂ gallons of salted water in a large pot to cook the pasta.

Heat the oil in a pan large enough to hold all of the spinach. Sauté the scallions for 30 seconds, then add the spinach and stock. When the spinach is wilted, add the parsley and dill and remove from the heat.

Warm a large, heatproof serving bowl and individual dishes in a 200°F oven or with hot water. (This will keep the pasta from cooling down too fast.)

Cook the fettuccine, drain briefly, and pour into the large serving bowl. Toss it first with the butter and chèvre, then with the spinach-herb mixture. Serve immediately, garnishing individual servings with hazelnuts or diced tomatoes or both.

Variations: Instead of spinach, use 1 cup of shelled green peas or 1¹/₂ cup of sugar snap peas cut into 1-inch lengths. Add the herbs when the peas are just tender. The dill can be replaced with ¹/₃ cup of chopped fresh basil or chervil.

🌿 Serves 4 as an entrée or 6 to 8 as an appetizer

SPINACH-HERB MIXTURE
- 2 tablespoons vegetable oil
- ²/₃ cup chopped scallions
- 1 pound fresh spinach, washed, large stems removed, big leaves torn into pieces
- ¹/₃ cup vegetable stock (page 224) or water
- ¹/₃ cup chopped fresh parsley
- ¹/₃ cup chopped fresh dill (1 tablespoon dried)
- 12 ounces dried fettucine or about 1 pound fresh
- 4 tablespoons butter, cut into small pieces
- 12 ounces chèvre (fresh goat cheese, not aged), crumbled or diced into small pieces

TOPPINGS
- ¹/₂ cup chopped toasted hazelnuts
- 1 fresh tomato, diced

CREPES

Crepes are an elegant, versatile dish for a starter course, brunch, light dinner, or dessert. A crepe can be a wrapper for any number of vegetable fillings; even leftover vegetables that are still presentable can be combined with cheese or a cheese sauce, and voilà!—an elegant brunch or dinner. Try one of the savory or sweet filling variations following the main recipe.

CREPE BATTER (SEE NOTE)

3 eggs

1¹/₂ cups milk

1 cup plus 2 tablespoons whole wheat pastry flour or unbleached white flour

¹/₄ teaspoon salt

3 tablespoons butter, melted

ZUCCHINI-LEEK-CHEESE FILLING

2 leeks, tender green and white parts, carefully rinsed, cut into strips ¹/₄ by 1¹/₂ inches

2 tablespoons vegetable oil

2 zucchini, cut into strips ¹/₄ by 1¹/₄ inches

¹/₂ teaspoon fresh thyme leaves (¹/₄ teaspoon dried)

Generous pinch of freshly grated nutmeg

Salt and freshly ground black pepper to taste

³/₄ pound grated fontina cheese (about 2¹/₂ cups)

To make the crepes, blend the eggs, milk, flour, and salt in a blender or food processor, or whisk in a bowl until just smooth. Whisk the melted butter into the batter right before cooking.

Heat a skillet, crepe pan, or omelet pan on medium-high heat. A heavy, well-seasoned cast-iron skillet works well. When the pan is hot, brush it with a very thin film of vegetable oil. This should be sufficient for cooking all the crepes, but if sticking should occur, brush the pan before each crepe.

For an 8-inch pan, use ¹/₄ cup of batter. For a smaller pan, use less. There should be just enough batter to thinly coat the pan bottom. Tilt the pan to distribute the batter, and cook for a moment or two, until the edges are light brown and lacy and the crepe is no longer runny. Flip it with a spatula and cook the second side just a moment, until it's speckled light brown. With the spatula, transfer to a platter and continue cooking crepes, placing wax paper between each one, until all the batter is gone.

Preheat the oven to 325°F.

To make the filling, sauté the leeks in the oil for a couple of minutes, until they begin to soften. Add the zucchini, thyme, nutmeg, and salt and pepper. Cook over medium heat until the vegetables are just tender, about 5 minutes. Remove from the heat.

Fill each crepe with about 3 tablespoons of grated cheese and an equal amount of cooked vegetables. Either roll the crepe up around the filling or place the filling in a strip down the center and fold the sides over.

Bake the filled crepes in a buttered baking dish, loosely covered to keep them from drying out, for 10 to 15 minutes. until the filling is heated through and the crepes are very lightly browned.

Note: Crepes can be made in advance and filled at the last minute for easy preparation. Crepe batter keeps in the refrigerator for a day or two. Cooked crepes keep for three days under refrigeration, or a couple of months in the freezer.

Savory Variations: Vegetables should be sautéed, steamed, or blanched until just tender. Bake only to warm through and melt the cheeses, if any.

- Asparagus spears and Parmesan cheese
- Sautéed spinach and mushrooms with toasted walnuts
- Cauliflower, scallions, and Cheddar cheese
- Sautéed broccoli and tofu seasoned with gingerroot and soy sauce
- Green beans, pearl onions, and Gorgonzola cheese
- Sautéed eggplant, zucchini, peppers, garlic, and fresh basil, topped with a tomato sauce

Dessert Filling Variations: Dessert or brunch crepes can be filled with lightly sweetened fruits (use all-fruit preserves, maple syrup, or honey) and do not need further cooking.

- Sautéed apples with raisins, walnuts, and cinnamon, topped with vanilla yogurt
- Fresh berries with ricotta cheese
- Diced fresh peaches with crème fraîche or sour cream and grated nutmeg
- Bananas or diced cantaloupe with cottage cheese

🦋 Yields 11 crepes using an 8-inch pan

SQUASH-APPLE CHEDDAR GRATIN

This is a homey casserole that will warm the chilly evenings of fall and winter. Tart apples, such as Granny Smiths, bring out the sweetness of the sautéed onions and squash. I prefer to use butternut squash because its unridged skin makes it easier to peel than other squash. One large butternut will make enough for this recipe.

2 cups sliced onions

1 teaspoon fresh thyme leaves
(1¹/₂ teaspoons dried)

2 tablespoons vegetable oil

2¹/₂ cups thinly sliced apples

1 tablespoon unbleached white flour

1¹/₂ cups grated Cheddar cheese

2 tablespoons bread crumbs

3 cups cooked, lightly mashed winter squash (see note)

Salt and freshly ground black pepper

Gently sauté the onions and thyme in the oil for about 20 minutes, or until the onions are soft and golden. Meanwhile, toss the apple slices with the flour. In a separate bowl, toss the cheese with the bread crumbs.

Preheat the oven to 350°F. Oil a baking dish, approximately 8 by 8 by 3 inches, and layer the ingredients as follows: the squash, with a sprinkling of salt and pepper if desired, the sautéed onions, the apple slices with a bit more salt and pepper, and the Cheddar–bread crumb mixture.

Bake covered for 30 minutes, then uncovered for 15 minutes, or until the apples are tender and the topping bubbly and golden.

Note: Peel, remove the seeds, cut into slices or cubes, and steam until tender.

❧ Serves 4 to 6

FRAGRANT BULGUR PILAF

Bulgur wheat is a nutty-flavored grain made from roasted cracked wheat berries—an interesting, tasty alternative to rice. This pilaf can be made with dried herbs, but it is far superior with fresh or even frozen herbs.

Preheat the oven to 300°F.

In an ovenproof skillet large enough to contain all the ingredients, sauté the onions, carrots, and peppers in the oil. When the onions and carrots have just softened, add the bulgur and sauté for a minute or two, stirring constantly to prevent scorching. Add the rest of the ingredients, except for the cheese, and bring to a boil. Cover and bake for 20 minutes, until all the liquid is absorbed.

Serve topped with the feta cheese if desired.

❧ Serves 6 generously

$3/4$ cup diced onions

$1/2$ cup diced carrots

$1/2$ cup diced red or green bell peppers

2 tablespoons olive oil

$1^1/2$ cups bulgur

3 cups vegetable stock (page 224) or water

$1/4$ cup toasted ground nuts (optional)

$1/4$ cup chopped fresh parsley

$1/4$ cup chopped fresh basil (1 tablespoon dried)

3 tablespoons chopped fresh spearmint ($1^1/2$ tablespoons dried)

2 tablespoons chopped fresh lovage or celery leaf (optional)

1 teaspoon soy sauce

$1/4$ teaspoon salt

Freshly ground black pepper

1 cup crumbled feta cheese (optional)

VEGETABLE LASAGNA

This lasagna relies on the flavors of the fresh vegetables and herbs and is lighter than a traditional lasagna. It's also quicker to prepare because the sauce is barely cooked.

1 pound lasagna noodles

4½ cups chopped fresh tomatoes

1 red onion, finely diced (about ⅔ cup)

5 garlic cloves, minced or pressed

3 tablespoons olive oil

2 teaspoons ground fennel

2 cups chopped leeks, white and tender green parts or onions

3 cups green beans, cut into 1½-inch lengths

3 red or green bell peppers, sliced

Salt and freshly ground black pepper

3 zucchini, cut into 1½-by-½ inch sticks

¼ cup coarsely chopped fresh parsley

¼ cup coarsely chopped fresh basil (½ tablespoon dried)

¼ cup coarsely chopped fresh oregano (½ tablespoon dried)

3½ cups grated mozzarella cheese

2 cups freshly grated Parmesan cheese

Cook the noodles in a generous amount of boiling water until firm but tender. Rinse in cold water to prevent sticking, and set aside.

Sauté half of the garlic in the olive oil for 1 minute. Add the fennel and leeks, and sauté for 2 minutes. Add the green beans and 3 tablespoons water, cover, and simmer for about 5 minutes or until the beans are tender. Add the peppers and a pinch of salt and black pepper to taste, cover, and simmer, stirring occasionally, for 3 minutes. Add the zucchini, cover, and simmer for 1 minute.

In a saucepan, combine the tomatoes, the remaining garlic, and the red onion. Bring to a boil and simmer to heat the sauce through, about 2 minutes. Add the parsley, basil, and oregano, then remove the sauce from the heat.

Preheat the oven to 350°F. Lightly oil an 11-by-14-inch baking dish.

Layer the ingredients as follows: half of the tomato sauce, a layer of noodles, half of the vegetables, a third of the cheese, a layer of noodles, the rest of the vegetables, a third of the cheese, a layer of noodles, the remaining tomato sauce and cheeses. It may not be necessary to use all the noodles.

Bake tightly covered for 50 minutes, then uncovered for 5 to 10 minutes, until the top is golden. Allow to sit for 10 to 15 minutes before serving.

🦋 Serves 6 to 8

SESAME BAKED TOFU WITH SNOW PEAS AND ALMONDS

This dish can be prepared a few hours ahead and chilled until serving time, but the snow peas will retain the brightest green color if you serve it soon after tossing with the dressing.

Preheat the oven to 350°F.

Place the tofu between two plates, weight the top plate with a heavy object, and press for 15 minutes. Drain, then cut the tofu into 1-inch cubes and arrange in a single layer in a baking dish. Mix the sesame oil and soy sauce together, pour over the tofu, and bake for 30 minutes. At three intervals, turn the tofu with a heatproof rubber spatula, being careful not to break the cubes, so all the surfaces become browned and crisp. Transfer from the oven and let cool.

While the tofu is baking, spread the almonds on a separate baking sheet and toast in the oven for 5 minutes. Transfer from the oven and set aside to cool. Blanch the snow peas in boiling water for 30 seconds and drain.

Combine all the dressing ingredients and toss gently with the tofu, snow peas, and almonds. Garnish with the scallions and serve at once, or chill for a couple of hours.

Variations: Asparagus, broccoli, green beans, or red and green bell peppers can be used in place of snow peas. Cut the vegetables into bite-sized pieces; you need approximately 2 cups. Blanch or steam until tender yet crisp.

❧ Serves 4 as an appetizer or 2 as a side dish

TOFU TRIO

1 16-ounce cake firm or extra firm tofu
1 1/2 tablespoons dark sesame oil
2 tablespoons soy sauce

1/3 cup whole almonds
2 cups snow peas

DRESSING

1 1/2 tablespoons vegetable oil
2 teaspoons dark sesame oil
2 tablespoons rice vinegar
2 teaspoons grated fresh gingerroot
1/2 teaspoon ground coriander seed
1 teaspoon honey or brown sugar
1/4 teaspoon salt

GARNISH

1/2 cup thinly sliced scallions

GRILLED VEGETABLES

Smoky flavored, crisp on the outside and juicy within, grilled vegetables are a highlight of summer meals. This is a treat that I've enjoyed at home, as Moosewood has no grill. Try roasting vegetables in the oven (see tip, page 222), regardless of the season, for a similar dish.

HERBED VINAIGRETTE MARINADE

1/4 cup vegetable oil

1/4 cup olive oil

1/4 cup balsamic vinegar

3 garlic cloves, minced or pressed

3 tablespoons chopped fresh herbs (choose a combination of 2 or 3: basil, tarragon, oregano, parsley, thyme, or rosemary)

🌿 Yields about 1 cup

SPICY CITRUS MARINADE

1/2 cup vegetable oil

Juice of 1 lime

Juice of 1/2 lemon

1 teaspoon chopped fresh cilantro

1 1/2 teaspoons grated fresh gingerroot

1 teaspoon minced fresh hot pepper, or 3 or 4 dashes of Tabasco sauce

🌿 Yields about 1 cup

Choose either marinade and combine all the ingredients in a small bowl. Cut the vegetables so that the pieces are large enough not to fall through the grill. Special grill baskets designed to hold smaller foods are helpful.

Marinate the following types of vegetables for 1 to 2 hours with either marinade before cooking:

Zucchini or summer squash. Cut diagonally across the length into 1/2-inch-thick slices.

Scallions. Peel the outer layer, cut off the roots, and leave whole.

Onions. Peel baby onions and leave whole. Slice larger, peeled onions from the top to bottom in 1/4-inch-thick slices, leaving some of the root end attached to keep slices intact.

Mushrooms. If larger than 3 inches across, slice into halves or thirds; otherwise leave whole.

The following vegetables will be soggy on the grill if marinated too long. For these, generously brush with marinade just 10 to 15 minutes before grilling:

Eggplant. Cut diagonally or lengthwise into 1/2-inch-thick slices. Thin Asian or "baby" eggplants can be cut in half lengthwise.

Green or firm red tomatoes. Cut into 1/2-inch-thick slices.

Sweet potatoes. Parboil until just tender; cut into 1-inch-thick slices.

Potatoes. Use whole new potatoes (about 1 to 2 inches in diameter) that have been parboiled until just tender.

Winter squash (smaller varieties such as acorn or delicata). Cut crosswise into 1-inch-thick slices and parboil until barely tender.

Greens. Individual leaves of kale, quarter heads of radicchio, or small fennel bulbs, whole or cut into 1/2-inch-thick slices.

Have platters of vegetables and tongs on a table close to the grill.

For a charcoal grill, the charcoal should be at the gray-ash stage for grilling. For a gas or charcoal grill, adjust the grill so the heat is in a medium range. You can test this by holding your hand at grill level: if you can wait 5 seconds before you must pull your hand away, it's just right.

Place sprigs of thyme, rosemary, savory, oregano, sage, or marjoram on top of the hot coals to add their smoky essence to the grilled food.

Most vegetables need 3 to 4 minutes per side. They should be just slightly blackened on the outside yet tender on the inside. Cooking times vary depending on the height of the grill and intensity of the fire.

Note: Vegetables will be crisper if salted *after* grilling.

🌿 Sauces, Butters, and Condiments

RED PEPPER SAUCE

A zesty sauce, featuring the smoky sweetness of roasted red peppers. It's a good companion with Crepes (page 250), pasta, or grilled or broiled fish. To roast the peppers, follow the method in North African Roasted Vegetable Salad (page 231).

$^1/_2$ cup dry red wine

$^1/_3$ cup chopped scallions, white part only

$^1/_4$ cup herb vinegar (tarragon, basil, dill) plus extra as needed

$^1/_2$ tomato, diced

4 red bell peppers, roasted

$^1/_3$ cup pine nuts or ground almonds

Salt and freshly ground black pepper

Simmer the wine, scallions, and $^1/_4$ cup of the herb vinegar in a nonreactive saucepan until the mixture is reduced by almost half, to about $^1/_2$ cup. Soften the diced tomatoes by simmering for a moment or two in the reduced sauce base. In a blender or food processor, purée the cooked ingredients with the roasted peppers and the nuts until smooth. Season to taste with salt and pepper, adding more herb vinegar if desired.

🦋 Yields 3 cups

SHALLOT-HERB BUTTER SAUCE

A creamy, tangy sauce that brightens steamed vegetables and grilled or broiled fish. It also makes a nice topping for Vegetable "Pasta" (page 245).

3 tablespoons finely chopped shallots

4 teaspoons herb or wine or fruit vinegar

3 tablespoons water

$^3/_4$ cup butter (1$^1/_2$ sticks), cut into $^1/_2$-inch pieces

1 teaspoon minced fresh tarragon ($^1/_2$ teaspoon dried)

1 tablespoon finely chopped fresh parsley

1 tablespoon finely chopped fresh chives or scallion greens

1 tablespoon fresh lemon juice

Salt and freshly ground black pepper

Combine the shallots, vinegar, and water in a small saucepan and simmer for about 10 minutes, until the volume is reduced by half and most of the liquid has evaporated.

Reduce the heat to very low and whisk in the butter, a few pieces at a time. The butter should soften but not separate. Low heat and continued whisking will result in a creamy, opaque sauce. Remove the pan from the heat when there are no butter lumps remaining; add the herbs, lemon juice, and salt and pepper to taste.

The sauce can be slowly reheated in a double boiler or on a flame tamer.

Variations: Instead of tarragon, try chervil, dill, basil, fennel, lemon balm, lemon basil, sorrel, thyme, or marjoram. Add a pinch of saffron or paprika for a golden hue and rich flavor.

🦋 Yields almost 1 cup

HERB VINEGARS AND HERB-INFUSED OILS

Herb vinegars and herb-infused oils offer cooks a convenient way to incorporate the rich essence of summer herbs all year round. Spiking a marinated vegetable salad in January with a splash of basil vinegar or rosemary oil adds a taste dimension that dried herbs can't achieve. Dressings, marinades, and mayonnaise prepared with herb vinegars are more deeply flavored. Add a splash to steamed vegetables, herb butters, soups, sauces, and stews. The sharp tanginess of herb vinegars also allows you to cook with less or no salt.

Vinegars Making homemade herb vinegar is a simple, rewarding task. Jars of vinegar make nice gifts from the garden.

First choose the appropriate vinegar for the herbs. I especially like the flavor of apple cider vinegar and white- and red-wine vinegars. Distilled white vinegar and rice vinegar are acceptable as well. Distilled white vinegar provides a clear, uncolored base for brightly colored herbs or flowers, such as purple basil leaves and the blooms of chives, nasturtiums, violets, roses, and carnations.

For the most intense flavor, pick herbs when the plants are beginning to bloom and the essential oils are at their highest concentration. Strip the leaves from the heavier stems. Remove and discard the bitter, green or white petal base from flower blossoms.

Stuff a clean glass jar with fresh, dry, clean herbs or flowers. Fill with vinegar. Cover and let sit in the sun, outdoors, or at the brightest window for 4 to 6 weeks. Residents of very hot and sunny climates (like the American Southwest) should place the vinegar in a partially shaded spot for a shorter time. Pour the steeped vinegar through a paper coffee filter into a nonreactive pot (stainless steel, enamel, or heatproof ceramic or glass) and discard the herbs or flowers; they've given their all. Gently heat until the vinegar just starts to simmer. Do not boil. Pour into hot, sterilized jars and cap to seal. Store in a dark place away from heat; it will keep for about a year.

Here are some favorite herb-vinegar combinations:

- Chervil, shallots, and white-wine vinegar
- Dill, chives, and apple cider vinegar

- Cilantro, chives, and rice vinegar
- Purple basil, garlic, and white vinegar
- Oregano or marjoram and red-wine vinegar
- Lavender buds and white vinegar
- Tarragon, shallots, and apple cider vinegar

Use one to two whole, peeled cloves of garlic, a few peppercorns, a small, whole, peeled shallot, or a fresh chile pepper for each pint of vinegar, if desired.

Infused oils Herb-infused oils have such a concentrated flavor, only a small amount is needed to enhance seasoning. At Moosewood, we use them for sautéing and in marinades, vinaigrette dressings, mayonnaise, sauces, and grain or bean salads, as well as tossed with pasta and drizzled directly on salads or cooked vegetables. When steaming, broiling, or grilling, just a bit of infused oil—as a marinade or final garnish—can impart a rich taste to low-fat meals.

Mild oils that do not compete with the herb flavors are best: canola, corn, light olive, safflower, or soy. For 1 cup of oil, use $1/2$ cup of chopped fresh herb. Let stand at room temperature for 4 to 5 days to infuse the oil with the herb's essence. The herbs will settle to the bottom. Carefully ladle or decant the clear oil into clean jars; discard the spent herbs. Tightly cap and store refrigerated for up to 6 months.

Basil, cilantro, dill, lemon balm, marjoram, mint, oregano, rosemary, sage, tarragon, and thyme have been our favorite fresh herbs to use.

🌿 Vinaigrette Dressings

Zesty vinaigrettes enliven salads. Be versatile and vary the types of oils and vinegars. Try an Herb Vinegar (page 260), red- or white-wine, rice, cider, and balsamic vinegars. Olive oil (extra virgin is rich and flavorful), peanut oil, soy oil, and corn oil are also recommended. Fresh or frozen herbs will yield superior dressings to dried.

Regardless of the recipe, the procedure for all vinaigrette dressings is the same. Combine the ingredients in a jar or bottle that can be tightly sealed. The dressing ingredients will separate on standing, so shake well before using.

Vinaigrettes will keep refrigerated for several weeks.

RASPBERRY VINAIGRETTE

$^1/_3$ cup raspberry vinegar

$^2/_3$ cup mild vegetable oil

2 teaspoons Dijon mustard

1 teaspoon fresh thyme ($^1/_2$ teaspoon dried)

1 teaspoon chopped fresh marjoram ($^1/_2$ teaspoon dried)

Salt and freshly ground black pepper to taste

We like to serve this dressing with a simple green salad featuring tender, buttery Boston lettuce. It is lightly fruity with a subtle raspberry flavor.

🌿 Yields 1 cup

BASIL-SHALLOT VINAIGRETTE

Wonderful on sliced ripe tomatoes.

🌿 Yields 1 1/4 cups

1/2 cup olive oil (all or part extra virgin)

1/4 cup fresh lemon juice

1/4 cup minced shallots or scallions

1/4 cup chopped fresh basil leaves (1 tablespoon dried)

Salt and freshly ground black pepper to taste

TARRAGON VINAIGRETTE

Good with mixed green salads or as a dressing for cooked vegetables.

🌿 Yields 1 cup

2/3 cup peanut oil

1/4 cup white wine vinegar

1 teaspoon dry mustard

1 tablespoon chopped fresh chives

1 garlic clove, minced or pressed

1 1/2 tablespoons chopped fresh tarragon

Salt and freshly ground black pepper to taste

DILL–RED ONION VINAIGRETTE

We especially like this as a marinade for potato and other cooked vegetable salads.

🌿 Yields 1 cup

1/2 cup vegetable oil

1/4 cup red wine vinegar

1/4 cup minced red onions

1 1/2 tablespoons chopped fresh dill

1 tablespoon chopped fresh parsley

1 teaspoon Dijon mustard

Salt and freshly ground black pepper to taste

🌿 Creamy Dressings

GOLDEN SESAME DRESSING

Carrots add a gentle sweetness to the rich, creamy tahini in this tangy dressing.

$^1/_2$ cup grated raw carrots

$^1/_4$ cup fresh lemon juice

2 tablespoons chopped scallions (white part only)

$^1/_3$ cup water

1 teaspoon Dijon mustard

$^1/_4$ teaspoon salt

$^1/_2$ cup tahini

Purée the carrots, lemon juice, scallions, water, mustard, and salt in a food processor or blender until smooth. Slowly add the tahini while continuing to blend. The dressing will thicken as it sits.

   Keeps refrigerated for up to 10 days.

🌿 Yields 1 $^2/_3$ cups

HERBED YOGURT

Tangy, flavorful, and low in fat, this sauce can be used as a dip or a dressing for greens, pasta, or cooked vegetable salads.

$^1/_2$ cup plain low-fat yogurt (we use an all-dairy, no-additive type)

2 tablespoons fresh lemon juice

3 tablespoons olive oil

1 teaspoon Dijon mustard

1 tablespoon chopped fresh parsley

1 tablespoon chopped fresh chervil or dill

2 teaspoons chopped fresh basil

Salt and freshly ground black pepper to taste

Combine all the ingredients in a small bowl and mix until smooth. Serve immediately or refrigerate, covered, until needed. Use within 1 week.

   Minted Cucumber-Yogurt Dip (page 275) makes a refreshing salad dressing as well.

   Thin Herbed Mayonnaise (page 266) with an equal volume of yogurt to make a rich, creamy dressing for cooked vegetables or leafy greens. Adjust seasonings if necessary.

🌿 Yields $^3/_4$ cup

CREAMY PARMESAN DRESSING

Good with all green salads, especially those with romaine lettuce, croutons, cucumbers, tomato wedges, and hard-boiled eggs.

Purée the Parmesan cheese, garlic, milk, and lemon juice or vinegar until smooth. Add the herbs and continue to blend, slowly drizzling in the oil.

Keeps refrigerated for up to 1 week. Reblend if separation occurs.

Note: Blanched garlic has a milder, nuttier flavor than raw. To blanch, drop the garlic cloves in boiling water for 1 minute. Drain and use. Raw garlic can be used for a more robust flavor.

❧ Yields 1 1/4 cups

1/2 cup freshly grated, good-quality Parmesan cheese

2 garlic cloves, blanched (see note) and minced or pressed

1/4 cup milk

2 tablespoons fresh lemon juice or white-wine vinegar or herb vinegar (page 260)

1 tablespoon chopped fresh parsley

1 tablespoon chopped fresh basil or oregano or marjoram (1 teaspoon dried)

1/2 cup vegetable oil (all or part olive)

Salt and freshly ground black pepper to taste

Herbed Mayonnaise and Mayonnaise Alternatives

Due to the increase in salmonella-related, foodborne diseases, it is wise to avoid using recipes that call for uncooked eggs. So here are some suggestions for enhancing store-bought mayonnaise, a recipe for a cooked egg mayonnaise, and a few eggless alternatives.

You can customize commercial mayonnaise with the addition of fresh herbs or herbal vinegars. To each cup of mayonnaise, add 2 to 3 tablespoons of chopped fresh herbs. Basil, chervil, chives, dill, nasturtium blossoms, sorrel, and tarragon are delicious alone or in various combinations. The addition of a tablespoon of curry powder or a pinch of saffron dissolved in a tablespoon of warm water to 1 cup of mayonnaise will add fragrance, warmth, and color.

For a Mediterranean-style aioli, add one to two cloves of pressed or minced raw garlic, 2 tablespoons of a fragrant extra virgin olive oil, and 1 teaspoon of Dijon mustard to each cup of mayonnaise.

COOKED MAYONNAISE

This rich dressing should satisfy the most ardent fans of homemade mayonnaise. The basic recipe may be "dressed up" using the preceding suggested enhancements for commercial mayonnaise.

4 egg yolks

1 tablespoon cornstarch

¹/₄ cup vegetable oil, all or part olive oil

2 tablespoons fresh lemon juice or herb vinegar (page 260)

¹/₂ cup hot water

¹/₂ teaspoon Dijon mustard

Salt and freshly ground black pepper to taste

Combine the egg yolks and cornstarch in a small saucepan. Slowly whisk in the oil, followed by the lemon juice and water. Cook over low heat, whisking constantly until the mixture thickens. Remove from the heat and add the mustard, salt and pepper, and any additional seasonings desired. Transfer the mayonnaise to a bowl. It will keep refrigerated for 3 to 4 days.

Yields 1 cup

TARATOUR

Laura Branca originated a version of this rich, creamy sauce at Moosewood Restaurant. We use it on vegetables, baked fish, in pita sandwiches, or as a dip.

Combine the almonds, bread crumbs, lemon juice, mustard, garlic, olive oil, and 1/2 cup of the water in a food processor or blender. (If using a blender, coarsely chop the almonds before blending.) Process until smooth. Add the parsley and the remaining 1/2 cup of water. Blend until smooth. Add salt and pepper to taste and stir in the herbs. Serve immediately, or store covered in the refrigerator for up to 1 week.

Note: To toast almonds, bake in a 350°F oven for 5 minutes.

🌿 Yields 2 cups

- 3/4 cup lightly toasted almonds (see note)
- 1 cup fine French or Italian bread crumbs
- 3 tablespoons fresh lemon juice
- 1/2 teaspoon Dijon mustard
- 2 garlic cloves, minced or pressed
- 1/2 cup olive oil
- 1 cup water
- 2 tablespoons chopped fresh parsley
- Salt and freshly ground black pepper
- 2 tablespoons chopped fresh chervil, chives, dill, fennel, marjoram, or mint

ROUILLE

Traditionally used as a spicy garnish for the Provençal seafood stew bouillabaisse, rouille makes a zesty dressing or dip for steamed vegetables, grilled or poached fish, hard-boiled eggs, and potato and other cooked-vegetable salads.

Briefly soak the bread crumbs in water to cover, then drain and squeeze dry. In a blender or food processor, purée with the pimentos, garlic, water, and oil. Stir in the parsley and seasonings to taste. Serve immediately, or store covered in the refrigerator for up to 1 week.

🌿 Yields 2 cups

- 1/2 cup French or Italian bread crumbs
- 2/3 cup chopped pimientos
- 2 garlic cloves, minced or pressed
- 1/2 cup water or vegetable stock
- 3/4 cup olive oil
- 1 tablespoon chopped fresh parsley
- A few drops of Tabasco sauce
- Salt and freshly ground black pepper

Herbed Pestos

In Italian, the word *pesto* means "pounded," a reference to the pre–food processor method of making pesto with a mortar and pestle. Pesto Genovese, the classic basil preparation, is the most well-known pesto but not the only one. The following recipes share Pesto Genovese's rich, concentrated quality but use different herbs, nuts, and seasonings. Many of our Moosewood cookbooks offer other pesto ideas and recipes.

These highly flavored mixtures should be served in moderation (just a spoonful or two for each bowl of pasta) to complement, not overwhelm, the foods they accompany.

All pestos are made in the same way: Place all the ingredients, except the oil, in a food processor or blender. Mix until everything is well chopped, and then slowly add the oil in a thin stream to form a fairly smooth paste. If you're using a blender, it may be necessary to prechop the herbs and nuts by hand.

Pesto will keep refrigerated for a couple of weeks. Keep in an airtight container and cover with a thin layer of oil, if desired, to prevent discoloration. When fresh herbs are plentiful, make extra batches of pesto and freeze in small jars.

PESTO GENOVESE

3 cups loosely packed fresh basil leaves

¹/₃ cup pine nuts

¹/₂ cup freshly grated Parmesan cheese

3 garlic cloves, coarsely chopped

¹/₂ cup olive oil

Salt and freshly ground black pepper to taste

We toss this pesto with pasta and top with additional Parmesan cheese and chopped fresh tomatoes. It's a wonderful enrichment as a final garnish for soups and added to cheese fillings for lasagna or stuffed vegetables. Fill mushroom caps with pesto and toasted bread crumbs, then briefly bake for a savory hors d'oeuvre. Top grilled or broiled fish with a dollop of pesto.

Yields 2 cups

CILANTRO PESTO

A spicy and tangy pesto that we serve in dollops to top beans, enchiladas, burritos, tostadas, huevos rancheros, and baked or grilled fish. It makes a zesty dip when added to avocados mashed with a squeeze of lemon juice. Use ²/₃ cup cilantro pesto for three small avocados.

🌿 Yields I cup

1 cup loosely packed fresh cilantro leaves

1 cup loosely packed fresh parsley leaves

¹/₃ cup whole almonds

1 small fresh chile (jalapeños are good), coarsely chopped

2 garlic cloves, coarsely chopped

2 tablespoons fresh lime juice

¹/₄ cup vegetable oil

Salt and freshly ground black pepper to taste

DILL PESTO

A rich, mellow blend that is nice by the spoonful to garnish potato or cucumber soups. We use it as a filling for rolled-thin fish fillets. Spread on crackers, canapés, or rye bread for sandwiches. Add it to mayonnaise-dressed salads for additional flavor.

🌿 Yields I cup

1 cup loosely packed fresh dill leaves

¹/₂ cup coarsely chopped fresh chives

¹/₂ cup grated sharp Cheddar cheese

¹/₂ cup coarsely chopped walnuts

¹/₄ cup vegetable oil

Salt and freshly ground black pepper to taste

TARRAGON PESTO

1 cup loosely packed fresh parsley
leaves

1/2 cup loosely packed fresh tarragon
leaves

1/4 cup coarsely chopped scallions or
3 tablespoons chopped shallots

1/3 cup pine nuts

1/2 cup freshly grated Parmesan cheese

1 1/2 teaspoons fresh lemon juice

1/4 cup vegetable oil

Salt and freshly ground black pepper
to taste

This pesto has the full, aromatic flavor of tarragon. I like to serve this at home, on grilled fish steaks. Toss a few tablespoons with steamed vegetables or a grain pilaf, or use as a garnish for a light tomato soup. Add a little to a cream or cheese sauce.

🌿 Yields 1 cup

HAZELNUT PESTO

Lemon and hazelnuts are wonderfully fragrant and combine here in a rich, yet delicate pesto. For an elegant side dish, toss with a small-shaped pasta or steamed vegetables. Use as a spread for fresh biscuits, rolls, or French bread.

1 1/2 cups loosely packed fresh parsley
leaves

1/2 cup loosely packed fresh chervil
leaves (if unavailable, use more
parsley)

1 tablespoon fresh lemon-thyme leaves

1/2 cup toasted, skinned hazelnuts (see
note)

1 tablespoon fresh lemon juice

1/2 teaspoon grated lemon peel

1/4 cup vegetable oil

Salt and freshly ground black pepper
taste

Note: Hazelnuts have a finer flavor if skinned. Bake on a cookie sheet at 325°F for 10 minutes. Cool for a few minutes, then rub with a small towel to remove most of the loosened skins.

🌿 Yields 1 cup

Herb Butters

Butter that is used as a spread, as an enrichment, or for sautéing can be easily enhanced with fresh herbs.

Toss toasted bread cubes with herb butter for savory croutons. Bread crumbs toasted in herb butter make a superb topping for steamed vegetables, casseroles, and simple pasta with grated Parmesan cheese.

Herb butter can be prepared in the summer and kept frozen in small packages for winter use. It will keep refrigerated for up to 1 month, and frozen for up to 6 months.

Herb-Infused Oils (page 260) provide a good alternative for people who are avoiding butter in their diets.

Use softened butter for ease of preparation. Cream in the remaining ingredients. For full flavor, before serving let the butter sit for at least an hour for the herbs to impart their essence.

TARRAGON-DIJON BUTTER

Dijon and lemon provide a sharpness that nicely accents mildly flavored foods.

$^1/_4$ **pound (1 stick) softened butter**

1 tablespoon finely chopped fresh tarragon

1 tablespoon finely chopped fresh parsley

2 teaspoons fresh lemon juice

1 teaspoon Dijon mustard

DILL-CHIVE BUTTER

1/4 pound (1 stick) softened butter

2 tablespoons finely chopped fresh dill

1 tablespoon finely chopped fresh chives

1 teaspoon prepared horseradish

We like to toss new potatoes with this herb butter. It's also good with steamed vegetables from the cabbage family: broccoli, brussels sprouts, cauliflower, cabbage, and kohlrabi.

BASIL-GARLIC BUTTER

1/4 pound (1 stick) softened butter

2 tablespoons finely chopped fresh basil

1 teaspoon finely chopped fresh oregano

1/4 teaspoon finely chopped fresh thyme

1 large garlic clove, minced or pressed

A robust butter for garlic bread, croutons, or steamed zucchini, or simply toss with egg noodles.

FINES HERBES BUTTER

1/4 pound (1 stick) softened butter

2 teaspoons each: finely chopped fresh chives, parsley, tarragon, and chervil

A classic combination used in French cuisine. Toss with steamed vegetables or use to top broiled or baked fish.

MINT BUTTER

Try this delicately fragrant herb butter with breakfast breads, muffins, and peas or carrots.

- ¼ pound (1 stick) softened butter
- 2 tablespoons finely chopped fresh spearmint
- 1 tablespoon finely chopped fresh fennel leaf
- 1 tablespoon finely chopped fresh parsley
- ½ teaspoon finely chopped fresh thyme or lemon thyme
- 1 teaspoon fresh lemon juice

SAGE BUTTER

This hearty blend goes well with bread cubes for stuffings or croutons, baked winter squash, bean and potato dishes, cornbread, and crusty loaves.

- ¼ pound (1 stick) softened butter
- 2 tablespoons finely chopped fresh sage
- 1 teaspoon finely chopped fresh marjoram
- 1 teaspoon finely chopped fresh thyme

 # Dips

Toss out that tired onion soup mix! Fresh herbs make perky, easily prepared, delicious dips. Use raw vegetables, crackers, chips, and toasted pita bread wedges for dipping.

CLASSIC CHIP DIP

Cool and tangy, yogurt makes this a lighter dip than those made entirely of sour cream.

1 cup sour cream

1 cup plain yogurt

3 tablespoons chopped fresh parsley

$^1/_3$ cup chopped scallions or fresh chives

2 teaspoons prepared horseradish (optional)

Salt and freshly ground black pepper to taste

Combine all the ingredients. Vary this classic by substituting some of the herb combinations listed for the dill and parsley in the Herbed Cheese Spreads (page 276). Keeps refrigerated for at least 1 week.

🌿 Yields about 2 $^1/_2$ cups

MISO-TAHINI DIP

Rich and savory, this dip also makes a good spread for rice cakes and can be added to stir-fried dishes to enrich the sauce.

3 tablespoons white or rice miso

$^3/_4$ cup cool water

$^3/_4$ cup tahini

1 teaspoon finely grated fresh ginger root

2 tablespoons chopped scallions

Mix the miso and water until smooth. Add the tahini and mix until smooth. (It should have the consistency of sour cream; add 1 or 2 additional tablespoons of water, if necessary.) Add the ginger and scallions. Will keep refrigerated for several weeks.

🌿 Yields about 1 $^3/_4$ cups

DIP OR SAUCE FOR FRESH FRUIT

This can be used as a topping for pancakes, French toast, and fruit-filled crepes (page 250).

Combine all the ingredients. Will keep refrigerated for at least 1 week.

🦋 Yields almost 2 cups

- ³/₄ cup sour cream
- ³/₄ cup plain yogurt
- 2 tablespoons chopped fresh lemon balm
- 1 tablespoon chopped fresh mint
- 2 tablespoons honey or maple syrup or brown sugar
- ¹/₂ teaspoon ground cinnamon
- Pinch of freshly grated nutmeg

MINTED CUCUMBER-YOGURT DIP

This refreshing dip could also double as a low-calorie salad dressing if you use low-fat yogurt. Use less lemon juice to reduce the tartness.

Combine all the ingredients. Allow the flavors to meld for at least 30 minutes before serving. Will keep refrigerated for up to 4 days.

🦋 Yields about 2 cups

- 1 cup plain yogurt
- ¹/₂ cucumber, peeled, seeded, and grated (about ¹/₂ cup)
- 2 tablespoons fresh lemon juice
- 1 tablespoon olive oil
- 1¹/₂ tablespoons chopped fresh mint
- 1 tablespoon chopped fresh cilantro
- 2 tablespoons chopped fresh chives or scallions
- Salt and freshly ground black pepper to taste

Herbed Cheese Spreads

Cheese spreads are familiar as appetizers with bread or crackers. Try these assorted lively spreads as fillings for sandwiches, omelets, crepes, or stuffed vegetables.

There are countless possible combinations of herbs; here are a few that we think work well: dill and chervil; basil and tarragon; mint and chives; thyme and lemon basil; cilantro and chiles; rosemary and shallots; marjoram and sage; summer savory and chives; and fennel leaf and parsley. Use small quantities of stronger herbs, such as cilantro, rosemary, sage, and thyme.

BASIC CHEESE SPREAD

- 1 1/2 cups grated firm cheese (Cheddar, Monterey Jack, Swiss, Jarlsberg, Gouda)
- 2/3 cup cream cheese or Neufchâtel or cottage cheese
- 1/4 cup or less chopped fresh herbs
- 2 to 3 tablespoons additional seasonings: chopped scallions, chiles or roasted red peppers, toasted nuts, roasted garlic, or edible flower blossoms

Allow the grated cheese to soften at room temperature or briefly microwave for easier mixing. Use a food processor or handheld mixer to whip the cheeses together until smooth and well blended. Add the remaining ingredients.

Yields about 2 1/2 cups

SPICY MONTEREY JACK SPREAD

- 1 1/2 cups grated Monterey Jack cheese
- 2/3 cup cottage cheese or cream cheese
- 2 tablespoons chopped fresh chiles
- 1 tablespoon chopped fresh cilantro
- 1 tablespoon chopped fresh parsley
- 1/2 teaspoon ground coriander seeds

Proceed as for Basic Cheese Spread (above).

Yields about 2 cups

HERBED CHÈVRE SPREAD

Cream the chèvre and ricotta until light and fluffy. Add the remaining ingredients. If the chèvre or feta is particularly salty, increase the quantity of ricotta.

Variations: Try some of the herb combinations listed on page 276.

🌿 Yields about 2 1/2 cups

1 1/4 cups fresh chèvre (mild goat cheese) or feta cheese

1/2 cup low-fat ricotta cheese

1/4 cup chopped fresh parsley

2 tablespoons chopped fresh basil

2 tablespoons chopped fresh tarragon

2 garlic cloves, minced or pressed

1/4 cup ground toasted nuts (optional)

Freshly ground black pepper to taste

BLUE CHEESE SPREAD

Reserve 1/4 cup of the crumbled blue cheese. Combine all the other ingredients and cream until well blended. Gently stir in the reserved blue cheese.

🌿 Yields about 2 1/4 cups

1 cup crumbled blue cheese

1 cup sour cream

2 garlic cloves, minced or pressed

2 tablespoons chopped fresh parsley

2 tablespoons chopped fresh dill (1 tablespoon dried)

1 tablespoon chopped fresh marjoram (1 teaspoon dried)

CHEDDAR-SAGE-THYME SPREAD

Combine all the ingredients until well blended.

🌿 Yields about 2 1/4 cups

1 1/2 cups grated sharp Cheddar, softened

2/3 cup cottage cheeseor cream cheese

2 teaspoons chopped fresh sage (1 teaspoon dried)

1 teaspoon fresh thyme leaves (1/2 teaspoon dried)

2 tablespoons chopped pimiento

 # Desserts

FRESH RASPBERRY SORBET

A very quick, vividly colored, and irresistible dessert with pronounced fruit flavor. It requires no special equipment and little or no sweetener besides fruit and fruit concentrates; use the larger amount of sugar if the berries are very tart.

About 2 cups fresh raspberries, or 1 (12-ounce) package of frozen

$^1/_3$ cup unsweetened frozen juice concentrate (I used a ready-made blend of cherry, grape, and apple)

1 to 2 tablespoons sugar

1 teaspoon rose water (optional)

1 tablespoon Amaretto or Cointreau liqueur (optional)

Pale rose petals, for garnish

Freeze the fresh berries in a tray until hard. Place the frozen berries in a blender or food processor with the other ingredients. Blend until smooth but not soupy. Serve immediately, garnished with pale rose petals. Any leftover thawed sorbet can be used as a dessert sauce or ice cream topping.

Variation: Strawberries can be substituted for the raspberries. Slice the berries into halves or thirds before freezing.

🌿 Serves 4 (small servings)

PUMPKIN CAKE

Pumpkin and honey have an affinity; the flavors harmonize without overwhelming each other. Use either the small pumpkins specifically noted as "pie pumpkins" or winter squash; either will make a moist, rich cake.

Preheat the oven to 325°F. Lightly oil three 9-inch cake pans.

Cream together the honey, eggs, oil, and pumpkin. In a separate bowl, sift together the dry ingredients and then add to the wet mixture, stirring until smooth. Fold in the nuts. Pour the batter into the prepared cake pans. Bake for 25 to 30 minutes, until the edges pull slightly away from the pan and the top springs back when pressed. Cool the layers on wire racks.

Whip the softened cream cheese with the maple syrup until light and fluffy. When the cake has cooled, spread the frosting between the layers and on the top and sides.

🍂 Yields one 9-inch triple-layer cake

CAKE

1¼ cups honey

4 eggs

1 cup mild vegetable oil

2 cups mashed cooked pumpkin (1 16-ounce can of plain pumpkin—not canned pie filling) or winter squash

2½ cups unbleached white flour (up to 1 cup can be whole wheat pastry flour)

1½ teaspoons baking soda

1½ teaspoons baking powder

1 teaspoon salt

2 teaspoons ground cinnamon

½ teaspoon ground nutmeg

1 cup chopped walnuts

FROSTING

8 ounces softened cream cheese

¼ cup pure maple syrup

BLUEBERRY-LEMON TART

Uncooked berries in the filling and a creamy, fragrant lemon custard topping make this tart the very essence of freshness.

BLUEBERRY FILLING

4 cups fresh blueberries

$1/3$ to $1/2$ cup sugar (depending on the tartness of the berries and your sweet tooth), sifted with 2 tablespoons cornstarch

LEMON CUSTARD

2 egg yolks, lightly beaten

$1/4$ cup plus 1 tablespoon sugar

$2^1/2$ tablespoons unbleached white flour

1 cup milk

2 teaspoons fresh lemon juice

1 teaspoon grated lemon peel

9-INCH PIE SHELL

$1^1/2$ cups unbleached white flour

3 tablespoons sugar

$1/2$ cup butter

2 egg yolks

$1/2$ teaspoon pure vanilla extract

2 tablespoons cold water

To make the blueberry filling, place 2 cups of the berries in a saucepan on medium heat. Set aside the remaining 2 cups of berries. With the back of a spoon, smash a few of the berries, and after a couple of minutes add the sugar-cornstarch mixture. Cook, stirring, for 1 to 2 minutes, until the mixture bubbles and simmers. Remove from the heat and chill for at least 2 hours.

To make the custard, combine the egg yolks, sugar, and flour in a saucepan, stirring to blend. Slowly whisk in the milk. Simmer on low heat or in a double boiler, stirring until the sauce thickens. It will be ready when it just begins to bubble; do not let it boil vigorously. Remove from the heat and whisk in the lemon juice and zest. Chill, covered, for at least 2 hours.

To make the pie shell, preheat the oven to 400°F. Combine the flour and sugar. Using a pastry blender, a food processor, or two knives, cut in the butter until the mixture resembles coarse meal (with pieces of butter no larger than baby peas). Stir in the egg yolks, vanilla, and water. Either roll out the dough or pat it into a pie plate. Prick the dough with fork tines, and bake for 10 minutes or until lightly browned. Cool on a rack before filling.

To assemble the tart, fold the 2 cups of uncooked blueberries into the chilled berry mixture. Pour into the cooled pie shell and serve right away or refrigerate. Top each serving with chilled lemon custard and an edible flower garnish.

🌿 Yields one 9-inch tart

PEPPERMINT BUTTER WAFERS

We like to serve these crisp, delicate wafers with tea or ice cream, or as a refreshing after-dinner mint. We've found that double-layered, insulated cookie sheets are good for avoiding unevenly baked or burnt cookies.

Cream the butter with the fresh mint, then let stand at room temperature for an hour to suffuse the butter with mint flavor.

Preheat the oven to 375°F. Cream the sugar into the butter and mint. Add the beaten egg and mix until well blended. Add the salt and flour, and mix just until the batter is smooth.

Drop teaspoonfuls of the batter onto a lightly oiled cookie sheet, 2 inches apart. The batter will spread and flatten as it bakes. Bake for 10 to 15 minutes in the center of the oven, until the wafers are light brown at the edge. Let cool on the sheet for 5 minutes, then transfer to a wire rack.

If desired, place a small piece of semi-sweet chocolate in the center of each cookie before baking for a classic mint-chocolate combination.

❧ Yields about 2 dozen cookies

1/2 cup sweet (unsalted) butter
1/4 cup finely chopped fresh peppermint leaves
1/2 cup sugar
1 egg, lightly beaten
Pinch of salt
3/4 cup unbleached white or whole wheat pastry flour

All Fruit Preserves or Jams

Naturally sweet preserves can be made using fresh fruit and fruit juice concentrates. White grape, apple, and cherry concentrates are versatile and blend well with other fruits. This recipe can be halved, doubled, or tripled.

1 quart fresh ripe fruit (strawberries, raspberries, blueberries, black-berries, peaches, apricots, sweet cherries, grapes, or plums)

1 cup unsweetened frozen juice concentrate (undiluted)

1 cup low-methoxyl pectin solution (see note 1)

4 teaspoons calcium solution (see note 2)

Honey, sugar, or fresh lemon juice to taste

Cut, peel, and pit the fruit as needed to make 4 cups of prepared fruit. Gently heat the fruit and juice concentrate. Add the pectin solution and stir to dissolve. When the mixture is near boiling, mix in the calcium solution. Add either honey, sugar, or 1 to 2 teaspoons of lemon juice to taste. Bring to a boil, pour into canning jars, and process for 10 minutes in a boiling water bath, or allow to cool and then freeze.

Serve as a spread, or add to cakes, crepes, or other dessert fillings.

Note 1: Low-methoxyl pectin is the only type that will gel with little or no sugar. Pomona's Universal Pectin is one widely available brand. Prepare the solution by placing 1 quart of very hot tap water in the blender. Turn it to low speed and add 4 tablespoons of pectin all at once. Whirl at high speed for several minutes to dissolve all the pectin. The mixture will thicken, then gel more upon cooling. It can be kept refrigerated for several weeks.

Note 2: Calcium phosphate comes in a small packet with the low-methoxyl pectin. It allows the pectin to gel without the sugar or acid used in standard jams. Add $\frac{1}{8}$ teaspoon calcium phosphate to $\frac{1}{4}$ cup water and stir well to make a calcium solution. Stir again vigorously when ready to use.

❦ Yields 1 $\frac{1}{2}$ quarts

Herbal Tea Mixes

We serve herbal teas for their taste and ability to soothe (like chamomile) or stimulate (like peppermint). The mints are our most popular teas.

Gardeners can expand their tea repertoire to reflect the full range of aromatic flavors in the kitchen garden: basil, bee balm, borage, chamomile, fennel, garden sage, lavender, lemon balm, lemon basil, lemon thyme, rose hips, rosemary, various mints.

Spices and herbs from tropical or frost-free areas give additional possibilities: cardamom, cinnamon, citrus peel, cloves, gingerroot, jasmine flowers, lemongrass, lemon verbena.

When making tea with garden-grown herbs, use the fresh or dried leaf. The exceptions are chamomile and lavender (bud and flower), fennel (seed), and rose hip (fruit). Generally, 1 heaping tablespoon of dried herbs (or 2 of fresh) is sufficient for each generous cup or mug of boiling water.

Selections from either or both of the above lists combine to create the following tea blends that are good either hot or iced. These proportions are for dried herbs and spices.

- 1 cup apple mint, $^1/_2$ cup rose hips, 1 tablespoon orange peel, 1 teaspoon ground cinnamon
- 1 cup lemon basil, 2 tablespoons lemon thyme, 1 cup lemon verbena
- $^1/_2$ cup chamomile, $^1/_2$ cup peppermint, $^1/_2$ cup lemon verbena
- 1 cup spearmint, $^1/_4$ cup garden sage, $^1/_2$ cup lemon balm
- 1 cup bergamot mint, 1 tablespoon ground fennel, 1 tablespoon ground ginger
- 1 cup peppermint, 1 cup lemongrass, $^1/_2$ cup rose hips

Be energy efficient! Make sun teas by placing herbs and cool water in a covered glass jar for a few hours in a sunny spot.

Note: NEVER make tea from any plant that you cannot identify with certainty as being one of the above.

Resources

BLUESTONE PERENNIALS
223 Middle Ridge Road
Madison, OH 44057
www.bluestoneperennials.com
Reasonably priced, young, flowering perennial and herb plants sold in packs of three or more. Catalog free.

W. ATLEE BURPEE CO.
300 Park Avenue
Warminster, PA 18974
www.burpee.com
Venerable catalog featuring flower, vegetable, and herb seeds, plus nursery stock, supplies, and beneficial insects. Many new introductions. Catalog free.

COMPANION PLANTS
7247 North Coolville Ridge Road
Athens, OH 45701
www.companionplants.com
Listings of more than five hundred potted herb plants.

THE COOK'S GARDEN
P.O. Box 5030
Warminster, PA 18974
www.cooksgarden.com
Excellent selection of culinary vegetable and herb seeds, with a particularly wide array of lettuces and other salad greens.

FEDCO SEEDS
P.O. Box 520
Waterville, ME 04903
www.fedcoseeds.com
A cooperative offering seeds for vegetables, flowers, and herbs that do well in cool climates. Groups are encouraged for the best discounts, but seeds are quite inexpensive for individual orders as well. Excellent, extensive selection, informative reading.

GARDENER'S SUPPLY
128 Intervale Road
Burlington, VT 05401
www.gardeners.com
Tools, garden supplies, season extenders, beneficial insects, organic fertilizers, furniture, and more.

GARDENS ALIVE!
Highway 48
P.O. Box 149
Sunman, IN 47041
www.gardensalive.com
Biological and botanical pest controls, beneficial insects, organic fertilizers, and garden supplies. Discount for members.

HARRIS SEEDS
355 Paul Road
P.O. Box 24966
Rochester, NY 14624
www.harrisseeds.com
Large selection of vegetable, flower, and herb seeds. Many varieties specifically bred for good results in the Northeast and Midwest.

EVERGREEN Y.H. ENTERPRISES
Box 17538
Anaheim, CA 92817
www.evergreenseeds.com
Over 250 varieties of Asian vegetables as well as books on gardening and cooking.

J. L. HUDSON, SEEDSMAN
Star Route 2 Box 377
La Honda, CA 94020
www.jlhudsonseeds.net
Features seeds from open-pollinated edibles and ornamentals. Their stock is from all over the planet, with American Indian, Australian, and African ethnobotany. Includes some rare and endangered species.

JOHNNY'S SELECTED SEEDS
955 Benton Avenue
Winslow, ME 04901
www.johnnyseeds.com
An excellent source of vegetable, herb, and flower seeds. Many new introductions are bred at Johnny's, but their selection of heirlooms is very good as well. Helpful catalog with good cultural information, garden supplies, and soil test kits.

J. E. MILLER NURSERIES
5060 West Lake Road
Canandaigua, NY 14424
www.millernurseries.com
Large selection of fruit and nut trees, ornamentals, and berry plants.

LEE VALLEY TOOLS, LTD.
Box 1780
Ogdensburg, NY 13369
www.leevalley.com
Season extenders, quality tools, books, and much more.

LOGEE'S GREENHOUSES
141 North Street
Danielson, CT 06239
www.logees.com
Potted herb plants and a vast array of ornamentals for indoor culture.

NICHOLS GARDEN NURSERY
1190 North Pacific Highway
Albany, OR 97321
www.nicholsgardennursery.com
Seeds for vegetables and flowers; many potato and garlic varieties. Plants and seeds of many herbs.

PARK SEED CO.
1 Parkton Avenue
Greenwood, SC 29647
www.parkseed.com
Seeds for vegetables and flowers plus nursery stock. Good selection for southern gardeners.

PINETREE GARDEN SEEDS
Box 300 Route 100
New Gloucester, ME 04260
www.superseeds.com
Reasonably priced seeds for vegetables, flowers, and herbs available in small quantities. Garden supplies, tubers, and plants as well.

RAINTREE NURSERY
391 Butts Road
Morton, WA 98356
www.raintreenursery.com
Disease-resistant fruit and nut trees plus unusual landscape edibles for organic growers.

REDWOOD CITY SEED CO.
P.O. Box 361
Redwood City, CA 94064
www.batnet.com/rwc-seed/index.html
Good selection of Native American corn, beans, and peppers as well as vegetables and herbs.

RICHTERS HERB SPECIALISTS
Goodwood, Ontario
Canada L0C 1A0
www.richters.com
Impressive collection of herb plants and seeds for all uses, from around the world, dried herbs and herb products as well.

SEEDS OF CHANGE
P.O. Box 15700
Santa Fe, NM 87592
www.seedsofchange.com
Specializing in organically grown, open-pollinated seeds as well as garden supplies, books, and tools. Many varieties suitable for the Southwest.

SEED SAVERS EXCHANGE
3094 North Winn Road
Decorah, IA 52101
www.seedsavers.org
Nonprofit seed exchange network of thousands of heirloom varieties of vegetables, fruits, herbs, and flowers—many not commercially available. An important international organization for promoting and conserving the genetic diversity of the world's food crops.

SOUTHERN EXPOSURE SEED EXCHANGE
P.O. Box 460
Mineral, VA 23117
www.southernexposure.com
Open-pollinated and heirloom varieties as well as newer high performers adapted to the mid-Atlantic region.

STOKES SEEDS
P.O. Box 548
Buffalo, NY 14240
www.stokeseeds.com
Wide assortment of vegetable, flower, and herb seeds for commercial and home growers. In-house varieties and generous cultural information are featured in their printed catalog.

TERRITORIAL SEED CO.
P.O. Box 157
Cottage Grove, OR 97424
www.territorial-seed.com
Flower, herb, and vegetable seeds for all regions, with many well suited to the maritime Pacific Northwest. Catalog free.

TOTALLY TOMATOES
334 West Stroud Street
Randolph, WI 53956
www.totallytomatoes.com
Vast array of tomatoes (what else?) in seed or plant form. Peppers too.

WELL-SWEEP HERB FARM
317 Mt. Bethel Road
Port Murray, NJ 07865
www.wellsweep.com
Large selection of potted herb plants, catalogued according to use and hardiness.

WHITE FLOWER FARM
P.O. Box 50 Route 63
Litchfield, CT 06759
www.whiteflowerfarm.com
Informative catalog lists many perennials, herbs, shrubs, and vines.

WOOD PRAIRIE FARM
49 Kinney Road
Bridgewater, ME 04735
www.woodprairie.com
Organically grown seed potatoes and other vegetables.

Bibliography

GENERAL GARDENING BOOKS

Brookes, John. *The Garden Book*. New York: Crown, 1984. Comprehensive, detailed information on garden design.

Bubel, Nancy. *The Seed Starter's Handbook*. Emmaus, Pennsylvania: Rodale Press, 1988. How to start a wide variety of plants from seed.

Creasy, Rosalind. *The Complete Book of Edible Landscaping*. San Francisco: Sierra Club Books, 1982. An excellent source of information on the design and selection of landscape material. Includes information on vegetable, herb, and fruit growing.

Druse, Ken. *The Natural Garden*. New York: Clarkson N. Potter, 1989. Text with beautiful photographs to illustrate gardens that work with the natural assets of a site.

Kourik, Robert. *Designing and Maintaining Your Edible Landscape Naturally*. Santa Rosa, California: Metamorphic Press, 1986. Techniques and detailed information on all aspects of gardening.

Lima, Patrick. *The Harrowsmith Perennial Garden*. Camden East, Ontario: Camden House, 1987. Informative text and attractive photos of perennial flowers.

Sheldon, Elisabeth. *A Proper Garden*. Harrisburg, Pennsylvania: Stackpole Books, 1989. Delightfully written, well-informed text on perennial flowers.

Smith, Miranda and Anna Carr. *Rodale's Garden Insect, Disease and Weed Identification Guide*. Emmaus, Pennsylvania: Rodale Press, 1988. Comprehensive book on plant protection.

Thompson, Sylvia. *The Kitchen Garden*. New York: Bantam Books, 1995. Wonderfully personal, passionately related, thorough text on kitchen gardens.

HERBS

Adams, James. *Landscaping with Herbs*. Portland, Oregon: Timber Press, 1987. Detailed information on common and unusual herbs.

Gladstar, Rosemary. *Family Herbal*. N. Adams, Massachusetts: Storey Books, 2001. Guide to using medicinal herbs by a well-respected herbalist.

Kowalchik, Claire and William Hylton, editors. *Rodale's Illustrated Encyclopedia of Herbs*. Emmaus, Pennsylvania: Rodale Press, 1987. Thorough discussion of the history, use, and cultivation of over 150 herbs.

Lima, Patrick. *The Harrowsmith Illustrated Book of Herbs*. Camden East, Ontario: Camden House, 1986. Herb lore, usage, and garden information.

Tolley, Emilie and Chris Mead. *Herbs: Gardens, Decorations and Recipes*. New York: Clarkson N. Potter, 1985. Beautifully photographed.

VEGETABLES

Ball, Jeff. *Jeff Ball's 60 Minute Garden*. Emmaus, Pennsylvania: Rodale Press, 1985. Good source book for beginning gardeners. It includes an efficient system for building raised beds, trellises, and growing tunnels.

_____ *Rodale's Garden Problem Solver*. Emmaus, Pennsylvania: Rodale Press, 1988. Environment-friendly controls for vegetable, herb, and fruit growing.

Bradley, Fern and Barbara Ellis. *Rodale's All-New Encyclopedia of Organic Gardening*. Emmaus, Pennsylvania: Rodale Press, 2002. A classic compendium, updated and filled with a wealth of knowledge.

Coleman, Eliot. *The New Organic Grower*. Colchester, Vermont: Chelsea Green, 1996. Techniques for every step of gardening. An excellent, thorough guide for market and home gardeners.

Coleman, Eliot. *Four Season Harvest*. Colchester, Vermont: Chelsea Green, 1992. How to extend the season for gardeners in cold climates.

Jeavons, John. *How to Grow More Vegetables*. Berkeley, California: Ten Speed Press, 1995. Extensive guide to the Biodynamic/French Intensive method of vegetable growing, a technique that achieves maximum yields from minimum space.

Ogden, Shepherd. *Step by Step Organic Vegetable Gardening*. New York: Harper Collins, 1992. Good information from the founder of The Cook's Garden seed company.

Riotte, Louise. *Carrots Love Tomatoes: Secrets of Companion Planting*. Pownal, Vermont: Garden Way, 1986. Nicely written, helpful guide to companion planting.

Weaver, William Woys. *Heirloom Vegetable Gardening*. New York: Henry Holt, 1997. An encyclopedic guide to 280 varieties of treasured heirlooms.

GARDEN TO KITCHEN

Cheney, Susan Jane. *Breadtime*. Berkeley, California: Ten Speed Press, 1998. Comprehensive guide to making bread includes accompaniments to create delightful meals.

Creasy, Rosalind. *Cooking from the Garden*. San Francisco: Sierra Club Books, 1988. Thorough compendium of information, including discussions with renowned cooks and gardeners.

Greene, Janet, Ruth Hertzberg, and Beatrice Vaughan. *Putting Food By*. New York: Plume Books, 1992. Helpful guide to preserving, canning, freezing, and storing garden produce.

Hayes, Joanne Lamb and Lori Stein. *Recipes from America's Small Farms*. New York: Villard Books, 2003. Members and fans of Community Supported Agriculture have contributed recipes that feature fresh produce.

Merrill, Richard and Joe Ortiz. *The Gardener's Table*. Berkeley, California: Ten Speed Press, 2000. A very comprehensive guide, with helpful details for kitchen gardeners.

Miller, Ashley. *The Bean Harvest Cookbook*. Newtown, Connecticut: The Taunton Press, 1997. A wealth of information on beans, with excellent recipes by former Moosewood chef.

Miller, Ashley. *The Potato Harvest Cookbook*. Newtown, Connecticut: The Taunton Press, 1998. Everything you've ever wanted to know about potatoes, with delicious recipes.

Moosewood Collective. *New Recipes from Moosewood Restaurant*. Berkeley, California: Ten Speed Press, 1987. Two hundred original recipes explore a cornucopia of garden produce.

_____*Sundays at Moosewood Restaurant*. New York: Fireside/Simon and Schuster, 1990. Each of eighteen chapters explores a different cuisine from around the world. Traditional and original recipes provide a wealth of ideas for using garden vegetables and herbs.

_____*Moosewood Restaurant Cooks at Home*. New York: Fireside/Simon and Schuster, 1994. Featuring over two hundred recipes that can be prepared in 45 minutes or less; a James Beard award winner.

_____*Moosewood Restaurant Cooks for a Crowd*. New York: John Wiley, 1996. Favorite recipes to feed twenty-four or more.

_____*Moosewood Restaurant Low-Fat Favorites*. New York: Clarkson Potter, 1996. A healthy approach to good food; a James Beard award winner.

_____*Moosewood Restaurant Book of Desserts*. New York: Clarkson Potter, 1997. Recipes for home-style and elegant desserts.

_____*Moosewood Restaurant Daily Special*. New York: Clarkson Potter, 1999. A collection of over 250 soups, salads, stews, and accompaniments.

_____*Moosewood Restaurant New Classics*. New York: Clarkson Potter, 2001. Recipes from starters to dessert, destined to become classics.

_____*Moosewood Restaurant Celebrates*. New York: Clarkson Potter, 2003. Festive meals for holidays and special occasions.

Stoner, Carol Hupping, editor. *Stocking Up*. New York: Fireside/Simon and Schuster, 1990 reprint. Definitive guide to vegetable and fruit selection and harvest, plus freezing, canning, pickling, drying, juicing, preserving, and storage.

Index

aioli, 266
almonds
  sesame baked tofu with snow peas
    and, 255
  taratour, 267
  toasting, 267
amaranth, 72, 78
angelica, 103
anthracnose, 210
aphids, 207
apples
  roasted, frisée salad with, 230
  -squash Cheddar gratin, 252
arugula, 73, 78
  gazpacho verde, 225
  salad, 229
  temperature preferences of, 191, 194
Asian vegetables, 10–13. *See also*
    individual vegetables
  companion planting and, 212
  insects and diseases of, 205
  succession crops of, 195
  temperature preferences of, 194
asparagus, 14–16
  companion planting and, 212
  fertilizing, 186
  insects and diseases of, 205
  placing, 163
  roasted, 15
  winter chilling for, 158
asparagus beetles, 207
astrological signs, planting by, 196–97

Bacillus thuringiensis (Bt), 204, 206
basil, 104–6
  companion planting and, 213
  drying and freezing, 100, 106
  -garlic butter, 272

head start for, 201, 203
pesto Genovese, 268
-shallot vinaigrette, 263
Batavian endive. *See* escarole
bay, 107
beans, 16–20
  companion planting and, 39, 212, 214
  fertilizing, 186
  head start for, 201
  insects and diseases of, 205
  Portuguese kale soup, 226
  Provençal, 239
  succession crops of, 195
  temperature preferences of, 194
  trellising, 161
  vegetable lasagna, 254
bee balm, 108, 163, 164, 213
beets, 21–22
  companion planting and, 212, 214
  insects and diseases of, 205
  succession crops of, 195
  temperature preferences of, 194
Belgian endive, 75, 194
bergamot. *See* bee balm
biodynamic farming, 211
blossom-end rot, 210
blueberry-lemon tart, 280
bok choy. *See* pak choi
borage, 146, 147, 213
bread
  garlic croutons, 120
  herbed croutons, 271
  and tomato salad, summer, 233
broccoli, 22–25
  companion planting and, 212
  insects and diseases of, 205
  temperature preferences of, 194
  winter growing of, 157

broccoli raab, 23, 24, 25
brussels sprouts, 25–26
  companion planting and, 212
  insects and diseases of, 205
  temperature preferences of, 194
  winter growing of, 157
Bt, 204, 206
bulgur pilaf, fragrant, 253
butter
  basil-garlic, 272
  dill-chive, 272
  fines herbes, 272
  mint, 273
  rosemary, 133
  sage, 273
  tarragon-Dijon, 271

cabbage, 27–28
  companion planting and, 212, 214
  fertilizing, 186
  insects and diseases of, 205
  succession crops of, 195
  temperature preferences of, 194
  winter growing of, 157
cabbage worms, 24, 208
cake, pumpkin, 279
calcium phosphate, 282
calendula, 109–10, 213
callaloo. *See* amaranth
cantaloupes, 53, 54
carnations, 147
carrots, 29–31
  companion planting and, 212, 214
  golden sesame dressing, 264
  salad, herbed, 227
  salad, minted, 227
  succession crops of, 195
  temperature preferences of, 194

vegetable "pasta," 245
Vietnamese rice noodle and
   vegetable salad, 232
cauliflower, 32–33
   companion planting and, 212
   insects and diseases of, 205
   pasta with, 33
   temperature preferences of, 194
   winter growing of, 157
chamomile, 111, 164, 213
cheese
   arugula salad, 229
   blue cheese spread, 277
   Cheddar gratin, squash-apple, 252
   Cheddar-sage-thyme spread, 277
   chèvre, fettucine with spinach,
      herbs, and, 249
   chèvre spread, herbed, 277
   crepes, 250–51
   frittata, 238
   Greek salad, 130
   John's pizza, 235–36
   Monterey Jack spread, spicy, 276
   mozzarella and tomato sandwich, 130
   Parmesan dressing, creamy, 265
   red, white, and green phyllo pizzas,
      246–47
   spread, basic, 276
   summer garden fajitas, 242
   vegetable lasagna, 254
chervil, 112
chicory, 73–74
chiffonades, 106
chiles. See peppers
Chinese cabbage, 10–11, 12, 13
   crisp-fried tofu and greens, 244–45
   insects and diseases of, 205
   spring rolls, 243
   temperature preferences of, 194
chives, 113–14
   classic chip dip, 274
   companion planting and, 213
   -dill butter, 272
chrysanthemums, 11, 12, 13, 148
cilantro (coriander), 114–15
   freezing, 100, 115
   pesto, 269
clay, 183
claytonia, 74
climate, 157–58
clove pinks, 147
club root, 210
collards, 34–35
   companion planting and, 212
   insects and diseases of, 205
   temperature preferences of, 194
Colorado potato beetles, 207
companion planting, 162, 211–14
compost, 186–88
container gardening, 178–80

cooking techniques, 221–23
coriander. See cilantro
corn, 36–39
   companion planting and, 39, 212, 214
   fertilizing, 186
   fritters, 38
   grilled, 38, 228
   head start for, 201
   insects and diseases of, 205
   roasted, 38
   temperature preferences of, 194
corn earworms, 208
corn salad. See mâche
cover crops, 186
crepes, 250–51
crop rotation, 200
croutons
   garlic, 120
   herbed, 271
cucumber beetles, striped, 207
cucumbers, 40–42
   companion planting and, 212, 214
   fertilizing, 186
   gazpacho verde, 225
   Greek salad, 130
   head start for, 202
   insects and diseases of, 205
   raita, 115
   temperature preferences of, 191, 194
   trellising, 161
   Vietnamese rice noodle and
      vegetable salad, 232
   -yogurt dip, minted, 275
curly endive, 75
cutworms, 208

daikon, 11, 12, 13, 194
damping off, 210
daylilies, 149
desserts, 250–51, 278–281
dill, 116
   -chive butter, 272
   companion planting and, 213
   drying and freezing, 100, 116
   pesto, 269
   –red onion vinaigrette, 263
dipping sauce, 240
dips
   classic chip, 274
   for fresh fruit, 275
   minted cucumber-yogurt, 275
   miso-tahini, 274
diseases, 203–5, 210
dooryard gardens, 171–72

earthworms, 189
eggplant, 42–44
   baked and stuffed, 43
   companion planting and, 212
   grilled, 256

head start for, 203
   insects and diseases of, 205
   North African roasted vegetable
      salad, 231
   emperature preferences of, 191, 194
eggs
   cooked mayonnaise, 266
   frittata, 238
   uncooked, 266
enclosed gardens, 167–68
escarole
   growing and harvesting, 76
   John's pizza, 235–36
espalier training, 167

fabric row covers, 202
fennel
   bulb-forming, 44–45
   grilled, 257
   as herb, 117
   Provençal beans, 239
fertilizers, 185–86
fines herbes butter, 272
flea beetles, 12, 207
flowers, edible, 17, 83, 145–55. See also
      individual flowers
frisée
   growing and harvesting, 75
   salad with roasted apples, 230
frittata, 238
fritters, corn, 38
fruit. See also individual fruits
   dip or sauce for, 275
   preserves or jams, 282

garden cress, 74–75, 78
gardens
   design plans for, 167–80
   location of, 160–61
   maintenance of, 163–64
   paths in, 163
   pattern of, 161–62
   plant placement in, 162–63
   raised beds, 197–98
   size of, 157
   winter, 157–58
garlic, 118–21
   -basil butter, 272
   companion planting and, 213
   croutons, 120
   roasted, 120
gazpacho verde, 225
geraniums, scented, 136–37, 163
germander, 121
grapes, 161
Greek salad, 130
green manures, 186
grilling, 222, 256–57
growing season, extending, 201–3
grow lights, 193

hardening off, 195
hazelnut pesto, 270
heirloom varieties, 8–9
herbicides, 199
herbs. *See also individual herbs*
  for bouquets, 98
  butters, 271–73
  cheese spreads, 276–77
  in container gardens, 177–80
  culinary tips for, 219–21
  drying and freezing, 98, 99, 100
  fertilizing, 186
  fragrant, 98, 163
  growing, 97–99
  as houseplants, 99
  -infused oils, 260, 261
  low-maintenance perennial, 164
  ornamental aspects of, 162
  pestos, 268–70
  potpourri from, 101–2
  propagating, 100–101
  shade-tolerant, 98
  spices vs., 97
  storing fresh, 99
  tea mixes, 283
  vinegars, 260–61
hillside gardens, 175–76
honeydew melons, 53, 54
hotkaps, 202
hot pepper spray, 206
humus, 184
hybrids, 8, 9
hyssop, 121–22, 213

insecticides, 204, 206
insects, 203–10
irrigation. *See* watering

jams, fruit, 282
Japanese beetles, 207
Johnny-jump-ups, 152

kale, 34–35
  companion planting and, 212
  crisp-fried tofu and greens, 244–45
  grilled, 257
  insects and diseases of, 205
  soup, Portuguese, 226
  temperature preferences of, 194
  winter growing of, 157
knishes, potato, 236–37
knot gardens, 169–71
kohlrabi, 46–47, 194, 205, 212

lady's mantle, 122, 164
lamb's ears, 123, 164
lamb's lettuce. *See* mâche
lasagna, vegetable, 254
lavender, 123–24
  low maintenance of, 164
  potpourri, 102

lawn beds, 174
leeks, 47–49
  crepes, 250–51
  Mama Flora's baked, 248
  sautéed, with thyme, 141
  temperature preferences of, 194
  vegetable lasagna, 254
  vegetable "pasta," 245
lemon balm, 124–25, 163
lemon potpourri, 102
lettuce, 49–53
  companion planting and, 212
  fabric row covers for, 202
  insects and diseases of, 205
  succession crops of, 195
  temperature preferences of, 194
  winter growing of, 157
loam, 183
lovage, 125–26, 213

mâche, 76, 78, 194
maple cider dressing, 230
marigolds, 150, 213
marinades
  herbed vinaigrette, 256
  spicy citrus, 256
marjoram, 126
mayonnaise
  aioli, 266
  alternatives to, 267
  cooked, 266
  enhancing commercial, 266
melons, 53–55
  companion planting and, 212
  fertilizing, 186
  head start for, 201, 202
  insects and diseases of, 205
  temperature preferences of, 191, 194
  trellising, 161
mesclun, 76–77
miner's lettuce. *See* claytonia
mint, 127–28
  butter, 273
  companion planting and, 213
  drying, 100, 128
  peppermint butter wafers, 281
minutina, 77
miso-tahini dip, 274
mizuna, 11, 12, 13
  insects and diseases of, 205
  succession crops of, 195
  temperature preferences of, 194
monarda. *See* bee balm
moon, planting by, 196–97
mulch, 189–90, 199, 201–2
mullein, 128–29
mushrooms, grilled, 256
mustards, flowering, 11, 12, 13

nasturtiums, 150–51, 162
neem, 204
nitrogen, 185
noodles
  summer rolls, 240–41
  Vietnamese rice, and vegetable
    salad, 232

oils
  herb-infused, 260, 261
  rosemary, 133
okra, 55–56, 205
onions, 57–60
  caramelized, 59
  companion planting and, 212, 214
  -dill vinaigrette, 263
  fertilizing, 186
  grilled, 256
  insects and diseases of, 205
  John's pizza, 235–36
  peperonata, 241
  potato knishes, 236–37
  red, white, and green phyllo pizzas,
    246–47
  roasted, 59
  sautéed, with thyme, 141
  temperature preferences of, 194
  winter growing of, 157
orach, 77, 194
oregano, 129–30, 213

pak choi, 11, 12, 13
  crisp-fried tofu and greens, 244–45
  insects and diseases of, 205
  spring rolls, 243
  succession crops of, 195
  temperature preferences of, 194
pansies, 151–52
parsley, 130–31
  cilantro pesto, 269
  companion planting and, 213
  freezing, 100, 131
  hazelnut pesto, 270
  tarragon pesto, 270
parsnips, 60–61
  and potatoes, puréed, 61
  temperature preferences of, 194
  vegetable "pasta," 245
pasta
  with cauliflower, 33
  fettucine with chèvre, spinach, and
    herbs, 249
  vegetable lasagna, 254
  vegetable substitute for, 245
patio gardens, 164–67
peas, 61–63
  companion planting and, 212, 214
  fertilizing, 186
  insects and diseases of, 205

snow, sesame baked tofu with almonds and, 255
temperature preferences of, 191, 194
peat pots, 191
peperonata, 241
peppermint. *See* mint
peppers, 64–67
  companion planting and, 212
  fertilizing, 186
  head start for, 201, 203
  insects and diseases of, 205
  North African roasted vegetable salad, 231
  peperonata, 241
  rouille, 267
  sauce, red, 258
  stuffed, 67
  summer garden fajitas, 242
  temperature preferences of, 191, 194
  vegetable lasagna, 254
  vegetable "pasta," 245
pesticides, 204
pestos
  cilantro, 269
  dill, 269
  Genovese, 268
  hazelnut, 270
  making, 268
  storing, 268
  tarragon, 270
pH, 184
phosphorus, 185
phyllo
  pizzas, red, white, and green, 246–47
  potato knishes, 236–37
pilaf, fragrant bulgur, 253
pizzas
  John's, 235–36
  red, white, and green phyllo, 246–47
planting. *See also individual plants* 97
  temperature preferences and, 194
  trans-, 195
polyethylene tunnels, slitted, 203
potassium (potash), 185
potato beetles, 70, 207
potatoes, 68–71
  companion planting and, 212, 214
  fertilizing, 186
  grilled, 257
  knishes, 236–37
  mashed, 70
  and parsnips, puréed, 61
  roasted, 70
  temperature preferences of, 194
potpourri, 101–2
potting mixes, 191
powdery mildew, 210
preserves, fruit, 282
progression planting, 163
pumpkins. *See also* winter squash

cake, 279
  head start for, 202
purslane, 77–78
pyrethrum, 204, 206

radicchio, 74, 78
  grilled, 257
  temperature preferences of, 194
raised beds, 197–98
raita, cucumber, 115
raspberries
  sorbet, fresh, 278
  vinaigrette, 262
rhubarb, 71–72, 158, 163
rocket. *See* arugula
rolls
  spring, 243
  summer, 240–41
root maggots, 208
roquette. *See* arugula
rosemary, 132–33
  butter, 133
  companion planting and, 213
  low maintenance of, 164
  oil, 133
roses, 153–54
  hips, 153
  potpourri, 102
rotenone, 204, 206
rouille, 267
rue, 133
rust, 210

sage, 134
  butter, 273
  companion planting and, 213
  tea, 134
salad dressings. *See also* vinaigrettes
  creamy Parmesan, 265
  golden sesame, 264
  maple cider, 230
  sweet and sour, 232
salad greens, 72–78. *See also individual greens*
  fertilizing, 186
  insects and diseases of, 205
  temperature preferences of, 194
  winter growing of, 157
salads
  arugula, 229
  cooked vegetables for, 218–19
  corn salsa, 228–29
  frisée, with roasted apples, 230
  Greek, 130
  herbed carrot, 227
  marinated, 219
  minted carrot, 227
  North African roasted vegetable, 231
  summer tomato and bread, 233
  sweet potato, 84

Vietnamese rice noodle and vegetable, 232
salsa, corn, 228–29
sandy soils, 183
santolina, 135
sauces. *See also* pestos
  dipping, 240
  for fresh fruit, 275
  red pepper, 258
  rouille, 267
  shallot-herb butter, 259
  taratour, 267
savory, 135–36, 213
scab, 210
scallions, 57
  grilled, 256
  succession crops of, 195
  temperature preferences of, 194
screened gardens, 167–68
seedlings
  buying, 193
  hardening off, 195
  indoor temperatures for, 193
  thinning, 195
  transplanting, 195
  watering, 192
seeds
  germination temperatures for, 191
  saving, 10
  starting, 190–93
sesame
  baked tofu with snow peas and almonds, 255
  dressing, golden, 264
  miso-tahini dip, 274
shallots, 79
  -basil vinaigrette, 263
  -herb butter sauce, 259
  temperature preferences of, 194
simmering, 221
slugs, 209
snails, 209
soil
  depth of, 184
  drainage of, 184
  importance of, 183
  microorganisms in, 185
  mulching, 189–90
  nutrient content of, 184–86
  pH, 184
  types of, 183–84
soil blocks, 192
soil cells, 191
sorbet, fresh raspberry, 278
sorrel, 78, 194
soups
  gazpacho verde, 225
  Portuguese kale, 226
spice potpourri, 102
spices, 97

spider mites, 209
spinach, 80–81
   companion planting and, 212
   crisp-fried tofu and greens, 244–45
   fettucine with chèvre, herbs, and, 249
   gazpacho verde, 225
   insects and diseases of, 205
   red, white, and green phyllo pizzas,
      246–47
   temperature preferences of, 191, 194
   winter growing of, 158
spoon mustard. See tatsoi
spreads
   basic cheese, 276
   blue cheese, 277
   Cheddar-sage-thyme, 277
   herbed chèvre, 277
   spicy Monterey Jack, 276
spring rolls, 243
sprinklers, 201
squash. See summer squash; winter
   squash
squash bugs, 208
steaming, 222–23
Steiner, Rudolf, 211
stir-frying, 223
stock, vegetable, 224
succession crops, 195
sugar, scented geranium, 137
summer rolls, 240–41
summer squash, 82–83. See also
   zucchini
   companion planting and, 39, 212
   fertilizing, 186
   grilled, 256
   head start for, 202, 203
   insects and diseases of, 205
   stuffed, 83
   summer garden fajitas, 242
   temperature preferences of, 191, 194
summer tomato and bread salad, 233
sunflowers, 154
sweet and sour dressing, 232
sweet cicely, 138, 164
sweet potatoes, 83–85
   fertilizing, 186
   grilled, 257
   head start for, 201
   salad, 84
   temperature preferences of, 194
sweet woodruff, 138–39, 164
Swiss chard, 85–86
   crisp-fried tofu and greens, 244–45
   insects and diseases of, 205
   temperature preferences of, 194

tahini
   golden sesame dressing, 264
   -miso dip, 274
taratour, 267

tarragon, 139–40
   -Dijon butter, 271
   freezing, 100, 140
   pesto, 270
   vinaigrette, 263
tart, blueberry-lemon, 280
tatsoi, 11–12, 13
   crisp-fried tofu and greens, 244–45
   insects and diseases of, 205
   succession crops of, 195
   temperature preferences of, 194
tea
   chamomile, 111
   mixes, herbal, 283
   sage, 134
terraced beds, 160, 175–76
thyme, 140–42, 164, 213
tofu
   crisp-fried, and greens, 244–45
   sesame baked, with snow peas and
      almonds, 255
   summer rolls, 240–41
tomatoes, 86–92
   and bread salad, summer, 233
   companion planting and, 213, 214
   fertilizing, 186
   Greek salad, 130
   grilled, 256
   head start for, 201, 203
   insects and diseases of, 205
   and mozzarella sandwich, 130
   North African roasted vegetable
      salad, 231
   Portuguese kale soup, 226
   Provençal beans, 239
   red, white, and green phyllo pizzas,
      246–47
   summer garden fajitas, 242
   temperature preferences of, 194
   trellising, 161
   vegetable lasagna, 254
tomato hornworms, 208
transplanting, 195
trellising, 54, 55, 161
turnips, 92–93
   companion planting and, 212, 213
   insects and diseases of, 205
   temperature preferences of, 194

vegetables. See also individual
      vegetables
   à la grecque, 234
   choosing varieties of, 7–9
   in container gardens, 177–80
   cooked, for salads, 218–19
   cooking techniques for, 221–23
   cooking times for, 218
   cutting, 218
   frittata, 238
   grilled, 256–57

heirloom varieties, 8–9
hybrids, 8, 9
   insects and diseases of, 205
   lasagna, 254
   open-pollinated varieties, 8–9
   "pasta," 245
   and rice noodle salad, Vietnamese,
      232
   salad, North African roasted, 231
   spacing, 10
   stock, 224
   temperature preferences of, 194–95
vinaigrettes
   basil-shallot, 263
   dill–red onion, 263
   dressing, 52
   marinade, herbed, 256
   raspberry, 262
   tarragon, 263
vinegars, herb, 260–61
violas, 151–52
violets, 155

wafers, peppermint butter, 281
watercress, 75, 78
watering, 192, 200–201
watermelons, 53, 54, 55
weeding, 199
whiteflies, 210
winter squash, 93–95
   -apple Cheddar gratin, 252
   baked, 237
   companion planting and, 39, 212
   fertilizing, 186
   grilled, 257
   head start for, 202, 203
   insects and diseases of, 205
   pumpkin cake, 279
   stuffed, 95
   temperature preferences of, 191, 194
   trellising, 161

yams. See sweet potatoes
yarrow, 142–43, 164
yogurt
   classic chip dip, 274
   -cucumber dip, minted, 275
   cucumber raita, 115
   dip or sauce for fresh fruit, 275
   herbed, 264

zucchini, 82–83
   crepes, 250–51
   grilled, 256
   stuffed, 83
   summer garden fajitas, 242
   vegetable lasagna, 254
   vegetable "pasta," 245